Love and War
in the WRNS

VICKY UNWIN

The
History
Press

First published 2015

The History Press
The Mill, Brimscombe Port
Stroud, Gloucestershire, GL5 2QG
www.thehistorypress.co.uk

© Vicky Unwin, 2015

The right of Vicky Unwin to be identified as the Author
of this work has been asserted in accordance with the
Copyright, Designs and Patents Act 1988.

British Library Cataloguing in Publication Data.
A catalogue record for this book is available from the British Library.

ISBN 978 0 7509 6304 6

Typesetting and origination by The History Press
Printed in Great Britain

Contents

Acknowledgements

[handwritten annotation:] THE LIVING DEAD
EVEN THE DEAD
SMELL

This book is a tribute to my remarkable mother, and also to all those women in the Second World War who, in many ways, took a greater risk than the men in leaving the sanctuary of their homes and country in order to serve.

When I found Sheila's letters bundled up in black bin liners after her death in 2009, I decided to fulfill her final wish, which was to write her memoirs. She had often told me that she was immensely proud of her war years: she had even begun to sort the letters herself, using recycled envelopes. However, our daughter's sudden death in 2011 put a temporary stop to the project. Louise and her Granny had always enjoyed a close relationship and so it became the clichéd labour of love to complete this book in honour of both of them.

I thank them for inspiring me: writing the book was the perfect antidote to the grieving caused by this double bereavement.

Thanks also to my friends and family – especially my husband, Ross, and our son, Tommy, who have supported me during the painstaking process of pulling the book together. And special thanks to Charlotte Blundy who transcribed the letters, cleverly deciphering my mother's difficult handwriting, and to Joanna Frank who gave me some excellent advice on an early draft.

Finally, thank you to Felicity Kendal for agreeing to write the foreword: I feel we share a bond via our two sets of eccentric parents. Felicity – your empathy through these difficult times has been a great solace.

Foreword by
Felicity Kendal CBE

It is no exaggeration to say that what we have in this volume is a treasure chest of letters.

They start with Sheila, as an innocent 'green girl', joining the WRNS at the beginning of World War Two. She writes home to her mother, begging for parcels to be sent, for silk stockings, nail polish, and her old fur coat. She seems from the start to be obsessed with dances, dates and young men, and is determined not to have her hair cut short. But as these letters, like a journal, continue through the war, we see her grow into the feisty, ambitious and independent woman she will become.

Assigned to the important work of monitoring via cyphers and signals the enemy and British fleets, she travels to Egypt, and in her words becomes an 'Invasion Addict'. She is promoted to Cypher Officer and as such has the knowledge of planned invasions and attacks. Her details of so many – now famous – turning points of the war are intriguing.

She lives a giddy life full of romance, hard work and danger, yet never loses her almost childlike wonder and excitement of the day-to-day social scene, the work she is doing, and her wonder at the Exotic East.

This is a chronicle of a time gone by, when in the midst of death and destruction so many women like Sheila, passionately committed to serving King and Country, were nonetheless equally committed to the important job of securing a suitable husband.

Sheila seems oblivious to her beauty, but not to the staggering number of young men who constantly pursue her. Like a modern-day Emily Eden, she enthrals us with details of her journey and adventures:

Saturday
Dinner at the Mena Hotel. It was just perfect – dining and dancing in the moonlight by the side of the swimming pool, all very gay – At about midnight we decided to walk up a hill to see the Pyramids, it was rather glorious – you walk out of the hotel garden up a hill which slopes round the foot of the Big Pyramid ... which I climbed ... and all in the bright moonlight ... beautifully cool!

Her letters chart the war almost weekly. By the end she has met 'unconventional' Tom. He is the opposite of the social and gregarious Sheila, yet he seems to see off with ease any competition for her hand and heart. At the end of the war they plan to marry, as she writes to her mother:

Dear Ma,

Please don't make too much fuss about anything – Tom hates it so – we shall get married I expect in a Registry Office – I honestly don't think Tom would survive a proper wedding with relatives and guests – he'd probably get up and say something awful or shocking – he's quite liable to!! And please don't rush around telling everyone I am marrying a Czech!!

This is an extraordinary and detailed portrait of an intelligent and passionate woman, and a fascinating read.

Felicity Kendal CBE

Chronology

1939	September	Hitler invades Poland on 1 September; Britain and France declare war two days later
1940	January	Rationing starts in the UK
	March	Bombing of Scapa Flow naval base in Scotland
	April	Germany invades Denmark and Norway
	May	Germany invades Belgium, Holland and France
		Churchill becomes Prime Minister
		Holland surrenders
		Belgium surrenders
	June	Evacuation from Dunkirk
		Italy declares war on Britain and France
		Norway surrenders
		France signs armistice with Germany
	July	German U-boats attack Atlantic convoys
		Battle of Britain begins
	August	First German air raids on London
	September	Operation Sea Lion (invasion of Britain) planned by Germany with Blitzkrieg bombing of British cities
		Italy invades Egypt
		British victory in Battle of Britain
		Germany, Italy and Japan sign pact
		Sheila joins up and goes to Dunfermline for training

	October	Sheila moves to Dundee
		Germany invades Romania
		Italy invades Greece and Albania
		Hungary and Romania join the Axis
	December	Britain begins desert offensive against the Axis
1941	January	Tobruk falls to the British
	February	Afrika Korps arrives in Tripoli, led by Rommel
		Benghazi falls to the British
	March	Benghazi falls to Rommel
		Tripoli falls to Rommel
		Rommel besieges Tobruk, the only part of Cyrenaica to remain in British hands
		Stalemate in the desert
		British forces land in Greece
		Sheila goes to Greenwich Naval College for Officers' Training Course
		Germany invades Greece and Yugoslavia
		Greece and Yugoslavia surrender
	May	British counterattack in Egypt
		Fall of Greece and Crete
		Sheila goes to Methil, Lundin Links, Fife
		Sinking of the *Hood* by the *Bismarck*, and then the *Bismarck* is sunk
	June	General Auchinleck takes over as Commander-in-Chief from General Wavell
		Allies invade Syria and Lebanon
		Germany attacks Russia
	July	Britain and Russia agree pact of mutual assistance
	August	Fall of Persia to British forces
		Battle for Western Desert begins
		Russia joins the war
		Siege of Leningrad begins
	September	First use of gas chambers at Auschwitz

	October	Germans advance on Moscow
	November	Aircraft carrier *Ark Royal* sunk off Malta by U-boat
	December	Bad period for the navy: loss of *Repulse* and *Prince of Wales* in Far east; *Ark Royal* and *Barham* hit by U-boats in the Mediterranean; *Valiant* and *Queen Elizabeth* sunk by human torpedoes in Alexandria harbour
Mid-1941 – mid-1942		Eighth Army in retreat in Western Desert
		Japan attacks Pearl Harbour
		US joins the war after Pearl Harbour
		Britain surrenders Hong Kong
1942	January	Sheila receives order that she is to report to Overseas Service Office in London
	Early February	Sheila sets sail from England, destination Egypt via the Cape
	End February	Sheila meets Robin Chater on board ship
		Fall of Singapore
		Tobruk taken by Rommel
	May	Sheila arrives in Alexandria and is attached to Office of the Commander-in-Chief Mediterranean
		Sheila meets John Pritty
	June	US Navy wins Battle of the Midway – turning point in the Pacific
		Sinking of the *Medway* at Port Said
		Germans advance on Alamein Line and two hours from Alexandria
		'The Flap' in Cairo and Alexandria, accompanied by mass evacuations of civilians and staff
	July	1st Battle of El Alamein begins
		British Army in the Western Desert in retreat: General Auchinleck replaced by General Montgomery

		Low point of war: Japanese sweeping through Malaya, Java, Burma, Philippines, Papua New Guinea and Borneo (1941–2)
	October	2nd Battle of El Alamein begins
	November	Eighth Army wins Battle of El Alamein; turning point of the war
		Operation Torch, combined landing of US First Army and Eighth Army begins offensive in North Africa with the aim of meeting in Tunis
		Axis forces defeated at Stalingrad – Germany's first major defeat
1943	January	Tripoli recaptured; Tunis falls to First (US) and Eighth Armies and Battle for Africa is won
		Casablanca Conference: Roosevelt and Churchill call for 'unconditional surrender'
	March	Sheila moves to Cairo to join Admiral Ramsay's planning team for Operation Husky, Royal Navy General Headquarters
	May	Sheila meets Major Bruce Booth-Mason
		German and Italian troops surrender in North Africa
	June	Sheila is promoted to 2nd Officer
		Sheila moves back to Alexandria now that Operation Husky planning is completed
	July	Allies invade Sicily, Operation Husky, the beginning of the Second Front agreed by Churchill and Roosevelt at Casablanca Conference in Jan 1943
		Sheila goes on leave to Beirut
	September	Eighth Army lands in Italy
		Italy surrenders but Germans rescue Mussolini
	October	Sheila moves back to Cairo to work for Admiral Waller, director of Combined Operations

		Rome falls to the Allies and Italy declares war on Germany
	November	Allied leaders meet in Tehran
1944	January	Allied landings in Anzio
		End of the Siege of Leningrad
	March	Sheila is transferred to Suez as Principal Cypher Officer
		Hungary occupied by Germany
	May	Germans surrender in Crimea
		Germans retreat from Anzio
	June	Allies enter Rome
		Operation Overlord: D-Day landings in Normandy
	July	Operation Cobra: Allies break out from Normandy
		Sheila goes on leave in Palestine with John Pritty
	August	Sheila on leave in Beirut, Baalbek and Damascus with Aenid Brothers
		Allies liberate Paris
		Germans abandon Bulgaria
	September	Sheila returns to England by sea; she remains in England for the rest of the war, stationed at Harwich
		Athens liberated; Rommel commits suicide
	October	Soviet army enters Prussia
	November	Surrender of Axis forces in Greece
	December	Germans attack Ardennes: Battle of the Bulge begins
1945	January	Germans withdraw from Ardennes
		Soviets capture Warsaw
		Auschwitz liberated by Soviets
		Japanese retreat to Chinese coast
	February	Yalta conference: the Big Three leaders meet
		US lands at Iwo Jima
	April	US army encircles Germans in the Ruhr

		Allies liberate Belsen, Buchenwald and Ravensbrück
		Roosevelt dies and Truman becomes US President
	May	Germany surrenders in Europe on 7 May
		Sheila is posted to Kiel to help with supervising the peace
	June	Sheila meets my father, Sub. Lieut. Tom Unwin, RNVR based in Kiel
		Leave in England
	July	Back to England for a three-week course at Petersfield Signal School
	September	Sheila is back in Germany: Hamburg, not clear what the job is
	October	Sheila moves to Plön; Bruce Booth-Mason awarded MBE
	November	New relationship with Captain Ken Millar of the Tanks
1946	Feb–March	Sheila is on leave in England
	April	Sheila is on leave in Brussels with Ken Millar
		Sheila moves to Kiel to do secretarial work
	June	Sheila celebrates the anniversary of V-Day sailing with Tom Unwin
	July	Sheila is on leave in England
	August	Japan surrenders after the US drop nuclear bombs on Hiroshima and Nagasaki
	September	Tom Unwin drives Sheila into a tree in Kiel
	October	The Nuremburg Trials
		Sheila announces her engagement to Tom Unwin
		Sheila goes on a three-week domestic science course to prepare for being demobbed
		Tom returns to London, having been demobbed
	November	Sheila is still in Germany but preparing to depart for England
	December	Sheila marries Tom Unwin in Durham on 23 December

Introduction

By the time of her death, aged 89, my mother had achieved her lifelong ambition: to be a respected member of the academic community. Recognised as the world's expert on Arab chests and Swahili culture, following the publication of her book *The Arab Chest* (Arabian Publishing, 2006), she had been invited to lecture at conferences and symposia and basked in the late recognition of her talents. It was an extraordinary achievement for a Norfolk girl whose education finished with the Higher School Certificate and a secretarial course.

But what was it that transformed her from a gauche, air-headed and rather vain, even if clever, young girl, into an intrepid adventurer, archaeologist and a collector of African artefacts, who travelled solo around India, the Persian Gulf and Saudi Arabia in the 1960s and '70s, like her heroine Freya Stark?

The Second World War proved to be a life-changing event for many young women, and for Sheila it was no exception. This collection of letters charts her rite of passage from childhood into womanhood. The letters sparkle with humour and observation, and paint vivid portraits of the hectic wartime social life – parties, riding, sailing, dancing – juxtaposed with gruelling night watches in both Egypt and Germany. Underlying this gaiety are undercurrents of mortality, combined with feelings of guilt at the forces' opulent lifestyle, and her passion for her work, for instance her pride in helping to plan the invasion of Sicily under Admiral Ramsay, a man she held in the highest esteem. Her first-hand accounts of 'The Flap', the sinking of the *Medway* and the Belsen Trials offer insights from a rare personal perspective.

Finding love and a husband seem to have been a major preoccupation – she had at least three admirers on the go at any one time – and
her 1946 whirlwind love affair and marriage to my father, a young
Czech-born intelligence officer in the RNVR, also based in Kiel,
underscores the desperation of many young women to emerge from
the war with a ring on their finger, negating a return to a home life
of suburban values and bourgeois boredom. The final letters on the
subject of the wedding fascinatingly reveal the often hinted-at ambiva-
lence of her relationship with her domineering and critical mother.

Sheila's mother, Grace, the recipient of these letters, was one of
ten children born to a middle-class Norfolk farmer, William Kemp
Proctor Sexton (1847–1946). The family grew up in Downham
Market; Grace, unlike her other sisters, did not marry immedi-
ately and, as was the way, became a governess/companion, to
Canon Harris's two children, Monica and Jack, from Appleby in
Westmorland. The fate of her first fiancé is unclear, although I was
always told that she sued him for breach of promise.

At some point, while travelling with the Harrises in Scotland, she
became engaged to a quiet and well-educated Scottish captain from
the Royal Engineers, who had been awarded the Military Cross in
the First World War, but who had been heavily gassed. Invalided
out of the army in 1922, he had the greatest of difficulty in finding a job – he sold dictionaries and vacuum cleaners among other
things, much to his wife's chagrin. Eventually they moved to Durham
in 1938, where he was Deputy Controller of the ARP (Air Raid
Precautions) and, later, secretary to the Durham County Hospital.
As my aunt Rosemary said, 'Daddy was never brought up to earn
money.' Indeed he was rumoured to be an illegitimate grandchild of
the Sackville-West family, the most likely candidate being Lionel, 2nd
Lord Sackville, who had a string of children with his Spanish mistress,
Pepita, among them Victoria Sackville-West (b.1862), Vita's mother.

This is quite possible: his father was born in Worthing in 1858 to
Harriet Mills, and baptised William Thomas Greenland (Greenland
being the name or, more likely, pseudonym, for his father). Sergeant
Major William Mills married Helen Horn Findlay from Rhynie,

Aberdeen, and together they moved with the army: first to Malta, where my grandfather Percival Findlay Mills was born in 1890. From there they set sail to join the regiment in Hong Kong, but William Mills died at sea two days out of Malta and was buried at Port Said (this strange coincidence was not lost on my mother when she discovered this fact in the 1990s). Helen and the young Findlay, as my grandfather was known, returned to Scotland, where a mysterious benefactor paid for his education at Edinburgh High School, before he joined the Royal Engineers as an officer. Quite an achievement for the son of a poor widow – unless he received help.

If you look at the photograph of him you will notice a great likeness to Vita Sackville-West, who was born only a couple of years later than him, in 1892. The mystery will never be solved, according to my mother, who spent years trying to track down her forebears. 'I can only comment that he physically resembled Vita Sackville-West, quite strikingly so, and was tall, with a long face and large high-bridged nose. He was tall quiet and reclusive, and certainly no match for mother who was overbearing and strong-willed. No wonder he didn't talk of his origins, which is annoying to us.'

Grace was a bossy, social-climbing bridge player, and in order to make ends meet she ran a boarding house in Glebe Avenue, Hunstanton (it had seven bedrooms and a live-in servant girl) which catered for summer visitors. During these months the girls were packed off to rich relatives. Two of Grace's sisters had married well: one, Aunt Rose, was childless and was keen to adopt Sheila (but Grace refused to agree as it was not the done thing), and the other aunt, Dorothy, had three children and would take the two young sisters on holiday with them to Skegness, Scotland and, once, to Jersey. Sheila was very close to her cousin Hazel as they were exactly the same age; Hazel told me that Grace had a 'terrible temper' and used to hit Sheila, but never Rosemary. I believe Rosemary was jealous of this friendship.

Sheila adored her father, who was bullied mercilessly by his wife. Before the First World War he had been an employee of the Crown Agents and had travelled widely, including to Iraq and West Africa.

He was an intellectual and I think she felt a great empathy for him and a solidarity born out of their shared victim status. Her occasional letters to him are warm, loving and more considered than those to her mother.

Both girls were bright, and attended Rhianver College; some of Sheila's schoolbooks survive, showing a talent for painting and art – something that she was to return to in later life and, indeed, in the occasional sketches contained in her letters – in the beautifully executed and coloured drawings of historical and Shakespearean figures amid the copperplate writing. Both girls won scholarships to St James's Secretarial College in London, where they went just before the outbreak of war to earn a living. Sheila excelled at shorthand and won the top prize of 140wpm, something she remained proud of for the rest of her life. Rosemary became secretary to the head of the department store Bourne & Hollingsworth.

Unwanted and unloved by her mother, bullied by her sister – Rosemary was pampered and adored – the sisters were never close. Sheila is frequently disparaging about Rosemary's tardiness at joining up and loose behaviour: perhaps she was trying to get her own back? Little wonder she escaped and joined up as soon as she was old enough, just after finishing college and a month after her 18th birthday.

Knowing this, I wonder why she devotedly wrote to her mother every week until the mid 1970s: Sheila certainly never forgave her for her unhappy childhood and, later, for taking my father's side in their messy divorce. This latent antipathy towards her mother surfaces occasionally as she chastises her for gossiping and not reading her letters properly. Her marriage to an idealist with no social standing in Britain may well have been a subconscious put-down for her mother's snobbery.

And yet Sheila confides in her mother and seeks her advice, perhaps out of a particularly British wartime sense of duty that we find hard to understand today. Maybe the sight of all her fellow Wrens devotedly writing to their parents influenced her notion of 'home' during the six years she was away, and undoubtedly she wanted to make her mother proud of her, to prove that she was the more worthwhile daughter. She is homesick too, frequently reminiscing about England and the countryside, contrasting the heat and dust of Egypt with the cool, green fields of home.

And, like many members of the forces posted overseas, there was a real sense of guilt at escaping the privations of the war at home. Ever the dutiful daughter and feeling ashamed about the abundance and excess of food, fabrics, cosmetics and all sorts of items scarce in England, she devotes hours to buying basics and packaging up parcels home. Given the ferocity of the naval battles raging in the Mediterranean, and the frequent sinking of the convoys carrying supplies and mail, there are frequent anxious mentions of letters and parcels going astray.

There are small hints of her future social conscience and liberal ideas – she visits injured sailors in hospital and is horrified by the extent of the destruction and suffering of the civilians in post-war conditions in Germany. Her letters demonstrate a growing fascination with archaeology and gift for travel-writing. She paints vivid portraits of the Musky in Cairo, of visits to the citadel, the pyramids, the City of the Dead, its mosques and ancient houses, and of her excursions to Beirut, Damascus and Palestine.

I believe this whetted her appetite for her later forays into the early Islamic culture of the Swahili coast, where she participated in several archeological digs, and her lifelong quest to discover the origins of the Arab chest.

Her rather unhappy childhood explains her yearning to be loved and to be happy, and the dominance of affairs of the heart in the letters often seem to put her work in the shade. But careful reading shows that she took her work and the war extremely seriously and was proud of her contribution. Censorship will have prevented her from writing much of the detail of her work, but there is a real sense of the long hours and the exhaustion, juxtaposed with absolute necessity of living every moment.

To the memory of my feisty mother, Sheila,
and my equally spirited daughter, Louise.

Give sorrow words; the grief that does not speak
knits up the o-er wrought heart and bids it break.
William Shakespeare, Macbeth

I have kept to Sheila's spelling and punctuation,
changing absolutely nothing. Sometimes this gives
rise to inconsistency or some political incorrectness,
but I wished to retain the letters' charm and
authenticity. Obviously I had to cut the letters
down by about two thirds, nevertheless I think what
remains gives a real flavour of Sheila's war.

1940

'Disappointed
with it all'

My mother, Sheila Mills, joined the Wrens just two weeks after her 18th birthday. She had only just graduated from St James's Secretarial College, and was working at Currey & Co, a law firm. By September 1940 the Blitzkrieg was in full swing; although the Battle of Britain had been won, London was suffering from air raids, France had capitulated, merchant ships were being torpedoed, Scapa Flow had been bombed, Italy had invaded North Africa, and the Axis – consisting of the Germans, the Italians and the Japanese – had been formed. Rationing had been in force since January. The future did not look bright.

To Sheila, as to many young people, it must have seemed logical to join up before being called up. In her case, as a well-educated girl with excellent typing and shorthand skills, she must have hoped for an early commission, something her letters reveal more or less from day one. Inheriting her father's wanderlust and, with her childhood sweetheart, Paul, already a naval officer, joining the Wrens must have been a natural choice.

Nevertheless on arrival in Scotland on 1 October, the enormity of what she has done begins to dawn on her. Her first letters from Dunfermline are a childlike mix of excitement, impatience and apprehension, and reflect her middle-class upbringing and values inherited from her snobbish mother:

W.R.N.S Quarters
St Leonards Hill
Dunfermline
Fife
2.10.40

My dear Mummy and Daddy

This is my second day here and all goes well. So far! I went into the town last night and bought an enormous torch, then got lost and had to ask twice before getting home. The 3 other girls seem most kind and helpful. They all LOVE the Wrens, say they have a super time, and wouldn't be out for the world. They seem to fraternise freely with all and tho' not a fast type really, pick up all kinds of people!

Yes Mama, we have to wear knickers 'closed in at the knees' for the morals of the Navy must be kept up! Also we have to have 'hussifs' to keep sewing in. Could you please send me the sleeve I knitted and which I left behind – and also my pale <u>nail polishes</u> (thick and clear) as we can't wear coloured polish. Hope I can use the Barbara Gould! I slept very well but was woken by furious snores from next door neighbour, which seemed strange after sleeping through all the guns of London. We had to get up about 7, had breakfast at 7.45 and then made our beds. At present I'm sitting in the rest room which is a huge, high windowed room, with wireless going. We're on a hill and the trees look marvellous – everything is very bright and light. I'm expecting to be called at any moment to be told where I'm going. I rather wish I wasn't a writer because you have to work from 9–6 every day, with one free day a week. As a telephonist, coder or a telegrapher you work half every day from 9–1 or 1–6, which seems much better.

Two rather nice girls have just spoken to me and they Signal. They work at C. in C. as I may do. They tell me they are going to be moved to some place or other where they will have to work underground. But then they have to work on during raids. Everyone seems terribly young. When they hear I type and do shorthand they think I'm most accomplished, which makes me laugh, and I feel quite a grandmother – at 20!

On top of this she is not impressed with her fellow Wrens:

> … I'm told that most of the Wrens are nice but some are pretty queer. They all appear to be honest I'm told … They are very young, or about 25 or 40 and missed their chances! I'm afraid I must be rather blasé or a terrible snob because I don't feel inclined to run around with any Tom Dick and Harry like these girls do. Any soldier or sailor does for them. But we shall see.
>
> Please don't think I'm wet blanketing it altogether; doubtless when I've sorted my friends and got my job sorted all will be well. People have been most kind, really, but they are terribly mixed. They keep coming and going, I believe, as this is a training and drafting depot.
>
> Tons of love
>
> Sheila

She is most amused to meet up with Miss Kidd, the secretary from St James's who 'remembered both me and R [sister Rosemary], that we had got scholarships and told the office, which may be useful. She also remembered we lived in Norfolk!'

Her work gets off to a rocky start, working in the Wren office part time and doing coding the rest. We should remember that this is only day 4, so she is showing an unreasonable amount of frustration and disappointment, probably exacerbated by anxiety.

This is compounded by an unpleasant incident soon after she arrives:

> W.R.N.S. Quarters
> St. Leonards Hill,
> Dunfermeline
> 5.10.40
>
> My dear Mummy,

I <u>was</u> reassured to get your letter and the papers. I had a simply horrid day and was feeling most depressed and they cheered me up no end. Yesterday I went to Mrs Henselgrew's office and worked there a bit (she's secretary to the Wren Superintendent) then I was transferred to coding which is rather fun but might be boring later on – not sure. Well I did that all this morning and then went to the Signals office (S.D.O) to help this afternoon. It was <u>awful</u>. All I did from 2:30–7 was file papers in pigeon holes. I nearly died of sheer boredom and fatigue for I had to stand up the whole time and had no tea at all. Then I had to go back to coding at the last minute as they were short. I don't know whether I'm going to code for good, but some of the Wrens here are awfully jealous, because they applied for coding and were told it was full and would they do telephone. This doesn't make me very popular, as you can see. But I've met several people I do like. Two Irish girls, the O'Neils, from Newcastle (I believe they were receptionists at the Turks Head and another girl from Darlington. (Funny they should all come from Durham!) On the whole I hate the girls here – Mary Diamond, whom I liked at first, is most queer now, hardly speaks to me at all. Nancy is quite nice tho'. But a <u>most</u> unfortunate thing happened last night which I'll tell you about.

We had a dance for members at the dockyard and Cochrane I. One horrible spotty man I was dancing with said he'd got some gin and lime and would I like some. I completely forgot Wrens and teetotal dances and said yes. Silly of me really, but I didn't think. We were in a small room downstairs and unfortunately a girl I dislike saw us there. The sum of the matter was that Mrs Crawley found a whiskey later in that room, made enquiries, heard I had been there and sent for me. She was very nice, but I felt such a fool, especially as he wasn't at all a nice man and on the face of it, it must have looked rather bad. I told her I had had gin and lime and she asked if I knew the difference between that and whiskey. Then she explained (!) why they mustn't have drink at parties and what might happen if men got drunk and made me feel a 2 year old. She was certainly nice and told me she knew that I wouldn't get up to tricks, and was surprised to hear such tales of me (!) but that she was afraid I might earn myself a bad reputation.

Of course, I apologised and said how silly I was – inwardly feeling furious, both with myself and that stinking girl. I bet a ghastly tale gets round to all the people I don't like, and they can be horrid I can tell you. However I may not remain here, but may be drafted.

I'm wondering if I should apply to be drafted as coder back to Newcastle. I think I'd like it better than this, or try for Glasgow. You see, I'm in such a muddle – no one knows what I'm meant to be doing and I can't see there's any chance of promotion (let alone a commission) for <u>ages</u>. Why lots of people who have been here in a year are still Wrens. I don't want to be pessimistic, or anything in these early stages, but I must say I'm terribly disappointed with it all. Any girl can do any of these jobs I'm doing, coding too, and I didn't like working on the Wren side at all. I much prefer messages about ships etc. I don't like being one of the hundreds doing work that hundreds could do, and it's horrid being ignored by people, whom, in ordinary life, one would fraternise with. No, I cannot mix with Mrs Kidd, or any of the officers. <u>Quite</u> taboo. And the men absolutely look through you. You might be dust. After a fortnight's probation, you are invited to enroll, provided they like you and you them. Well, if my work isn't settled, or I haven't found my particular type of work, and I still dislike all these people so, I shall seriously consider not signing on. It's an absolute waste of one's abilities, really. I feel I could be more useful elsewhere – and anyway, it's the dullest type of office work. Tho' I find messages about ships, and sending out real coded messages to them rather fun. It's all very secret tho' and one must be careful not to say anything.

I'm awfully sorry I find it all this way. I simply hate people who always grumble, but I think I really have cause to – for I've been brought up here under false pretences. Whether this coding will lead to anything remains to be seen. I worked from 9 until 7 today, I am terribly weary. I came home to go to bed, and am now told I've got tomorrow off. Thank heavens. Therefore I shall probably go to Church with Ines in the morning (there's a military service at the abbey) and ring up these people to see if I can go and see them later on. I've not done anything about Rosemary's Clive, but I had better do something quickly, before I develop an acute inferiority complex.

I should probably be calling him 'sir'! Mrs Crawley married a Crawley from Brancepeth. Surtees doesn't come into it.

I'm keeping a diary which ought to be rather fun, only I mustn't let it fall into enemy hands! Oh dear me no – I must keep it as safely as the codes! (Can't write any more tonight – eyes much too tired!)

Ines and Hayne came in last night very hilarious and we had a tremendous laugh. They had been on the spree and had had a very gay time. It really cheered me up no end and now I've got the day off which is a good thing. And it's a lovely day too. Mrs Crawley has just asked us all if we'd like to go to church and so we are most of us going. I'm told that that horrid girl who made all the row is most hated here, and has been shifted around a lot because she is a bad character. There's a girl in this room called Kinloch who knows Durham very well and all the people we know. She is rather a queer girl - and I'm rather surprised.

I've been sewing on my name tapes. We are allowed to send 8 articles to the laundry every Sunday. I haven't sent anything off this week. We can do most of our personal washing here, but I don't like to put it out in the drying room.

I'm writing this in the ironing room for peace and quiet. There's a terrific gale brewing, but it's a lovely sunny day.

You never told me if you knew anyone in the D.L.I [Durham Light Infantry] up here. I'm told it's the 14th. Do find out because it would be terribly nice to know someone here. Please, also, rack your brains and try and think of anyone you know in Edinburgh or near here. We have to pay 2/5d to get there which seems a lot to me, but as soon as we get into uniform and present a pay book we get a reduction.

What do you think about this whole thing? I think it seems most unsatisfactory. Do you think it would be a good idea to ask for a transfer to down to Newcastle? It would be nice to be near home and come home more often. It is 3 months before we get 7 days leave with free pass. I don't know how weekends run, but people always seem to be getting home (those who live here) and I feel most envious. Or do you think I ought to stick it out here? I expect I shall make some friends, in time ... Please don't think I'm being frightfully down on the place. I really loathe grumblers, but what worries me is loathing it so and having to sign up for duration. I think I should tire if it stays on at this rate and I have no chance of getting out. You can buy yourself out of the W.A.A.F.s so I'm told, but not the Wrens! Senior Service and all that. That obnoxious girl has come in and asked me if I got into a row. I told her quietly and firmly that it was an unfortunate mistake. So hope she knows she's squashed.

We've just been to church and then walked to get coffee, but couldn't. Rather a jolly girl came with us. I was most annoyed. Had to clean silver this morning. Oh, I rang up the people in Dunfermline and I'm going to see them this afternoon. She sounded rather Scotch. I hope she's nice. I get very tired of Scotch voices around, and long for even a few Cockneys. There's a YMCA concert tonight I may go to. Now do write soon and let me know all the news – try and find out some people around here – I'm sorry if this has been rather a horrid letter – I just feel I run out of steam sometimes and doubtless shall settle down again soon.

It's very pretty round here – must do some exploring.

Lots of love to you both –

Sheila

She does make one friend, a girl from Doncaster, Ines Gillespie:

… blonde and very kind, looks like Aunty Maud. I'm told she's 40 tho' looks 20 … and like me, doesn't seem to cotton on with the other girls much … She has made lots of friends up here (mostly officers) and we are going to have some fun – I hope – but all the other girls are terribly jealous of her and therefore not awfully pleasant … I like Ines very much, but she's what you might call 'man mad' which is rather sickening. However, she seems to meet with great success even among the Scotties[?].

Sheila is desperate for company from a similar social background, and pesters her mother for contacts, especially among the Durham Light

Infantry who are stationed in Dunfermline. But, for whatever reason, Grace fails to produce results until Sheila moves to Dundee at the end of October when she effects an introduction to a friend of the owner of respectable Durham coffee shop, Greenwells. This turns out to be Elizabeth Clayhill, who lives with her wealthy uncle at Invergowrie house 'almost a castle, with turrets … and a bed Bonnie Prince Charlie slept in'. Elizabeth in turn introduces Sheila to some of the local people, and together they go out to supper and to the cinema.

After Ines is posted to Methil (where Sheila goes herself in 1941), she makes friends with 18-year-old Maureen Pritty:

> a very attractive dark girl … She's definitely a cut above most Wrens, and feels she ought to have a commission too, but is only 18 … Tall, like me, she knows a girl whose brother is on the same ship as Paul and she tells me she puts into Rosyth very frequently, which, if true should be grand.

By strange coincidence Maureen is the sister of John Pritty, destined to be Sheila's great love in Egypt.

This dissatisfaction and uncertainty with life in the Wrens is set to continue throughout her career – always hankering after promotion and a desire to be anywhere but where she is – with the exception of Cairo as we shall see. For the first couple of weeks in Dunfermline she agonises over what to do, asking her mother over and over what she thinks: should she transfer to Newcastle or elsewhere in Scotland or chuck it all in? She is loath to return to Durham and for everyone say 'I told you so'.

Then 'just as prospects were brightening', and as she is beginning to resign herself to staying, she is sent to Dundee 'rather to my grief' to help them with secretarial work.

Life in the Wrens is a bit of a culture shock for pretty Sheila Mills. First of all the 'diet is unbalanced … a lot of bread and potatoes … lunch, soup, stewed steak, beans and potatoes, rice, apples and prunes and weak coffee' and she asks for apples to be sent from home, where there is a glut, although she seems to enjoy a slap-up tea given half a chance (I counted no fewer than twenty-three mentions of 'having tea' in her first three months in Scotland). Scotland is 'the land of cakes. The shops are full of the most marvellous buns, scones etc – much more than iced, or cream cakes. I always buy something for tea,' although the 'cake shops aren't so good in Dundee as in Dunfermline, mediocre' even, with the exception of 'such nice cakes and scones' and 'marvellous hot pancakes with maple syrup', good for 'cold feet'. No wonder she put on weight!

Like all young girls she wants to look good and the delay in getting kitted out in uniform means she can wear mufti:

Today I've been wearing my red jumper, lipstick and nail varnish to match. Miss Overy [her boss] at once asked me when my uniform was coming. She doesn't like to have her Wrens looking at all glamorous … When I am in uniform life will be hell, tho! No lipstick or nail polish, hair cut short; even tho' it's very tidy now, and skirt to my ankles, and you're not even allowed to wear your hat at an angle. Oh, I'm thoroughly fed up with them all. Surely, if you're willing to serve your country they should let you look at attractive as possible?

She is highly amused by the rumour going round at Dundee that she is an ex-chorus girl and puts it down to her red jumper and lipstick.

There is a constant to-ing and fro-ing between her and her mother requesting clothes be sent, in particular evening dresses for the dances, and an ongoing saga over her beaver lamb fur coat (which I still have):

13.10

As I shall be in uniform soon, I don't suppose I shall want any more clothes. Though I'm getting rather tired of these, I'd better have my pink frock sometime tho' because if you go away for the night, or anything, you can change if you like.

17.10

I wonder if my pink frock is ready yet. <u>Please</u> let me know how much it is, and also my watch. You see, if Roddy [friend from home] comes up here, we might have parties, and I should be able to change to go to them. Do you think I'd better have an evening dress sent up? If so, which? Do you think I could get into my black? I do love it so, and it is still very smart. My blue is very pretty, but rather summery. I might need my fur coat then – I really think it ought to be out of London, but can't get R. to say anything about it.

18.10

Yes, I believe I'd better have an evening dress and coat, would you have my fur coat or evening coat if you were I? Some of the girls are going for a dance (dressed) tonight. I'd love to go dancing again.

29.10

About my evening frock – Joy and I have been discussing it and we came to the conclusion evening dresses don't date very much. No, I wouldn't like mauve feathers, they wouldn't go with the silver very well. I would like some clip-on black velvet straps, not very wide, and some more white flowers, I think. Yes, I agree about lace frocks, but why bother about buying another? This will do if it's let out a bit. Do you think the dressmaker can manage all right?

When the evening dress finally arrives the 'swine' of a dressmaker has removed the gardenia flowers, much to Sheila's annoyance: 'Yes, I'm rather disappointed about the frock – the flowers on the skirt were so sweet – can you get them back for me, please? I've tried it on and it doesn't look too bad, but not so nice as before'; she now knows what became of the missing lamé on another frock!

In wartime, because of clothes rationing there was a lot of mending and making do, so this obsession with repairing and altering clothes and sending them around the country is quite understandable. The pay in the Wrens was 18s a fortnight, 'which isn't bad really', rising to 23s or 24s as a Leading Wren, the rank below 3rd Officer. If you think that the cheapest pair of stockings – not silk – were 3/4d per pair, it must have been quite hard to make ends meet. The beaver lamb coat would have been an extremely expensive garment and it is little wonder that so much anxiety is attached to its whereabouts. Apart from anything else, Sheila must have worried about it going up in smoke in the London bombing:

30.10

About my fur coat – I'm not sure what to do. I wondered if you would have liked to borrow it, but now I hear I may not have my uniform for ages – they are very short here because the store has been bombed in Deptford. So I may need lots more clothes, as these are getting worn out, but I'll let you know as soon as I hear what is happening to me. I left quite a lot at St. Leonard's [Dunfermline], including my costume skirt, so it's lucky I've got these two navy ones. I exist on only two jumpers, a navy one and a pink one, which is miraculous for me. Stockings are indeed a problem, because all mine have gone at once, and I've only got two pairs left and can't get any more. So I'm having some of them mended ... I think I may need my pink frock, if it is finished. I can always pack things up in a box and send them to myself, if I get switched suddenly. I wonder if my nice brown American shoes would be useful. The only thing is I haven't got anything else brown. I don't know what to say. No, I think my new navy ones (which have been mended very well) will be enough.

———◆———

29.11

I've asked Rosemary to have my fur coat sent here. It's very cold and I need it to go out in, if and when I'm asked again! How shall I manage at Xmas I can't imagine!

———◆———

2.12

Rosemary had my fur coat sent up here last week, and it really is a great boon; it's so useful to have to slip on when dashing out in the evenings, and really it's got quite cold lately

———◆———

10.12

I can't believe it's Xmas time – I'm still running about in my little check jacket and shirt, though it has been very nasty, and I've been glad of my fur coat. No sign of uniform yet, thank heavens! I shall look a frump.

What with all this stodgy food, Sheila seems to be putting on weight (later letters reveal she was a buxom 11 stone!) and takes great offence to her uniform fitting sessions:

Mayfield
7/11

We were having kitting, of course, and had to tear in and out of clothes at the rate of about 10 a minute. Really, everyone did look funny. Joy and I nearly passed out with laughter. Everything was so big. I was given a WX suit to begin with, which annoyed me intensely.

The jacket's not bad, but I could nearly get into the skirt twice. Then everyone said 'that's just the size for you' and I nearly passed out. I was given 7 shoes, broad, when I have a narrow foot and a 15 shirt, but I jibbed at these, and also my hat – 7 1/4! I will <u>not</u> have these – but shall wait until the next issue. I did get some very thick Lisle stockings, 10 1/2, and some gloves. Which I'm hanging on to – but apart from the suit, nothing else – and, whilst all this chopping and changing was going on, my arm was hurting like hell [she had just had her inoculations]. It was all terribly funny – I haven't laughed so much for years. Working at an orphanage[1] and then dressed in navy from head to foot (I had a navy jumper on) and everything too big – I really looked like an orphan. The hats are terrible – so cheap looking …

I took my Wrens costume to be altered to Hector Powe – and now learn is will cost over £1! Isn't that dreadful? I'm sure I could have worn a smaller size and shall investigate. And, to crown all the A/C officer isn't paying more than 10/- for any alternations, but Miss Overy has let mine go through, luckily.

Stockings were in short supply during the war, and silks were particularly prized:

---

1 Wrens, as part of the Royal Navy, either worked on real ships, like HMS *Unicorn*, an old ship in Dundee dockyard, or in offices named after ships, like HMS *Ambrose*, which was in fact situated in an old orphanage.

28.10

There's a little puppy here belonging to a Dutch officer. He is very fond of tearing stockings and laddered 2 very fine pairs of Joy's. She was very annoyed and told the officer to keep the dog under control. He said he'd give her 2 more pairs, which he did, lovely Aristoc ones – black – and wanted her to go out and celebrate, but she pretended not to hear. Very amusing.

1.11

I'm terribly worried about stockings because you can't buy any here and mine are all dying fast.

7.11

About those stockings. I don't think I'd be allowed to wear them in black. The girls here are wearing fine cut silk ones which look very nice – if they have them in my size. I do like the ribbed ones though.

10.11

I bought some silk stockings yesterday. Not black, so don't think I shall need any more ordinary ones – just black as and when I can get hold of them. We have very nice fine cut SMK ones in shops here at 3/3*d* but only in 10's, and as they don't give like silk, I don't think they'd be much good for me. I may try a pair to see.

14.11

I haven't done anything about the stockings but have bought another pair of black silk. It's quite easy to get anything you want here in 10's. They have excellent stocks – so if you want any Mummy, let me know, but I don't think you can get anything under 5/11 now. I shall get some ribbed Lisle – they'd be nice to wear with my suit.

17.11

I've been buying up black stockings. I've got six pairs now, hope they last me out!

2.12

I'm simply furious; one of those nice pairs of stockings Rosemary gave me has disappeared. I thought I'd tracked it down, in fact I'm sure I have, but there's no evidence beyond the fact that I know that it's mine. The person in question was very clever about it and beyond saying I know it's mine and you're telling a lie, I can't very well get my stockings back. It's funny isn't it, that people like that always have eyes very close together? The infuriating part is that they were only 10 1/2 pair I had, all my others being 10's as no one seems to stock the big ones up here. I did her [Rosemary] a very good turn, I consider; I got Draffens to reserve her four pairs of Aristoc 258 stockings until she sent them a cheque. They are very difficult to get just now. I just can't get anything in 10 1/2 in black so expect I shall have to wear Lisle in the end. Artificial silk is all right, but unless they make them large enough I can't wear them.

13.12

Another thing, which will prove most useful – [Paul's] promised to get me all the stockings I need from Canada, so I won't have to be a plain Jane in lisle after all. Oh goody goody!

It is hard to imagine that a letter posted in the morning would sometimes arrive on the same evening, hence the habit of writing daily which give the letters a conversational stream-of-consciousness quality. One thing my grandmother was good at sending was parcels. She used to send me her famous Be-ro (a type of flour from Newcastle) fruit-cake to boarding school, completely forbidden, and we would have midnight feasts. It must have been immensely cheering for Sheila to have parcels from home at this rather bleak time:

St Leonards Hill, Dunfermline
9.10.40

My Dear Mummy,

I was terribly thrilled to have the parcel, and everyone was most inquisitive and jealous. The cake went down well (we had some last night) and the apples are just what I've been wanting – I adore chocolate fingers too! Now I can go skating which will be great fun; the rink is half ice and half dancing. Another great thrill was to have a letter from Paul. He's still working hard, and doesn't think there's much chance of having leave yet a while; however, it will be quite easy to come and see me if I am still here. So these two things cheered me up no end, and I felt very gay the whole afternoon and evening. But somehow getting up at 7 o'clock dims one's high spirits!

———•———

St Leonards Hill
Dunfermline Fife
11.10.40

My dear Mummy –

I don't know whether I thanked you for everything you sent me,
corselette etc. But here goes! I know I've asked for my slacks but I'm
wondering whether they are suitable for hockey and should I have my
navy blue shorts as well (if I can get into them) and my hockey pads.
Not stick also, as Ines has. I think I'd better send you some laundry
tomorrow, when Ines is free and can post it. I may not though because
we can send laundry to a place here.

It is extraordinary to think of sending washing home by post!

St Leonards Hill,
Dunfermline.
17-10-40

My dear Mummy –

Thank you very much for your two parcels and notes. The skirt I
wore this afternoon. I shall take the biscuits with me when I go on
early watch. As for the stockings, I don't wear any at all for hockey so
far, but anyway, they'll be useful to wear with uniform. I think that's
all but if I have left anything out, don't get worried – it's only my
bad memory.

Mayfield
Arbroath Road
Dundee
28.10.40

My dear Mummy,

I must now thank you properly for the parcel – the chocs are divine and Joy and I are having grand feasts. The towel came just in time – I'm wondering whether I ought to have another in case I'm here for some time. Miss Smith's successor is coming in tomorrow, and so Miss Smith will probably go with her. I wonder, then, what will become of me. There isn't a lot of typing, but it's all much more informal than at Rosyth.

Mayfield Hostel
Dundee
5.11.40

My dear Mummy.

Thank you for your letter and the parcel with the jacket – I was so thankful to get it as it's much colder here and I haven't much to wear. I've finished my cardigan, but haven't got it sewn up yet. We loved the chocolate – it was most welcome.

Mayfield
10.11.40

My dear Mummy,

Thank you so much for your letter enclosing the £1 and the parcel of clothes. I'm writing a separate little note to Daddy. No I won't wear the slacks for hockey – I wear my navy skirt which is just about right, tho' a little long. I suppose gym slips were given away ages ago. My lilac frock is marvellous – I INSIST on knowing how much she charges and also the black evening frock. Why should you pay for my things? Yes, my clothes are warm enough – we have central heating.

Mayfield
10.11.40

My dear Daddy –

Thank you so much for the £1 – as a matter of fact I was getting rather short as Cochrane II owe me 18/- and haven't sent it to me yet. It's nice to feel £1 in your pocket in case of jams!

Well, how's Durham these days and the 'A.R.P.' We've had a lot of bombs near here, just up the road to be exact, but they did very little damage. But they did hit a power station to the North of Dundee and did a lot of damage I believe. We sit tight in the cellar, and everything is most dull – I hate being below ground for fear of being buried, but Mayfield is a huge building and certainly wouldn't fall down like a pack of cards.

Apparently, unless there's lots of work to be done, I get Sunday and Saturday afternoon off each week, which is grand. We play hockey on Saturday afternoon, but everyone is terribly bad, I quite shine!

I'm looking forward to Xmas leave – whether I shall get it bang at Xmas I don't know – but shall get some, anyway, unless there's a major Wren crisis. I really think I'll have to rush it's 9:20 and service at 10 and I haven't even got up yet <u>and</u> I've got to go down to the house. So sorry this is so scrappy. I told Mummy all the real news I think.

Lots of love and thanks,

Sheila.

❖ ❖ ❖

Despite her reservations about the move to Dundee, she finds it 'very nice'. They are billeted at an enormous old house, Mayfield, and work in an old orphanage, known as HMS *Ambrose*. She lets slip, as a sort of by-the-by, that she did enrol despite her gloom at being a rating, and the long wait for a commission:

> ... very difficult because I am not 21 yet. I don't think for one moment they'll give me one before I'm 21 ... I think I'm resigned to staying in the Wrens now pretty well. I <u>do</u> wish I could get a commission – the people would be much nicer and I know I should enjoy it more. I don't mind being a rating at all if I thought I should get a commission eventually – it's the hopeless feeling of being a rating for ever that gets me down.

———

Mayfield Hostel,
Arbroath Road
Dundee.
21.10.40

My dear Mummy,

Here I am at Dundee and I'm liking it very much at the moment! I'm working for 2nd Officer Smith in the Drafting Office – she's very amusing: vague, friendly and going to be married shortly. The typewriter is appalling and consequently I have great wrestles with it. I arrived this morning in the pouring rain and got soaked. Mayfield is an <u>enormous</u> house – mansion really – there are very few Wrens here at present but there will be shortly. I'm sharing a large room with another girl, Joy Fisher, who is very sweet. She's feeling rather miserable. She's been here since Saturday, as a steward, because she wasn't qualified for anything else. Stewards work very hard – just housework actually. Joy is married to a film producer in London who has volunteered for the Navy. They have given up their flat off Sloane Square. We have had our supper, bathed and come straight to bed. The other girls are rather house-maidy – but we get very good food, and my room looks out on to the sea – the river I should say. I like Dundee, but don't really want to stay here as it's such a long way away. I may of course, be transferred here permanently.

On the other side of the house lots of Dutch officers are living (hush). Soon, however, they are going to be moved and English officers are going to be sent here.

Oh, I forgot to tell you, I've enrolled – rather unwillingly I'm ashamed to say. But I really couldn't get out of it. I don't know when I shall get my uniform, but I would like those shoes please, because all mine let the water in. I don't suppose I shall be kitted till I get back to Dunfermline.

We went to a concert last night which was rather fun – rotten really, but was amusing. There were lots of Poles there.

Please would you send me some bath towels and a face towel, because we have to have them here. Actually one of each might do, as I don't expect to be here very long. Of course, you never know tho'. But I've left half my clothes at Dunfermline.

I really must stop now. It's 10:20 and I've been in bed since 8:30. Joy wants to go to sleep I think. I may add more tomorrow if I've time.

Tons of Love

Sheila.

No time: off to work. Thank you for your letter. Will write tonight.

She and Joy become inseparable; it's fascinating that Joy, who is obviously middle class, is working as a steward, along with all the 'very young – domestic servant types – and rather rough'. Sheila is still hankering after people from a similar social background (her mother's upbringing beginning to show perhaps?):

I do wish we could meet people of our own kind whom we could visit or go out with. Life is so mundane and dull mixing with the servant class the whole time. Not that they aren't nice people – they are. But you get so tired of living with them and they scream about the place so.

Good company appears in the form of the Dutch naval officers referred to in Sheila's letter of 21 October, billeted in the other half of Mayfield House, and she seems content at last:

133 Ferry Road,
Carolina Port,
Dundee
30th October 1940

My dear Mummy,

I was pleased to get your two letters this morning … I had to rush off to work in the rain, and so didn't have time to read them. But now I have (not the enclosures, though) and so here is a quick answer, until Miss Smith arrives.

This is a very funny typewriter, so don't mind if my typing isn't all that can be desired. Apparently it was dropped when they brought it up from the base here and it hasn't been the same since.

Well, things look a little brighter. Joy and I decided we'd go skating on Sunday, so off we went. She had never been before, but proved very brave and got on terribly well. There were millions of people there; we thought if we went on a Sunday, it would not be so crowded, but it turned out to be cheap night. However, round we went. Joy saw one of her Dutch officers whom she valets, and he took her round. Then a little Pole helped her, and whilst this was going on, the Dutchman sailed up to me (metaphorically) and said could he take me round. So off we set in grand style, for Dutchmen are marvellous skaters. Soon it was time to go home, and so I found Joy and we put our things on. Just as we got to the door, however, the sirens went, and though a commissionaire put us on the road, he didn't tell us that the trams all stopped, and so back we went again. The first person we saw when we got there was our Dutchman. He was very sweet, and took us for a drink; lots of other Dutch officers appeared, and said they would get us a taxi home, as they live in Mayfield too. This, however, was impossible, so we went back to the rink. Everyone had disappeared, so we had the place to our-selves. We said that as soon as we put on our skates again the All Clear would go, and so we didn't bother. But after about an hour we decided to do so, and sure enough, off the All Clear went. But the Dutchman and I went on and had a marvellous time. We were the only people on the ice, on this enormous rink, and it was grand. He could do all sorts of tricks, but I could only just go round, and backwards, but I felt terribly courageous and did all sorts of things. Eventually the taxi arrived and off we went home. It was frightfully funny when we got to Mayfield, because we went to the back door, it being nearly 12, and we had not got a late pass to 11. We tiptoed in, bursting with laughter, and hurriedly bid each other good night. When we got to the Wren side of the house, who should we see but Robinson, an elderly steward, who had had to come in a taxi from Oxford Street, 7/6d. This was terribly funny, and we all accused her of being drunk. All she could say was 'it was only cheese' and we nearly split our sides. Chapman was there too, for she has to be up till the last people come in. Poor Robinson, it was a great shame really. Mother's ruin was what we put it down to. Luckily there were no warnings in the night.

Yesterday I had great fun. Joy and I went into Dundee at lunch time as we usually do, for it makes a good change. In the afternoon Miss Smith was interviewing prospective Wrens, and I had to take them down to the Surgeon Lieutenant for medical examination, and stay there and chaperone them. There were three of them, and it took a whole afternoon. When eventually I finished work, I rushed out, posted some letters, and then met my Dutchman coming home on his bicycle. We walked up the drive and he asked me to go to the pictures with him on Thursday, when he said he would meet me at the front door in a taxi, as it wouldn't be seeming to appear in the Officers' quarters, somehow. When I got in I remembered it was Miss Smith's party and had to write him a note telling him I couldn't go. Then I went to help Joy with the blackout, for she'd hurt her leg playing hockey. There are lots and lots of awfully nice Dutch officers, and I saw my friend, who was playing the violin marvellously. The other officer who was at the skating rink and who came home with us was a Baron, though he didn't look it!

... In the evening I promised to go shopping for Chapman and Joy, so out I went into the pitch black. Unfortunately I took the wrong turning, and went miles down the opposite way of the road. Eventually I found the shop and made great pals with the little man in it. I've ordered myself a Telegraph – we haven't a wireless, and there's never one in the shops here.

... I'm sorry I haven't had time to write so much lately, but really life is one long rush. I get up at twenty to eight, have breakfast at eight, and finish about twenty past. Then I have to bolt upstairs and make my bed, brush my clothes, and then dash off to work. The Orphanage is quite near, but I have to go down a very long drive, over the lawns down a short cut to get to it, and be at work at nine. If I'm lucky I can then rush off a note on the typewriter, but have to work till 12, when I dash off for lunch. If it's a nice day, I try and get out, either for a walk, or into Dundee to look around the shops. They really are very good, but I can't manage to get my stockings at all – apparently the chances of getting into mufti here are very good. So I shall need all the light stockings I can get hold of. Then back to work at 1:30 till five or six, it depends on the work, after which we have supper at 6:30. Then I either go to bed, iron, write letters, or read a little, but generally straight to bed, for after all this I'm quite worn out! Sometimes we go to the pictures, and skating of course, which I love, and am getting very keen. I think I'll have some lessons to get my style better and then learn to dance. I'll try and get my Dutch officer to learn to dance too, for he's very good and should pick it up easily, and then we could go together, which would be fun. He is very tall, fair, nice blue eyes, and pleasant looking, though not terribly handsome; such nice manners too. No don't worry, he's not cutting out Paul, though I haven't heard from the latter for ages, and am rather worried. I knew where his ship was when I came here, but haven't been able to ascertain anything since I arrived. I should be furious if he arrived at Rosyth all of a sudden and found I was not there. They are goophs at St. Leonard's, they'd probably say they had never heard of me. I'd hate Paul to be set loose amongst those voracious Wrens – they'd do anything!

I do wish I knew whether I am going to stay here or not; I really want to now, because when I think of Dunfermline and all those horrible girls, and the quarters, I'd much rather be here; besides, there is much more doing here, and more chance of promotion, I think. I have to do all kinds of things, it isn't just a secretarial job; you never know what is going to appear next, which is exactly what I like. The only things is that I'm afraid the secretarial work is rather limited, and they may not need a secretary, though they could always find other work for me to do as well, I'm sure.

Tomorrow I am going to play hockey – Miss Smith has promised me. They aren't very good here, so perhaps with my long ago experience, I may be able to do something for a change. I see they are short of left wings, which is my usual place, and the most difficult side, so I ought to be lucky. We are provided with sticks.

About my evening frock, once more! Please, I like it, and everyone young who has seen it has loved it too, and said it suited me very well, and wasn't a bit old. I don't want it altered really – black suits me anyway. But I don't suppose there will be many dances here ...

I didn't realise I'd written so much – so I think I'd better not waste a whole sheet. Please give my love to all those who send love to me ...

... Apparently Rosemary has been having a super time in London with Tim and half the Air Force. I'm glad – it's good for her to get out and enjoy herself once in a while! [this, I think, is heavily sarcastic]

Must fly now,

Lots of Love,

Sheila

Mayfield Hostel
Arbroath Road
Dundee
1.11.40

My dear Mummy

Thank you for your note. This will only be a short one too as I have to be back at work shortly.

Yesterday Miss Smith gave a farewell party to all the Wrens at Mayfield. It really was great fun and we all enjoyed it immensely. There were about 80/90 people there. We danced, played games, and ate and ate, and really made merry. I met a girl I used to know at Rosyth who's up at the Unicorn as C.P.O. [Chief Petty Officer]. She's rather nice, and we are going to the flicks next week. The party lasted till about 10.30 and then we had to clean up. There were apple cores all over the place – we'd had community singing, which was most rowdy, and when we danced you couldn't possibly hear the gramophone. Miss Smith made a farewell speech – very nicely and we all gave her a present, a rather lovely pig skin jewel case, which she seemed to like. In her confusion she forgot to introduce Miss Overy, but most people know her so it's all right.

I really think I'm being drafted here which I shall like. Apparently the Chief Officer fixed up about me on Sunday when she came over. Miss Overy is rather nice, a little abrupt but I expect that's because she's shy. I shan't be getting any uniform for ages I expect so may need some more clothes. I'd like my little check jacket (blue) to wear with an odd shirt and my tartan skirt if it can be shortened. It seems dreadful having all these clothes but uniform is so short. (scarce!) I'm terribly worried about stockings because you can't buy any here and mine are all dying fast.

Tonight I'm going out to the flicks with my Dutch officer. He wrote me a dear little note which he gave to the Baron to give to Joy to give to me. Joy had been taken off the Baron's room and met him running round the corridors flicking the note about terribly worried in case he should miss her. I'm being met at the main door in a taxi.

We had squad drill yesterday: several Dutchmen were playing golf which made things perilous. Then it poured with rain and we all got soaked. This afternoon I'm going to play in a hockey practice. There's a match tomorrow, and if I play well, I may play.

Joy has been given this weekend off and so we are planning to go across the ferry to Newport on Sunday afternoon. They say it's a lovely place and very good for walking. We think we'll go to Tay Port, get a motor boat ferry back to Broughty Ferry and then home. It should be rather fun I think.

I've been working very hard lately ...

I really shall have to fly now. Otherwise I'll be late for work. Which would be bad. Please write soon.

Lots and lots of love to you and Daddy

Sheila

Air raids seem to have been a common occurrence and someone was killed nearby as a result of a huge bomb:

In the middle of the night – 3.30 to be exact, we had an air raid warning. We went down to the cellar and discovered a bed put there for Red Cross purposes. This we bagged and fitted together like spoons, were fairly comfortable. I might have gone to sleep, only all the other Wrens, hearty as they are, would sing very loudly, so you can imagine how ghastly it was! We were there for two hours.

This bed becomes a habit, and they end up managing to sleep 'end to end'. Joy's Dutchman, Welter, gives them chocolates to munch in the darkness. Nevertheless, she is afraid: 'I hate being below ground for fear of being buried, but Mayfield is a huge building and certainly wouldn't fall down like a pack of cards.' One such air raid almost spoiled Sheila's date with her Dutch officer:

Mayfield Hostel,
Arbroath Road,
Dundee
3.11.40

My dear Mummy –

… did I tell you about going out with the Dutchman with an unpro-
nounceable name? Just as I was getting ready, the sirens went so downstairs
I tripped with all the rest. 3/4 hr later a head peered round the door and
I realised the Dutchman had been waiting all the while, plus taxi, expecting me still to appear. So I dashed out, with guns nattering and bombs
dropping, and we went to the pictures. When I got back Chapman had
been rather worried because no one had any idea of where I was. It never
occurred to me that they were all sitting in the cellar thinking my last hour
had come! He's going off on patrol tomorrow, hope everything is all right.

Yesterday I was to have played in a hockey match. In fact we drove
off in fine style in a Naval lorry, but it came on to pour with rain.
The other side, however, insisted on playing, and we got soaked to the
skin – literally. We only played half-time, but I had to take my skirt
and jumper off and come home in undies and a coat I was so wet.
My clothes aren't properly dry yet! We felt so miserable that Joy and
Chapman and I went into town and had an enormous high tea!

This morning Joy and I were both free so we took a bus to Broughty
Ferry and walked on the beach. We went in some forbidden part and
had soldiers chasing us off! In the afternoon we collected another
Wren, Eleanor Sherwen, whose father is a vicar in Cumberland and
knows the Harris's [where Sheila's mother was governess], and went
across the ferry to Newport. It's a sweet little place, and the country is
very pretty. Joy's leg is still very painful, so she couldn't walk far and I
had a horrid cold, so we didn't stay long, but came back to Dundee and
had tea. When we got back to Mayfield we saw a new moon, which we
bowed to; I went barging into the middle of a service the Wrens were
having – the old parson looked so astonished. It's been a lovely day –
but cold. I even wore my long-legged pants, and liked them!

Nothing much happened here of late except that it has got very cold and all my warm clothes are at Dunfermline. I shall send for them tomorrow. I had a letter from Lena, who says she will send me some pears which would be lovely. The food here is <u>excellent</u> – lots of variety and very well cooked.

Joy and I have made up our minds not to be dull, so we are going to the Palais, skating and cinemas as much as we can. We want to try and meet some nice people and have lots of fun. Otherwise things might get us down. We are having lots more English officers here, but they all seem to be terribly snobbish about Wrens. Which is more than the Dutch are: they are very sweet really and I feel very sorry for them.

Miss Smith goes tomorrow and Miss Overy and I take charge. She doesn't know a lot, and nor do I, but if I try hard I may be able to make a good impression. I'm just longing for gold buttons! and proportionate increase in pay!!

I've nearly finished my navy cardigan – I never seem to get much time these days. Any evening we don't do anything we go straight to bed.

No more now – for I must now do some knitting.

Tons of love

Sheila

Welter, who is Joy's 'admirer', is:

[the] queerest of men – he <u>insisted</u> on buying her a complete set of Elizabeth Arden face things, and when she protested said 'I will do what I like, don't try to change me'. He knows she's married, but still insists on showering gifts upon her. He even wanted to buy her a new pair of shoes because he didn't like the ones she wears. But Joy stuck at that. We've certainly had a good laugh out of poor Welter – he writes the most amusing letters, but doesn't mean them to be funny of course. We feel so sorry for these Dutchmen – it must be dreadful to be away from home and friends and not even knowing where they are, or whether they are safe.

The only remaining photo of Sheila's first serious boyfriend, Dutchman Jaap Drijfhout van Hooff

Sheila's beau is a submarine officer, 'Jacob (not Jewish) but is short-ened to Jaap (Yarp)' Drijfhout, who is musical and dances – and skates – 'extremely well'. He is often on patrol, and Sheila worries about his safe return as German U-boats are patrolling the North Sea. For Christmas 1940 he gave her 'a lovely original etching of 3 Scotties [dogs] and I have it on my dressing table'. I still have this etching today.

So life settles into a routine of girliness, work, hockey, little excursions, the 'flicks', tea and going out with the Dutchmen:

Dundee
17.10

… Up at the crack of dawn again today for work at 7. This afternoon as I told you, we went to play hockey against the crew of a ship in harbour. And we had great fun. I really wasn't too bad as I hadn't played for years. Then we went down to the dockyard and boarded a drifter which took us to the ship for tea. This was terrific fun, but sad to say I only had French knickers on, so had to be terribly careful! When walking up and down ladders I sandwiched myself between two knowing Wrens, so hope all was ok. We had tea with the team and a marvellous one it was too. There was a friendly coxswain who was most amusing. And we thoroughly enjoyed ourselves. I've never seen such a spread since I came up here. Well, we demolished a good part of it, and then were shown round the ship – I can't tell you what it was for obvious reasons, but it was very remarkable. We went into the galley, the crew's quarters, captain's quarters, quarterdeck, bridge, boiler rooms and everywhere and had a very jolly time. The men were so nice and friendly, and are going to ask us over again if possible, to dance and play pingpong. We then sailed back on the drifter. The cox-swain was terribly funny. He insisted on calling 'all Wrens muster on deck' all over the ship or blowing a whistle because he said he'd never shouted for Wrens before.

H.M.S. Ambrose
133 Ferry Road
Caroline Port
Dundee
25.10

Joy and I spend most of our spare time in our room, which is very large. We keep a supply of biscuits which are kept crisp by putting them on the radiator. Grand idea! A girl has just come in and brought me my tea, it's only twenty to three, but I dare say I'll like it – it's rather fun really, sitting here, and making out passes and shoe cleaning vouchers, and having people coming to ask.

... I tried on a Wren hat this morning and looked pretty terrible. McRobbie wears a jack tar's hat – the little round affair – and it looks so nice. I tried hers on and it looked awfully nice. I do wish all Wrens were allowed to wear them – but I expect they're too skittish.

Tonight I'm going to see 'Gone with the Wind' which is on up here. I've got to have a special pass to go, because it doesn't end till past 11 and we're supposed to be in at 10! Terrible isn't it? And only 2 late passes a week. I'd rather like to live in approved lodgings because you can be in when you please, and even get out of uniform when off duty. That would be much nicer.

Mayfield
7.11.40

Joy and I are going to give ourselves egg packs tonight. Joy went down to the kitchen to get the eggs, and met Welter, who at once twigged, so he asked for the eggs to be put on his mess bill, and so we've got two lovely brown ones for the pack. Rather a waste these days, really we get plenty of eggs really, boiled and scrambled for breakfast, but never butter, always margarine. Will have to go into the bathroom for the packs – the new girl would just pass out if she saw us!

H.M.S Ambrose
18.12.40

We have started having dancing lessons at Mayfield: some girl has kindly offered to teach the Wrens and we had our first lesson last night, and I relearnt the waltz and the foxtrot! Also some Scottish country dancing which was rather fun. So when I went out with Jaap and we went to the Palais, I was well practised. It was rather amusing; he thought I'd be most annoyed at the suggestion, but I'd always had a hankering to see what the Palais was like, and was pleased to go. He dances very well indeed. Extremely well.

———

Also 18.12

Have been terribly busy lately, hence scarcity of mail. Went out with Jaap last night. Last time for 2 weeks I'm afraid. He's nice. We wined and dined and went to the Palais! Good band and floor.

Spent all Saturday with Elizabeth [Clayhill] and Uncle Charles who were so nice. I'm meeting E. tonight. She's going to try and find a nice family to take me in as p.g. when I have to leave Mayfield. There are nearly 100 N.O.s [Naval Officers] here at the moment. Oh boy!!

———

Mayfield Hostel
Arbroath Road
Dundee
20.12

On Wednesday I went to see 'It's a Date' with Deanna Durbin and Elizabeth came too. She's been very kind and written off to the Bishop's wife about me and also to some people called Pilcher who do a great deal of entertaining in Dundee, especially the Dutch officers, and asked them to look me up whilst she's away. Also a Lady Wedderburn Ogilvy who lives at Alyth is going to ask me out for a whole day later on. People are most kind if they all remember me!

I've sent Elizabeth a big box of Morny bath powder – French Fern – and hope she likes it. She won't be back until the middle of January. I'm trying to arrange for us to go to our dance together in a party. Jaap says he'd love to come if he's not on patrol and so he might be able to find a friend to go with Elizabeth.

Life also improves on the work front, although she finds working for Miss Overy rather a trial:

Miss Overy and I sit opposite each other, firing questions and getting into terrible muddles, but things seems to work out all right in the end. We neither of us know a lot, but at present, I think I take the cake! McRobbie [their predecessor] came over the other day, very disgruntled because she's been ordered to wear an ordinary hat, and not her little sailor's cap. She asked me how we were getting on 'oh, going from mess to mess, you know'. She was furious. 'We thought we left everything in perfect order' she said. If she only knew – we find out 3 or 4 mistakes of theirs everyday.

Miss Overy seems to be looking out for Sheila, asking when she will be 21: 'I wonder if this means a commission in view?' More importantly she gives Sheila her first taste of working for the navy proper, on board a battleship:

Great thrill: I'm to be the writer to go on board the ship that put in here requiring someone to do secretarial work … Miss Overy daren't send me full time in case I was withdrawn by Rosyth on the grounds that I haven't enough work to do … So I'm to go down in the afternoon from 2–5, as they need me. It will be tremendous fun working on board a real ship – especially one I've heard about. I wonder when I'll start. I shall be furious if they suddenly find they can manage without a writer – it would be just my luck!

This experience is to inspire her for the rest of her naval career:

Mayfield
18.11.40

Dear Mummy –

I've had such a good day I must write and tell you about it – but one long rush as usual I'm afraid. I got to work this morning to find the ship wanted me this afternoon. Great thrill. So after lunch I dashed down to Unicorn to be told where to go. Unicorn is a very old ship, like the Victory, the other naval establishment here. It's marvellous on board old beams and what not – I'd love to work there. Everyone was so nice to me – even the Sub-Lieutenant who gave me my pass and sub-Lieuts are often so hoity-toity. So I rushed off to the decks with my pass to go on board. One of the Dutch submarines was in – I hope it's the one my Dutchman is on. However to return to the B.S. (the ship!). It had been struck by a sound mine and very badly damaged, so has been brought here for repairs. Everyone was expecting me and an office had been rigged up in the Wardroom. I had to run up and down companion ways so was glad I'd got on my passion-killers! An awfully nice Warrant Officer was in charge when I arrived – a dear little man, and so helpful – tho' hopeless seated at the typewriter! Then there was an awfully nice rating, definitely public school etc. who was a great help. So between us we got some work done. Apparently a sentry had accidentally shot another one, and there's been a hell of a row about it and its made much work for them all. Commander Anderson, the Captain, came in and was so nice. He apologised for the state of the ship, as it really is in rather a mess, but I didn't mind. Apparently he was a very leading light at Dunkirk, but no notice was taken of him at all. I may have to do my work on Unicorn later on, as he think's it's too cold for me on board, but I hope not. The B.S. was in an amazing state – she's only 9 months old, and everything was absolutely of the latest type. The mine had cracked the iron (or steel) castings and buckled them in places, so that it will have to be almost entirely reconstructed. Five men were hurt, 4 with broken ankles and one badly scalded as he was making a cup of tea. You'd like it on board mummy, for they use

nothing but tinned milk and brown sugar … I love it. My nice little
W/O was struck over the eye – next time I go he's going to take me
to see the engines, but really the whole ship's in such a mess. I do wish
Wrens were allowed on board on patrol – it would be marvellous and
would cheer up both parties. I can't get over how polite and nice everyone was – after six weeks in the Wrens I've got used to being treated
as a rating. The whole atmosphere was so nice – the officers and men
got on so well and there was no sort of 'barrier'. Of course, it's only
a little ship, really – so I suppose it makes a difference. But she's very
important and did a lot of good work at Norway in April. I shall be
dreadfully sorry when their writer comes back. Oh how I wish I could
be a sailor and go aboard on patrol – it would be so much nicer than
being ashore. I do think they ought to have Wrens aboard. Still, I'm
really very lucky, for lots of Wrens have never even been inside a ship.
The Unicorn people were very jealous. I've hardly told a soul here – it
might create a bad feeling. I believe I'm going again on Wednesday,
but don't know yet. Miss Overy may not want to spare me.
…We are busy kitting at the moment – my second suit is going to be
a size smaller! I insisted! I may not get all my kit by Christmas tho' as
the demand hasn't been put through yet.

Please don't tell people about this ship, and why it is here etc. It
doesn't matter saying I'm working on board, but please don't tell
anyone anything else as you never know! I don't really think I've said
anything I ought not to, but you can't be too careful.

Lots of love

Sheila.

But it's not all good news; just as Sheila was beginning to settle down,
Miss Overy drops a bombshell and says that Joy is being transferred
to Deptford as a telephonist, the reason being that:

> … as a messenger she's too much in the public eye and officers notice her
> and stare at her. Joy was furious, especially when Miss Overy said that

she'd watched her and found her manners perfect and that she could find no fault at all with Joy. 'But' she said 'you must be hidden. You can't help being attractive – it's not your fault so we're transferring you as a telephonist to Devonport'. Have you ever heard of anything so horrid? We think that the Wrens Officers are jealous of anyone good looking being about the place and have kicked up a fuss. Joy's so upset, especially as she's tried so hard, and been through an awful lot – steward's work is terribly wearing, especially if you haven't been used to such things.

Luckily Sheila has Jaap and her new 'posh' friend, Elizabeth Clayhill.

At the same time, the downsides of communal living become apparent: things start to disappear; in addition to Sheila's stockings, Joy lost some 'camminicks and 2/6. Also, soap flakes disappear like magic. We are all very annoyed.' This gave rise to a reprimand from Sheila's mother.

It is hard to believe that her mother was complaining about Sheila never writing, as Sheila wrote every other day; it's a shame that Sheila never kept her mother's letters, despite the exhortation to 'keep my letters you'll get a complete picture of life in the Wrens. They're much better than my diary, as I'm generally too tired to write much.' They would have revealed much about their spiky relationship, which Sheila's letters skate over unless, as on this occasion, she is pushed too far:

Naval Quarters,
133 Ferry Road,
Carolina Port,
Dundee
10.12.40

My dear Mummy,

I was pleased to get your letter last night, but really I think you are very hard on me. The last twice you've written it's been nothing but complaints about me – how careless I am with my things and that I never write. I'm only able to write now because Miss Overy is away

today. I start work at 9 in the morning, and have lunch at 12. Unless I
get out during my lunch hour I never get any fresh air at all, so I can't
write then. I work from 1.20 till 5.30 or 6, and we have supper at 6.30,
which finishes at about 6.45 if we're lucky. Then I can write letters,
but not every night – so you see my time's very much taken up, tho' I
always manage to write at weekends don't I? As for being careless with
my clothes, I'm very careful indeed and try and mark everything. But
I can't vouch for other people's dishonesty can I?

And to her father, rather more measured, as she knows he will sym-
pathise with her for getting a ticking off:

I've just had Mummy's letter of admonition – but it's quite uncalled
for, you know! Naturally I'm very careful about all my clothes and
keep all precious things away in my suitcase, but where there's a will,
there's a way, and anyone can break into a case. Walton, one of the
girls in my room, was quite indignant at the insinuation that I was
careless and threatened to write to Mummy telling her how careful I
am! Nothing else has gone – so far!

There were other drawbacks to life in a dormitory, but luckily Sheila
maintains a sense of humour on this one:

Mayfield
14.11.40

My dear Mummy and Daddy –

…Well today has been 'a day!' To begin with, 2 girls found visitors in
their hair, and so we all had to be inspected by the Surg. Lieutenant.
Joy and I were ok – apparently I'm not the type that has 'nits' or my
hair isn't, so the Dr. said. But 5 girls have to be disinfected – one, the
'bearer' is my next door neighbour at table, and a dirty looking girl, so
I'm not surprised. She is the originator – does this make you tickle? I
itch all over even tho' I haven't any!

Then I had to take a girl down to be medically examined – quite a stranger, not one of us, and she had them too, so it was a horrid tickley day. Miss Overy and I have been sitting scratching ever since. Still – it's nice to know the bugs don't like you isn't it?

Lots of love

Sheila.

Even after a few months there are early signs that Sheila is headed for promotion. First of all, over Christmas, she has to 'hold the fort' at the Wren office when Miss Overy takes ten days' leave, something she is justifiably nervous about. As it is Christmas there are several parties to organise and she is:

Frantically busy … I do hope nothing drastic happens in her absence. Today I've been coping with hospitality for Wrens and believe me it's a very difficult task. Phone call after phone call keeps coming through, letter after letter and I've been nearly upside down! There's a supper concert and dance on Tuesday – also on Thursday. We've been invited to a lunch on Boxing Day and we are having a party ourselves on Xmas Day, with a tree and presents. The WVS have given presents for every Wren here; isn't it wonderful? Then we are having a concert on New Years Day and one dance on the 24th. I wish I didn't have to cope so much – it wears me out, what with leave, tickets, ration cards etc. Dreadful!

As a result of her efficiency she is voted on as Secretary to the Wrens Club committee, which was formed just before Christmas. She says she won't have time 'what with typing out minutes and what not', but somehow she is appointed. They are to organise a 'swish' dance in the New Year, and a concert, at which she is to sing with another girl - 'Heaven help the Wrens! I only hope I don't get stage fright and fade out.' There is a bit of a to-do over the dance, as she wants the tickets to be 5*s* 'to make it a bit more select' – but it's 'no good' and she loses out to 3*s* 6*d*. They also arrange talks from the naval commanders on station.

Christmas 1940 was the first of many war Christmases spent with fellow
Wrens, and it was a jolly affair. Sheila tells how she and the captain's
secretary opened one of the WVS's gifts to see what was inside – 'soap
and sweets' – and how 'furious' he was as they 'smelt [sic] out his office':

Mayfield
25.12.40

My dear Ma and Pa

Thank you very much for your wire and also for the parcel of things
that arrived today. I hope you had a <u>very</u> good Xmas – as good as I have
had. I rose at 7.30 and went to church, then came back for breakfast
and then went to church again. After that, work not very much but just
enough to keep me busy. Then the phone went asking Miss Mills to go to
the Capt's secretary's office immediately. I dashed down in trepidation
to be seized by Steve and heartily embraced under the mistletoe – there
were 3 Sub-Lieuts. They're all very amused. Pat and Marjory had done
the same too and then another Sub-Lieut Simmons, who thought I was
a chorus girl (!) dragged me there too – oh it was funny! Then I slid
down the bannisters to celebrate and got stuck, we <u>did</u> laugh.

We've had a marvellous party today. Much too much to eat and I'm
going out to my 2nd Xmas dinner tonight with Pat Whittons. Now must
away there! Everyone got 2 presents off the tree, very good I thought.

Going out tomorrow, Friday and Saturday to various troop dances
- <u>HOPE</u> to go to Ambrose dance on N.Y. Eve.

Tons of love

Sheila

Harry sent me 2 pairs of lovely silk stockings

After Christmas Sheila is allowed a weekend off: Elizabeth has arranged for her and another girl to go and stay with a Scottish Minister and his wife at Arbroath, where they have breakfast in bed – 'a great luxury'.

On New Year's Eve she is looking forward to going to HMS *Ambrose* (where she works, along with HMS *Unicorn*) big dance with a party of naval people; Jaap is coming back from leave, and there is rumour of an 'important visit and I imagine it is the King and Queen, but of course no one will tell you anything. Must remember to give my shoes a polish and yank my hair up. What fun; hope they come round *Ambrose*, if it is them!'

Most of all she is looking forward to her leave, and the possibility of meeting up with Paul, even though she is seeing Jaap – 'Don't know about leave yet but may land myself in soup as Jaap may have leave in Jan and want to come and Paul may be here too! Would you mind a cosmopolitan household? But the navy's very unreliable so you never know – just warning you tho!'

Paul who, despite intermittent correspondence as he is on a ship, seems to be a bit of a hero: 'Apparently, his ship was one that stopped a non-British merchant vessel taking goods to Germany at the beginning of November, and Paul was the second of the two officers who went on board. I'm dying to hear all about it.'

She is still champing at the bit to get a commission, but at least she seems more settled, and manages to get an end-of-year dig in at her sister: 'I had a letter from Rosemary today. I think she ought to join up, don't you? It would be dreadful to be called up.' Despite the ups and downs of the first three months in the Wrens, she has the satisfaction of being able to look down on her older sister from the moral high ground.

1941

'It would be marvellous to feel one was doing something'

1941 was to be a bad year for the British army. The war in the desert hotted up with the arrival of Rommel and the Afrika Korps, followed by the invasions and subsequent losses of Greece and Crete, and the surrender of Yugoslavia. By August, Russia had joined the war and, by December, so had the US, following the bombing of Pearl Harbour.

It must have been frustrating for Sheila to be part of the war machine but to feel so helpless. She has not even received her uniform yet! She is unhappy about the lack of any clear pathway to a commission – aside from attaining the age of 21 – a theme that recurs constantly through the coming year.

Dundee, where she moved in October, is pleasant enough, and she has her Dutchman for company, plus boyfriend Paul, who is on convoy duty aboard HMS *Sheffield*. Nevertheless she is hankering for adventure and begins to show leadership qualities that will stand her in good stead when the time comes for promotions.

Letters – and sometimes the lack of them – continue to be central to her life.

The new year starts well with the New Year's Eve party (it seems Jaap didn't make it in time) and home leave to look forward to, despite a spat with sister Rosemary. This must have been after she wrote the friendly New Year's Day letter, although Rosemary's Christmas present is dammed with faint praise:

Mayfield
1.1.41

My dear R.

Many many thanks for the lovely sweater and also for the stockings which shouldn't excite the roving eye of the Navy too much. So sorry not to have written before; believe me I've been up to my eyes in work.

Thank you also for your note – I had EIGHT letters that day! One of them was from Walter Frisler, a nice Canadian Capt. we met at the O.S. who wrote to me. Remember, a tan face and good looking. Also one from Elizabeth Clayhill's uncle, signed 'Charles'. He's 74! Most improper.

Well – so glad you had a great Xmas. I ate much too much, in fact had about 5 Xmas dinners to be exact! I got up at 8 and went to Kirk and then again at 9.20. Then I went to work, only to be caught under the mistletoe by 2 Sub-Lieuts! Most annoying. Then a huge dinner; then a huge party, Xmas tree and presents given by the Capt and wife, then tea, then dancing reels etc. and then out to supper! I staggered home.

Meanwhile we had to arrange various invitations for the Wrens, one, sometimes 2 every day. I went to one dance and won a spot prize with the Chief Writer based at the Base.

I went to Arbroath for the weekend and stayed in a house. They were so kind. C of S [Church of Scotland] and we had breakfast in bed and a grand time. That night *Ambrose* gave a N. Year's Ball (officers only) and I went in a party with Steer and 5 or 6 other officers. It was fun, we drank the N Year in with rum punch. Lovely. I wore my black and I let it out and put stiff lace (Woolworths!) round the top and everyone admired it! Steer was rather a stick, but we had a grand time. One of the Sub-Lieuts got very tight. Most amusing.

Woke up this am to find snow on the ground, very hard and crackly. Simply lovely. I've been working all day. We had a 5 min siren at 1.30 but nothing happened.

Jaap came back at lunch time and has asked me out to dinner tomorrow night. He gave me an adorable etching of 3 Scotties (original) + it stands on my dressing table. Chapman has been most curious.

Am furious, why am I not just a little older. Miss Overy is sending up names for commissions and said if I had been old enough she would have sent mine. Nine b-y months to wait! My work is terribly responsible in a way. Wish they'd give me Wrens buttons of a sort. I've got to M.C. a Whist Drive tonight as everyone is going to be out. I don't believe anyone will be there much tho'.

All the shops are shut today and tomorrow. Pay day on Friday, thank heavens. The uniform has arrived so shall appear in it when on leave, but haven't got it yet. Don't know when I'm coming, haven't heard a word from Paul, but Miss O. says I can have it when I like under the circs, which is good, I think.

Am expecting to be told to have my hair cut soon. It really does (ahem) look awfully nice now – long page boy sometimes tied in a bow, but I don't think Penman will have much mercy on it!

We have to be inspected before we're allowed to appear in the street.

… Please, if you will, send this letter on to Mama, as I've been so busy lately and haven't had much time to write.

Really must away to this whist drive.

Heaps of love

Sheila,

Hope you are safe and OK.

Mayfield
3.1.41

My Dear Mummy,

… No time for a proper letter as I only have 10 mins. About this leave. R. says she is coming from the 9th to the 18th but I had such a rude postcard from her yesterday I don't feel at all inclined to come whilst she is there at all! Miss Overy says I can go whenever I like now. I could come from the 9th or part of the following week, but then I should miss Paul, whom I haven't heard from since. In fact I'm wondering whether it is worth while waiting as the Navy is so unsure, but in a way it seems a pity to miss him after so long. I went out with Jaap last night, who is going on leave on Friday (today I think) and seemed disappointed because I wasn't going on leave, for it's a shame. I don't think he has anywhere to go and is so nice. I'll probably ring up on Sunday night when you will have got this and we can have a discussion. The mails are very bad as regards ships, but I rather feel that Paul may soon be here as I haven't heard for about 3 weeks. We shall see …

Heaps of love

Sheila

Had 8 letters on Monday!

The next letter is dated 22 January, so we assume she went on leave as planned around 9 January; history doesn't relate the whereabouts of sister Rosemary. On her return she is rushed into preparations for the Wrens' Club dance, which she is organising – 'tons to do' – and to the welcome arrival of her uniform, although her hair is problematic:

I've really got quite a nice hat – smallish but my raincoat nearly touches the ground – shows up the shortness of my costume skirt. We measured it last night – it's 18" – so I expect someone will have something to say about it! I spent ages putting on my collar and tie and ruined one collar, and expect I'll have to be inspected tonight ready for wear tomorrow. The Chief Officer Rosyth is inspecting us on Friday when she comes to the dance – so it's just as well I've got my uniform … Heaven knows what I'm going to do with my hair. It seems to be getting longer and longer and I look terrible in a hat with it tied back –

... everyone seems to think I look quite nice – except for the hat! The shoes are terribly uncomfortable, but are beginning to look a little better now. By the way, I'd love another shirt size 14 or 14 1/2 (my linen ones are 14 1/2 but I thought perhaps 14 man's size would be big enough) as you said you'd like to get me one? They have only given me three, and I really need four I think. Anyway, I'd be absolutely pleased with one. My collars are too big, I think, but am told they shrink.

26.1

... I've not had my hair cut – it's in a net and looking quite tidy. I will not have it cut and have been OK so far, but got told quite a thick pair of silk stockings were too thin! I was very annoyed.

This is tempered by the unwelcome news that Jaap is off on patrol again and her one remaining friend, Chapman – who never seems to have a first name, perhaps because she was the Chief Petty Officer – is being commissioned shortly 'so there won't be anyone for me to talk to at all'.

However the dance was a 'great success' and she thanks her mother for sending her the 'frock, which everyone admired. I really must send a parcel of civvies home soon, I've got many too many clothes':

Mayfield Hostel
26.1.41

My dear Mummy –

... Several of us went there early to see that things were OK – there were tons of people there – really too crowded – and many too many Wrens of course. I met several Polish officers who were quite nice, but as soon as I was getting on nicely Miss Overy came to ask me to do things which was annoying. My mainstay, however, was Lt-Com Cowell, the senior engineer, whom I'd met at the Pilchers. He rescued me and was most amusing. About half my size incidentally! In the end I arranged for him and Osborne (Guns; a darling old 62 year old fellow) to come home in our bus to Mayfield and they made the whole show. Actually I've just had the most terrific row with one of the Wrens who said it kept the ratings off the bus to have them but I arranged it all and they paid for their tickets so I just let fly at her. She's been honey ever since. One of the Wrens got so tight she had to be taken home, and another violently sick! Mrs Boyd, Chief Officer at Rosyth, was there. I'd met her before and had to take her from Orphanage to Mayfield which was a good opportunity to talk to her. They are wanting cypher officers urgently and I hoped if I made a good impression they might take me on before I'm 21 but I don't know. Miss Overy said the other day she hoped for my sake the war would carry on a bit longer so that I could go to OTC Greenwich!

... I had a letter from Rosemary the other day, but haven't had a moment to answer it yet. Yours was the only letter I've been able to write this week.

It's thawed terribly here and everywhere's in a terrible mess. We've had 2 raid warnings during the last 2 days and we've all got to pass through the gas chamber and wear our gas masks for 1/2 hour every day! Heavens!

Please send me my nail brush! I'm lost without it.

Heavens – nearly tea time!

Heaps of love to you both.

Sheila

Meanwhile life in Dundee continues, despite reminders of the war from the air raids: Wrens' Club, hair, shoes, uniform, work, hopes of weekends away to alleviate the routine and, of course, grumbles about commissions and some good middle-class sanctimony:

Mayfield
28.1.41

My dear Mummy –

There's really not much news, but I'm just writing to thank you for your letter which on rereading, I have just been able to decipher!

I think I'll start by telling you that it is frightfully cold and does nothing but sleet the whole time. My shoes are damned uncomfortable (I've had to put plasters on my heels) and they squeak.

I've written to Roddy asking if I may go there this weekend, but of course haven't heard yet. I hope she will be able to have me. I shan't be able to go down till Saturday afternoon, but may be able to stay till Monday morning.

I went to a marvellous Naval talk on the war on Sunday night. I very much enjoyed it and met dear old Lieut. Osborne as I was coming out. We always seem to be bumping into one another. There has been a hell of a row over that girl who got tight, but I believe she's not going to be derated. They certainly don't do it to the ratings, but anyway I think it was horrid of her. Apparently most of the stewards here get as drunk as lords. Isn't it filthy?

… I still have great difficulty putting on my collar and tie. I always seem to get it bent somehow. There's going to be a parade through the streets on Saturday in connection with War Weapons Week, and they want some Wrens to be there, but thank heavens I'll be away, anyway I hope so!

I even wore lisle stockings yesterday! They didn't look too bad. It's just heaven to get into comfy shoes at the end of the day tho'.

Apparently there is a new rule that Wrens may be promoted at 20 1/2, only providing they've been in service over a year, so that doesn't include me – I'll be 21 first …

Well I must stop, as it's nearly time to go off again. To hell with this wet – you should see the mud!

Heaps of love to you and Daddy

Sheila

Sheila's sprits are raised by hopes of being billeted out and a visit to stay with Roddy, her grand friend who is living in a house in Dundas Castle grounds. Jaap comes back from patrol, and 'unfortunately I have no late pass and have to go out in uniform which he hasn't seen yet, so it will be a bit of a shock'. Mother is still coming up trumps on the parcel front:

Mayfield
3.2.41

My dear Mama,

Thank you so much for your letter and parcel with the shoes, stamps, nail brush etc. The shoes have been much admired and needless to say the stamps are marvellous.

Oh I've had such a good weekend. I went down to Dalmeny on Sat afternoon and Roddy met me plus bikes. It poured with snow tho'. Chapel Acre is really lovely. On the side of a hill looking towards the Firth and all country around. It's most beautiful and Roddy and I shared her room together. She's just the same; great fun. We went for a heavenly walk in the sun on Sunday and found a large loch completely covered with ice. So after lunch we went off skating and had a marvellous time. We had it all to ourselves too which was lovely. I got quite brave and went backward and did all kinds of tricks but not as well as Roddy who is very good. I am going away there in a fortnight's time.

I rang up Mrs Mackey re today and I am going there very soon I think. She seems a dear and I think I shall like it very much.

… A 14 shirt neck with 14 1/2 collar would be big enough I think. Can you get that do you think? I hope so. I really don't think 13 1/2 shirt would be big enough, tho' it might if it didn't shrink. I rather think it might, though.

… The choccies were lovely by the way – where did you get them? Please don't send me any more. We have a canteen remember.

How are you and Daddy? Well I hope. We've had a lot more snow – I'm off to the Naval dentist on Friday. I hear he's quite gentle! Hope so.

Really must stop and get ready to go out …
With heaps of love

Sheila

The might of the German invasion in North Africa was just beginning to alarm the British and, combined with the continuing air raids, it is not surprising everyone has 'the wind up'. Nevertheless the mundane still manages to dominate the letters, mainly because it was impossible to mention details of the work she was doing, except that there's a lot of it:

Mayfield
9.2.41

My dear Mummy

Thank you so much for your letter with the stamps and also the £1 from Daddy with which I was very pleased – Do thank him for me. I also have had the shirt which really is half a size too small so I am going to change it here. Otherwise it is very nice. All my Wren ones have shrunk – most annoying! Did I even thank you for the gloves? They are really awfully nice and I have worn them once.

As you see I haven't moved yet and I don't know when I shall. I must really make them decide soon. Actually I think everyone here, too, has the wind up for we have all been through the gas chamber and are having to put fire spotters on the roof in four shifts every night now. But of course that is all under your hat.

I'm rather fed up really because I've been working like a black this week.[2] I've had to attend 2 courts of enquiry and make verbatim reports of each as well as do my ordinary work. Also I had to work yesterday afternoon and this morning and it's such a lovely day.

2   While language such as this might seem shocking today, it must be remembered that it was common parlance at the time.

However, I get paid for the reports at the rate of 6*d* per 100 words so I shouldn't do too badly as they were really quite long and took the whole day to do.

I went out with Jaap again on Thursday, but he had a dreadful cold and I was terribly tired after a very busy day, so we didn't go skating as planned. He has gone off skiing this weekend, but I wouldn't be surprised if he didn't get any as all the snow has melted again thank heavens. It was terribly thick on Thursday, nearly a foot I should think.

I had a letter from Joy who is still at Greenwich just about to begin her W/J course. I do wish she was still up here – I miss one good friend very much. Actually Chapman has been all over me these last few days. I'm certainly wondering why but she really has been awfully nice.

Oh – (blast – sirens!!!) we had a kit inspection on Thursday and I was told I had many too many civilian clothes – so I shall have to send some home unless of course I move to the Bishop's tomorrow.

I do wish they would tell me because I don't want to send my things home and then have them back again.

Well I must stop. I've got so many letters to write. Somehow I never seem to get them done these days.

Heaps of love

Sheila

Sheila is never downhearted for long: the men in her life provide good cheer. There is news of Paul, who has been on HMS *Sheffield*, which had been on convoy with the *Ark Royal* in the Mediterranean, and Jaap meanwhile provides great company. She even manages to make light of some of the other realities of wartime.

Mayfield
12.2.41

My dear Mummy,

... Well they say you have to experience everything in life once, and I certainly had the shock of my life on Monday, when I saw a creepy-crawly running (or malingering) up my skirt. So away I dashed and washed my hair and clothes – and bolted for sister who examined my head and found nought! However, I caught three more in my clothes and were told they were 'body lice' (!!) so we 'Dettolled' the room thoroughly (I put all my washed wet clothes and my costume, out on the window coping all night and the dye came out of my stockings on to my shirt and collar and made one hell of a mess) and retired. I had to get up at 1am to do two hours fire spotting. Oh dear it was a game, and we've had the room fumigated and scrubbed out with disinfectant – it's never been so clean since we came here!

Apparently Dundee is alive with such things and you can pick them up in buses or anywhere and they say they always go to the cleanest people! So one up to me! However I've treated it as a tremendous joke and am none the worse for my unfortunate adventure.

Anyway, it meant that I was able to go about in civvies all day yesterday. I met Jaap in the morning and he was very intrigued, so I told him the story at length and he said 'we must go out tonight as you're in civvies' so out we went – and had a terrific time. He is a dear. This afternoon he came to bid me farewell in my office as he's off again, and I watched them sail out later on. Miss Overy has been at Rosyth all day. Provided I appeal to the board of examiners I shall definitely get a commission at 21, unless of course I disgrace myself in the meantime. She asked me whether I'd rather be a cypherer or a secretary when commissioned. I said the former, I never liked secretarial work very much – it's such a long time to wait though – nearly seven months.

Isn't it thrilling about the 'Sheffield'?[3] Perhaps it'll mean Paul will be back soon after such a marvellous performance. They've been abroad for five months – I'm sure they ought to come back for boiler cleaning or something quite soon! The wireless account at midday was terrific. Did you hear it?

I've just been issued with a greatcoat which is terribly nice and I feel most smart. I've only got to adjust the belt at the back and it will be a perfect fit. I changed the shirt at M&S for a 14 1/2 which is very nice; they tend to shrink and I loathe them tight.

Tomorrow I've got to attend another board of enquiry – rather a special one, as I've got to be there 1/2 hr early to see one of the officers, and they took my full name for some unknown reason. Miss Overy doesn't know about it yet; she will be furious – but I've got a lot of my tomorrow work done. So she can't really grumble.

With lots and lots of love to you both.

Sheila

Life in the Wrens is one long rollercoaster: now everything is falling apart. She isn't being billeted and Jaap is leaving 'going somewhere <u>very secret</u> so must say no more, only how disappointed and sorry I am that he is going as we did have such fun together and things will be very boring for me after next week.' They are trying to arrange a final evening before he goes, 'but he has so many farewells to bid that we may not be able'.

However, she has heard that Wrens are being called up for 'services overseas'. She asks her mother what she thinks: 'I'd very much like to go … it would be marvellous to feel one was really doing something.' She feels her work 'isn't so terribly important. Of course it might mean foregoing a commission (if I ever do get

---

3   The *Sheffield* had been involved in the shelling of Genoa, and operations against Vichy convoys and supporting air reinforcements in Malta. She played a large part in shadowing the *Bismarck*, which was eventually sunk in May 1941.

one) but I feel the experience would be wonderful.' She must have felt pretty desperate to consider giving up a commission for going overseas.

She gives vent to her frustration in her next letter:

I am very annoyed. Here I am slaving (!) for my country miles from anywhere and nobody writes to me! I've just been haranguing the postman but with no results I'm afraid – I haven't had a letter since Tuesday. That's very unusual for me and your last was written six days ago. VERY cross!

In a later letter she writes:

I don't think your homily to the family did the slightest bit of good – I've not heard from one of them, and really, with the little time I get, I don't feel like starting writing to them all over again, except of course, Granny, who has tons of people to write to. But Aunty Rose and Hazel etc. I don't think deserve letters as they never write to me, and Aunty Rose never even answered my last letter, written nearly two months ago! Perhaps I'll send them all Easter cards, just to remind them. Perhaps when you go down south you could enquire into the subject.

In wartime, far from your home and family, letters must have been of paramount importance: those she is complaining about were all civilians, although cousin Hazel was recently married to a naval officer, and obviously were not aware of how the sending and receiving of letters could have such an impact on morale. This whole collection of Sheila's letters to and from her mother demonstrate this; even her crabby mother understood the need to support her daughter in this way.

Her gloom continues with Jaap's departure: 'Jaap has gone … he went on Sunday and strange to relate I never saw him to speak to again. Well, we always said the Dutch were funny – I really believe they are!!'

Rosemary is an easy target for her ire. She feels she should go to the Admiralty or air ministry and 'sound them out about commissions. It's no good waiting until the time comes – there wouldn't be an earthly then.' Later she has a further swipe at her sister:

I had a letter from Rosemary too, yesterday, telling me about her rise. I have been working things out, she says she gets £3.10.0 a week sheer profit, with upkeep and insurance and income tax paid, I suppose. I get £3.10.0 a month. Still, you know, I manage very well really – I just can't imagine what I'd do with all that wealth. It would be fabulous ... I wish Rosemary would join up – I wrote and told her she ought and she replied that tho' she quite saw my point of view (I told her Rome burned while Nero played the fiddle) B+H [Bourne & Hollingsworth] couldn't possibly get on without her. I do feel that an older person could easily do the job and it's not essential to the nation's war effort anyway.

It is not surprising that Rosemary did not want to join up, seeing how well off she was compared to a services salary.

Sadly the call to go overseas does not materialise:

Nothing has come of that Near East rumour. I don't feel an awful lot of use here (tho' they couldn't do without me!) so am wondering if I should ask for a transfer. Might get sent somewhere miles worse tho'! This would be a marvellous place if I had lots of friends.

However, Sheila and Chapman seem to having fun. She 'dressed' her for a date with a Dutchman, and they went to supper 'and had a good chinwag. She is being nice to me – heaven knows, one needs a few pals these days!' Some people called the Mackenzies have invited her to tea and promise to introduce her to some more people –'so it should be much better'.

Never one to be downhearted for long, in the same letter (26 February) she writes:

Oh we had such fun yesterday. We went down in the gunnery store and are being taught rifle shooting. Strange to relate, I was very good and got 16 out of 17 rounds on the card with 6 rolls! So you'd best beware not to displease me! We are going every week and hope to get good. Unfortunately the range is very small, only 20 yards so you really can't help getting them on the card (!) but no one else was at all good. Cockadoodledoo!

Work, however, still has to be done:

I am having a very busy time what with one thing and another, but I'm not terribly fond of my type of work, forever running after people. Tho' I like being in Dundee. But it's no good asking for another job in Dundee – I'd never get it and it would put the old girl's [Overy] back up. So must just wait.

She is – justifiably perhaps – a little miffed when a long-planned weekend away in Perth is cancelled at the last minute:

Mayfield
2.3.41

My dear Mama –

I had arranged to go away for the weekend with another girl to Perth. A message came through from Commander Stack saying I had to attend a confidential enquiry on Saturday am and take shorthand notes. He loathes Miss Overy and would do anything to get a rise out of her. So I had to go and he said it would all be over by 12 am [presumably she means pm]. However, it wasn't. I spent all Saturday afternoon working and have had to come in this morning (Sunday) and this afternoon to get it all done – so of course I couldn't go to Perth! Everyone has been very nice about it so I feel quite a martyr, especially as the 2 writers in the secretary's office have had very little to do and have only been on one at a time the whole weekend! Com.

Stack of course, just daren't look my way, he knows I'm furious and that it's his fault. Miss Overy says I can have next weekend off, though as she's got to be here, Miss Penman is away, and Overy is living in, much to our horror.

… Help, I must get a move on as it's nearly 2 o'clock and I've got to rush back to do that report. I expect I'll be about the only person working in the whole orphanage. Me thinks I deserve an extra stripe for this! But I won't get it. I was rushing round in Chapman's coat last night and everyone thought I was a C.D.O. [Command Duty Officer] No such luck!

Sorry this is so dull. Really no news at all. Just work!

Lots of love

Sheila

In mid-May the King and Queen pay a visit to Dundee and inspect the *Unicorn*: 'it was great fun and they stopped bang in front of me for quite a while and talked for quite some time':

15.3

We had several photographs taken for the papers but the one I've seen was in Tuesday's Scotsman of the Queen signing the visitors book. The King was a bit grumpy and wouldn't let the Queen inspect us as thoroughly as she would have like to have done and speak to us. He was in a terrific hurry and they didn't even walk up both files. Thus nearly leaving the ship without signing the book – there was a terrific scramble and they signed it just before they left. There were pipes on board with bo'sun's whistles – a terrible squeak which made us all want to laugh. Miss Overy was terribly thrilled as she had to conduct the Queen round.

Life continues with a mixture of work, air raids, dances and some new admirers:

> On Thursday we went to a dance for Forces in the Marryat Hall and I met a sweet Pole called Feliks. He is very musical, has been in a concentration camp in Germany, but escaped through Hungary, Yugoslavia, Italy and France. I am meeting him tonight.
>
> On Wednesday we were in the middle of a club night when the sirens went and I went on fire duty. Likewise on Thursday, when we were dashing up and down stairs half the night but managed to get some sleep. Last night I met Elizabeth and her cousin Grizelda something or other and went to the flicks and the siren went again – so we all dashed out and I got a bus home. We went up and down to the shelter house, and at 11 up to bed. But had to keep our clothes on. Horrid. It lasted from about 9.30 till 2.30 – not bad for Dundee!

Finally Sheila has some really good news: 'Paul is home!' She won't be able to meet him for three or four weeks, by which time she hopes to have leave, but she is very 'excited – it was grand to hear him again after 8 months!' She reminds her gossipy mother that she is not meant to know which ship he was on, 'and I'm not saying where he is'.

Meanwhile she has a chance to shine in front of the Chief Officer of Rosyth, Mrs Boyd, who is attending the Wrens' Club meeting, where Sheila has to read the minutes and the report. Life generally seems to be looking up and you can sense the vitality in her writing again. It also interesting to note the emergence of her responsible attitude and leadership qualities; she doesn't seem even to be upset by the threat of all leave being cancelled, on account of the fall of Greece and Yugoslavia and British preparations for a counter-attack in the Western Desert:

Mayfield
30.3.41

My dear Mama

Well Chief Officer came on Wednesday and we had our general club meeting. I had to read out my report and was subsequently re-elected secretary!! Miss Overy was very kind, and thanked me publicly for all my hard work and excellent report and Mrs Boyd was charmed. She has asked for a copy of it and wouldn't believe I had written it all myself! So it was certainly a stroke of luck that she was there for the meeting as that is the kind of thing that impresses them – especially when I was re-elected unanimously! Well well, Miss Overy apparently told Mrs Boyd that I wanted to do cyphering and not secretarial work. Mrs Boyd is wanting a new secretary herself, but I should loathe to be at Rosyth and anyway I have to wait till I'm 21. The Superintendent is coming here shortly and we are expecting the Director later on, so here's hoping. Mrs Boyd is a <u>dear</u> and everyone loves her.

On Tuesday I went out to supper with Rachel with a girl I met at the Steggalls, who is rather nice. Friday was a terrific day. We had a hectic phone call asking for Wrens to go to a concert given to some soldiers who aren't allowed to move 100 yards from the gun emplacements in mid Craigie so I rounded up a small party and went. There were 100s of soldiers and 8 (no 9) Wrens. The concert was very very good and they had an item which the actors played and then 4 of the audience had to play so P.O. Swire and I decided to go up on the stage. Oh it was terrific fun – and of course everyone died of laughing. I was the mother and my 'husband' (I found out after he came from Norwich) was 1/2 my size. Anyway at the end of the play the C.O. had Swire and I on the stage again and said how pleased he was to see Wrens there, and asked us all to come again. They then gave us a huge feast and we were driven home in grand style in an army van. I met a man from Holt beach (!) and he gave me a copy of the Free Press which I have read from cover to cover!

I have had to work this weekend. Chapman has gone off to OTC [Officers Training Course] at last and whilst walking in the downs on Saturday evening I met Feliks. We went to a canteen and had supper and half the Wrens were there and on to the Empress Ballroom to dance. It is a very nice place. Lovely floor, good band and plenty of room and I quite enjoyed all. He's a dear really. Though rather solemn. Tho' it's not to be wondered at after all he must have been through.

I have been working today quite hard and although it has been a heavenly day, I've not been for a walk. I had to do fire watching from 3/5 and slept till 9, so missed my breakfast, so I've been trying to catch up since.

I've had the room to myself this weekend thank goodness. It's bad enough now, what will it be like in Summer? When I came back on Friday night there was an adorable little gray mouse flopping about the room. I thought I was seeing things, but no, it was a mouse. I have since got a trap for it, but haven't had the heart to set it. Anyway, haven't seen or heard the mouse since.

Please don't get me new face towels, but send me those I had in London, the orange and the green. It's no good having anything new here. The laundry is very hard on them. May I please also have my camera? There are plenty of things I would like to take here.[4]

Must fly – oh we may not be getting leave now – all the men's has been stopped, but the steward starts tomorrow. Will let you know.

Heaps of Love

Sheila

Can you please find and send me McCall pattern for knickers? It should be in my knitting bag.

Club life seems to have played an important part in keeping Sheila, and no doubt the rest of the Wrens, sane. They had a club night in

---

4 The lack of camera explains why there are so few photographs in the first few months of service.

the Marryat Hall in Dundee and she took Jean Stobie and Feliks and another Pole, Joseph. This is followed by a ping-pong tournament against the *Unicorn*, but she says:

> It really is most difficult to think of these Club evenings. Next week we are having a party to celebrate the commissioning of the ship. Then Commander E is giving us a talk. He is a star. We hope to go over to a submarine soon and also another large ship in dock here.

The visit to the ship was a great success, as she writes to her father on 9 May, in one of her affectionate letters to him giving a round-up of all the news:

> On Wednesday it was our Club Night, and we had arranged with Captain Hellingman to go over the 'Columbia' a huge luxury liner in harbour here at the present. It was really great fun – we were taken over by the stewards. Perhaps you have heard of her – she was a liner on the Holland–West Indies route, and is beautiful inside. After we had been taken round, we were taken to the first class lounge, where a lovely meal was arranged for us – I've never seen such a luscious cake since before the war, and they were all made on board. Then we had a sing song, and one of the Wrens was most amusing. I met a Dutch officer who had just come back from Newcastle that day, and had spent the night before staying with the Taylors, who are great friends of the Simpsons. I think he knew Sandy [her ex-boyfriend from Durham], but was a little vague. It was great meeting someone like that, and the Engineer, who was sitting at our table, had been in Newcastle too. They say they will invite us all again, and want me to drop in anytime I like, but of course it wouldn't be quite the thing, an 'umble Wren boarding this luxury liner whenever I pleased, though they couldn't see it. I do hope they ask us again though. The only silly thing was that they provided drink ad lib, and some of the Wrens were rather foolish, and took too much. But I haven't told Miss Overy about that side – and hope she never gets to hear about it, otherwise she'd be furious.

Last night we had a meeting of our Gardening Club, and had our plots of land allotted to us. I am sharing with the C.P.O. [Chief Petty Officer] Cook and another P.O., and we are hoping to grow lettuces, radishes, onions, and all kinds of things. I'd adore to grow a marrow, but I think it would take up too much space, and we haven't got room. Tonight Rattray, the C.P.O. and I are going down to Broughty Ferry to sail. Jean Stobie and I met an old man who looks after the Yacht Club last week, and he said he would arrange for us to go out with two youths. Unfortunately Jean is going on leave tonight, so Rattray and I are going. It will be fun, though it has turned rather dull. He says we can go over to Newport or Tayport, or where we like, and of course we can get into civvies (slacks, I suppose) which will be lovely.

I spent all Wednesday at a Board of Inquiry, which I love. It really is most interesting, and of course I love doing any secret or confidential work. Also, it means extra cash for me, as I get paid at the rate of 6d. per 100 words. Not bad, when you do lots and lots of pages.

Last night when I was ironing, I found a confidential signal lying on the table, and meant to give it to Jean [Stobie] to deal with, as I suppose one of the stewards had left it there when pressing an officer's suit. However, I forgot, and so gave it to the Secretary this morning. I happened to mention it to Miss Overy, who naturally thought it was a very serious thing to happen, and said I'd probably get into a row too, though I'm not quite sure why, as I never showed it to anyone, though of course appreciate that I ought to have told someone last night. The officer concerned had seen the signal, and had just left it in his suit, I suppose. Anyway, we shall see. The Secretary mentioned that the Wren concerned would get a bottling. I feel rather sorry, but of course there was no other way out. It's a very serious thing to let confidential documents lie about – especially when they concern the movements of ships.

How simply lovely if you were to go to Sierra Leone – though I must say the heat would be very trying. However, if you do, make sure that if there are any Wrens there, that I must go too. It would be glorious. I'm simply dying for the opportunity to go abroad – though they haven't sent many ratings yet. They may do, of course, in which case I shall certainly volunteer.

Mummy has been to Hunston, I see from a letter forwarded by Rosemary today, and has seen nearly everyone worth seeing, including the gorgeous Pompey [cat]. What fun.

I went to Woolworths today, and was able to buy slabs of chocolate, which was a score. Our Canteen has at last given out, and we can get no more, but we are having apples instead, which is really much better for us. I had a letter from Joy yesterday asking if I could send her some chocolate, but there's not much hope now, as we are only able to buy a limited amount. How do you manage for cigarettes? We are able to buy lots and lots here in our Canteen here, but they are H.M. Ships only, and I'd get a devil of a row if I were to send you any. They do all kinds of things to prevent such things happening – they even have special forms about it.

I must now pack up and go back to Mayfield, as I want to buy my daily apple from the Canteen, and also get ready for going out tonight.

With lots of love,

Sheila

Looking through her scrapbook, I found a letter dated 21 June from the Hon Sec of the Carolina Club, as the Wrens' Club was called, enclosing a brooch and engraved cufflinks 'as a small token of appreciation for all the work you did for the Carolina Club while you serving in Dundee'. To her mother, she writes:

I had a lovely surprise yesterday when some gold cuff links SFM and WRNS and an anchor on them, and a naval hat badge broach [sic], arrived as a parting gift from the Carolina Club Wrens of which I was secretary. I feel so smart in them, and am very touched.

She had kept these for the rest of her life, and I found them after she died, along with many other wartime mementoes.

Meanwhile affairs of the heart are still uppermost in Sheila's mind: her mother has forwarded on a letter from Jaap, sent home to avoid the nosy-parkers at Mayfield. 'Poor Jaap! He is having a very miserable time and has been in a "horrible bad mood" since he left Dundee. I do wish they would all come back here – we did have such fun and I did like Jaap so much.' As for Paul – her leave has been cancelled and as 'things are so uncertain these days' she's not sure if they will coincide. 'He will just have to come to Dundee and see me. That seems the only thing to do, and I have written and told him so.'

Paul does eventually get leave and they manage to meet in Edinburgh in June.

Following the pattern of her relationships yet to come she adds, 'as usual we scrapped and disagreed but made it up in the end.' He was due back again in November.

All romantic thoughts quickly disappear when in mid-May she tells her mother that there will be a post for a Wren writer abroad:

Mayfield
14.5.41

Dear Mummy and Daddy –

This is in a terrific hurry – and I want an answer straight away – Miss Overy told me in the strictest confidence that there will be a post for a Wren Writer abroad very shortly and would I like to go. If so, she is prepared to recommend me. It is terribly interesting, and I'd be the only one, but she can't tell me where it is. The only thing is that I'd be recommended for a commission very shortly – probably anytime now as the Chief Officer says I'm eligible. What on earth am I to do? You see abroad, I wouldn't have a commission and wouldn't do so well off, but would have a special subsistence allowance anyway. I think it wouldn't matter as regards social activities whether I had a commission or not of course the work would be much more interesting than as a Cypher Officer, which gets very boring. Now, I don't want you to decide for me, but just to say as soon as you possibly can whether you would allow me to go as I am not 21. It would be a great honour – the Superintendent may not of course consider me suitable, but the Chief Officer and Mrs Boyd are with me.

Now I must fly – please let me know BY RETURN, as it is <u>very</u> important we know at once. Wire if you like, but don't divulge anything as it's a dead secret.

Heaps of Love,

Sheila

We never hear the response, and the next letter is from the Royal Naval College, Greenwich where she is taking an Officers' Training Course in Cyphering. It seems she got an unexpected summons to a Selection Board at Rosyth on 22 May. 'If you are successful in passing that Selection Board, you will probably be required to attend an O.T.C. at Greenwich on 28 May.' This memorandum is pasted in her scrapbook.

It appears all went well and she left in a great hurry, calling in to see her parents at Durham, where she boarded the sleeper and, in true scatty Sheila style, managed to leave her gas mask, post office book and haversack behind. This was quite serious, she simply 'dare not arrive without a gasmask, and with great trouble managed to buy one' by giving an address of somewhere that had been bombed!

There are 49 of them on the course, and they sleep in dormitories. Her room overlooks the river. They are instructed in cyphering and teleprinting until 6.45pm each day, and also have lectures. Their only 'relaxation' is the meals, which they take in the Painted Hall, and which are 'excellent – we are even allowed to have dinner with the Naval officers, so we are coming on.'

Her mother has forwarded a letter from Jaap, with an 'awfully nice' photograph of himself enclosed. He is still depressed. Apparently clothes rationing has just been introduced; she can't resist a quick barb at her flighty sister: 'Just serves Rosemary right, and people like her.' At least in the services, most of your clothes are provided free of charge!

She has made a new friend, Marian, whose mother is later to lend Sheila her bike in Methil, her next posting, and together they manage to 'have a good laugh' at being waited on and called 'ma'am'.

Stopping in Durham en route to the OTC; Sheila with her father in the garden.

The course is a precursor to being promoted to Third Officer, provided she passes of course – as she tells her father on 5 June:

Royal Naval College,
Greenwich S.E.10.
5.6.41

Telephone: Greenwich 0606.
Telegrams: College, Greenwich.

Dear Daddy,

Thank you very much indeed for sending me the £1 via Mama – as a matter of fact expenditure to date has been very low, but I expect the pull will come when we are drafted and get no pay at all until we are commissioned.

Am very much enjoying my course, and so hope I pass out all right. I have finished with Cypher at the end of today, completed my 2 lessons on one special machine, and go on to teleprinting tomorrow.

Yesterday Moss Bros came down to fit us for uniform, and I have placed an order with them. And they are supposed to be very good. And also are most reasonable. I've ordered 2 suits, one bridge coat and a hat, and if I don't pass out all right they take responsibility. The suits I have ordered in superfine as I hate serge and the difference in price is negligible, and Hall, Gieves and Lillywhites have also been but are much more expensive.

I am hoping to spend next weekend in London, as I have it free, but may return here on Saturday night. I don't know yet. Then on Monday we have our board – and learn the fateful news.

Today we had to take squad drill personally, and my goodness it was dreadful, but I managed to get through some of the commands all right. On Monday the Director selects certain girls to take it – heaven help us!

I may be able to get some leave, as a notice has gone on the board asking us to give dates of our last leaves, but nothing is guaranteed. Tonight is guest night, and we have to be very proper and behave well – tons of courses – all very good. I am getting enormous!

A raid last night – nothing much but we repaired to the shelters. We went up to the top of the chapel dome and got a marvellous view. I took some photos! Hope they come out. It is very sultry and Thursday looks like rain – hope it clears up by the weekend.

Lots of love

Sheila

Sheila was hoping to get sent back to Scotland as the 'nicest people are up North' and indeed she ends up in Methil, near Fife. At first she thinks she will like it 'very much'. She has her own room in the Victoria hotel, Lundin Links, overlooking the sea, and it is 'marvellously bright and airy'. She likes the officer in charge, and Mrs Boyd, Chief Officer, is on hand to welcome her. An added bonus is that they have a more relaxed attitude to 'discipline' and civilian clothing is allowed, except at meals, 'so I think I'll be wanting some more clothes please … Definitely, a frock, slacks, navy swimming suit, a cotton frock.' She is wary, however, of ordering up too much stuff, plus an extra suitcase, until her probation is over in case she moves elsewhere.

But this turns out to be a false hope; she is soon complaining that she 'loathes' Miss Jameson, the Wren in charge, 'and I think she loathes me'. Moreover, they do very little cyphering and no teleprinting, which is a 'great disappointment … in fact I told them so yesterday so we should see whether I stay here or not'. The officers are all 'rather old and RNR [Royal Naval Reserve] and not very interesting'.

The letters written between June and November are missing, but by 9 November she is writing:

Things aren't going at all well here – we are all getting on each other's nerves and I hate the sight of several of us. Cowser goes tomorrow I am sorry to say she is a dear and we shall miss her very much.

I went to a dance in Leven but didn't enjoy it very much. I find I'm getting extraordinarily particular who I go out with – and there's not even a Bert to tell one's troubles to! I heard from Bert this week; he has sailed now poor old boy. I think he was very depressed about it all, and had a feeling it would be his last trip as he is quite old for our seas. None of his records, which I packed, broke though!

This is all rather depressed – I'm sorry. Somehow one always grumbles, but really, anything would be nice after Methil, I feel. I have just written to Michael Carter [a POW] and feel rather ashamed at grousing when I think of what they must be putting up with.

Heaps of love

Sheila

I have been trying to work out who Bert is: I think she must have met him during the missing letter period. He re-appears in Alexandria and again in Beirut and seems to have been a great source of comfort to her,

With friends at Lundin Links: Sheila and (left to right) Alice West, Chief Officer Boyd, Kay Way, Madge Cowser, Diana Fletcher and Vicar the dog.

and very kind. It would be amusing to know exactly how 'old' he was as refers to him constantly as 'old Bert', but I expect he was barely 40!

Contrary to her letters, life does not seem to have been too bad: there are sherry parties, hockey matches and long walks on the beach, and she bought a gramophone with her birthday money. 'I've always wanted one and I'm very pleased with it. It is a Decca.' It certainly cheers her up – 'it is a great boon ... I have a wonderful new recording of Night and Day which I'm afraid we play day in and day out – but it is grand'. She was in fact rather musical and later took singing lessons in Alexandria.

It was at Methil she met a number of Wrens who were to make the journey to the Middle East with her and who were to become her great friends: Kay Way, Mary Dugdale, Sybil Hoole and Diana Fletcher.

In June she wrote that she had not yet received confirmation of her appointment to Third Officer, but in September she celebrated her 21st birthday in some style, with a large dinner party for at least twenty-four (from Commanders, Lieutenant Commanders, and their wives, downwards), as counted on the signed menu. Bert was also there; his RSVP reads:

21st Birthday dinner menu.

9th September 1941

Menu

Grapefruit Cocktail

Consomme Julienne

Roast Sirloin of Beef,
Horseradish Saude,
Baked Potatoes   Green Peas.

Scotch   Trifle

Coffee

9th September 1941

Sheila parachuting.

To our Gert
Wishing her very many happy returns of the day on her 21st birthday from
The Three Berts

The menu was signed by all and is stuck in her scrapbook.

We know Sheila had been promoted by then as the formal RSVPs refer to her as 3rd Officer Mills.

Never short of admirers, there seem to have been a number of Polish officers stationed nearby, and one of them, Edward, promised to take her to the parachute tower to make a jump. 'I've always wanted to do it, but don't know if I will be brave enough.' Well she was – as there is photographic evidence to prove it! Again in her scrapbook is pasted a note from him 'I can only hope – your admirer'.

November and December are dark days for the Royal Navy: first the *Ark Royal* and the *Barham* are torpedoed off Malta by U-boats in November; then in the Far East the *Repulse* and the *Prince of Wales* are also sunk, while the *Queen Elizabeth* and the *Valiant* are sunk in Alexandria harbour. The theatre of war has also shifted very firmly to North Africa and the Middle East.

So it is hardly surprising that in early December she writes an excited letter to her mother:

Lundin Links
10.12.41

My dear Mama –

I'm terribly sorry to have been so long in writing. Honestly there has been such a lot to do one way and another I haven't had a moment for writing to anyone. However, thank you for your letter. I hope Daddy got the cigs. I thought I'd better register them.

Well things are on the move I think at last. Chief Officer came over the other day and I asked her about going abroad, and she seemed most agreeable, but said as I was young, I'd better get my parents to write a consent addressed (No. Alice says doesn't have to be addressed to anyone) saying you are agreeable to my serving abroad, and it will be attached to my papers. She says I'd probably be sent in the beginning of the year in March maybe. Piddocke then spoke to her and she told her that whether I go abroad or not I'll be the next one to leave Methil after Kay goes abroad in January. This is all very thrilling, and I take to it well …

We had a grand party last night, one of the officers from an HMT [Her Majesty's Trawler] came ashore and asked me for tea, and so I took Alice with me. Also in the party were the C/O and No 1 off one of the A/A escort ships. Very nice. Then the doctor from the ship arrived, and a sub.[5] from the trawler, so we had a good party. They all came back to dinner (we managed it somehow!) and then they left about 9.30. It's a pity they won't be here for the dance tomorrow. I am in the soup well and proper because I'd really expected Paul to be here for it, and also asked the HMT man mentioned above as I thought they would be here too; so the others asked 3 Air Arm people from Donibristle, now neither of my possibilities will be coming, I can see, so I'll have to go with Lieut. Porteous and his party (all the duds of Methil Base) as he's been asking us to go for about a month now. But he assures me he'll have a young army Lieut. from Kincraig for me, so I hope it will be OK. I don't feel very keen about the dance really. But know I must go!

… I've just had my hair done and look rather queer – for the dance tomorrow. My watches have been changed so I'm not going on till 7 tonight. Oh no, I forgot I've got to go on at 5, what a nuisance! However, Mary and I are going for a walk this afternoon.

I've got quite a good selection of gramophone records now and the C/O of the A/A ship says he'll lend me some of his if I'm careful. Hope he remembers!

Must stop now and go out.

Heaps of love

Sheila

5 Sub was the abbreviation for Sub-Lieutenant, the equivalent of 3rd Officer; many subs were RNVR (Royal Navy Volunteer Reserves) like my father.

———

Lundin Links. Fife

17/12/41

My dear Mama –

Thank you for your letter – I'm sorry you are so much against my going abroad because I feel I want to go very much, though less so now than I did a week ago, because Jaap is home and I have been hearing from him what it would be like – however it will be necessary for me to have a letter to forward to Rosyth whether to go or not, and I can always withdraw my application – so I do hope you or Daddy will give me one!

I had such a lovely surprise on Monday because Jaap phoned up to say he'd arrived home and could we meet – so of course we could, on Tuesday luckily, as it was my day off. So I went up to Edinburgh (meeting Jaap on the train by some extraordinary coincidence) and we had tea, went to a flick, then to dinner at the Aperitif and on to the Dequises, where we danced. He is still a great dear, though he doesn't look so well, he weights 200 lbs (help that's 16 stone, tho' he doesn't look fat – but of course is very tall 6ft 3"). He is coming over here on Friday and spending the night at Lundin Links hotel – we are invited to a party here, so I hope to get Jaap an invitation too. Then we shall go up to Edinburgh on Saturday and I shall probably come down south [i.e. home for Christmas] on Sunday – I don't think I shall go to London as travelling would be terrible. Jaap is going down south whenever his luggage arrives – maybe we'll even be honoured with his presence for Xmas – but I've not broached the subject yet – as I believe he has arranged to stay with relations in London. However, if he did come, would you object, and would it make a lot of extra work?

I am very upset because Mary Dugdale has been transferred to Greenock – all of a sudden, and I have lost my best friend once more! We have had such fun – especially with one of the Poles called Nicholas who often takes us out. He came to the dance with me, and we had a grand party of farewell. She didn't want to go one bit – in fact she was most upset about it. We used to have such fun – long long walks together and we had the same taste in all things, music, dancing, etc. It is all very sad. Sybil and I were walking on the beach on Sunday when we discovered a duck all oil lying on the sand, so of course we brought him in, rubbed him down, and kept him warm until we though he was better. He was saturated in oil, but I think we managed to get most of it off – we set him free yesterday.

If I get a moment when I am home, I want to meet Joy who is still at Scarborough. I don't think she will be coming to Fife after all and I would so much like to see her.

Well, no more tonight.

Hope you are feeling better.

Much love

Sheila

So ends 1941, Jaap back on the scene, Paul away at sea on the *Sheffield*, and Sheila's parents objecting to her going abroad. Her relationship with her mother has remained prickly despite the flow of letters. Here is a typical explosion in response to her mother listening to bridge-table gossip and accusing Sheila of not knowing what she is entitled to:

> You make me very cross when you say that the Johnsons are very quick on the uptake, as if I were not. The Navy does not give an allowance for plain clothes ever, and it's just hard luck. One can't break King's regulations, you know.

Sheila did not join the WRNS to serve out the war in Scotland – she was yearning for adventure and was determined to go abroad given the opportunity, whether mother agreed or not.

'Work, sleep ... and a little pleasure thrown in'

1942 was a critical year for the Allies. Japan had joined the Axis and the US had responded to Pearl Harbour by declaring war on Germany, supporting the British and Russian armies against the relentless Nazi advances throughout Europe: they were besieging Leningrad and had advanced as far as Moscow. The Germans were putting in place their plans for the 'final solution' and the gas chambers had been in use in Auschwitz since September 1941 – indeed my Czech family were all to be exterminated there in that year.

In early 1942 'invincible' Singapore surrendered to the Japanese and so began the building of the Burma railway, one of the cruellest POW events of the war; 90,000 Asian forced labourers and around 13,000 Allied prisoners were beaten and starved to death in its construction. I visited the war cemetery in Kanchanaburi in August 2014, and paid tribute to those brave souls.

In North Africa, Tobruk fell in February and the Afrika Korps began their advance towards Cairo and Alexandria, with the intention of taking Egypt and cutting off the British forces with a pincer movement, to join their victorious troops in Greece and Italy.

For Sheila, stuck in Scotland, the war is about to become interesting at last. Her parents' objections to her going abroad have obviously cut no ice with the Navy. She was, after all, 21. Practical to the last, even if a bit scatty – she still remembers to sort out her fur coat and finances, not forgetting the superstitious exchange of coinage for the scissors (something I still do if I give knives to people). She had no idea then that she was to be leaving England for the best part of four years:

L. Links
29.1.41

Dear Mama,

Did you get my wire yesterday? Because you didn't ring – anyway this is what I wanted to say to you … I have to go to London this weekend in connection with overseas service, have to travel back on Monday night and will probably <u>have</u> to call in at Durham to collect my trunk. Where will you and Daddy be? Because if I go I'll be sent off almost immediately and don't want to miss you.

It couldn't have come at a more awkward time – with <u>NO</u> notice at all and Mrs R. J. on leave.

Now, you are not to fret – whatever happens it will be for the best. I have to go to HQ to report and also order my tropical kit from Austin Reed …

Please don't worry about this, I haven't gone yet – But if you can manage to be at home on Tuesday (and I know what a bother it is) it would be marvellous. There's no time for me to stop on the way as I MUST be back here by Wednesday or Thursday. I hate having to write this in such a hurry, and without a lot of careful thought, but there's nothing else for it as when I'll get a moment today I can't say …

By the way, this is most confidential – almost secret so please don't tell everyone, though I know it will be very hard to keep it to yourself. I have told Daddy and Rosemary – and will try and get in touch with you as soon as possible.

With very much love, Mummy,

Sheila

—————

Lundin Links / [destination scribbled out]
12/2/42

My dear Mama –

… I am now 'en route' together with Mary Dugdale and Sybil Hoole
– it was a terrible rush getting off, but I think I've got everything.

Now listen, Mary is probably coming to join me in a month or so,
and I have asked her to write to you before she goes in case you would
like to send any letters out by hand, and also my wee watch which is
at the menders, and which I have asked to be forwarded to you. I'm
afraid I've no idea what was wrong with it or how much it will cost,
so I'm afraid that will be an outstanding debt, which I'm sorry about.
But apart from that I can think of nothing.

Friday has been such a rush. I rose at 7.15 to take divisions for
the last time – and have been doing things up to the last moment. I
packed off 2 suitcases and golf bag and sent them by rail so they will
be arriving in due course. My fur coat I've had sent to Draffens and
I've told them to surrender it to no one except you and me.

As I told Daddy last night, if I am not able to take any spare cash
I have away with me, I will send on a money order to him and he is
allowed to send £2 on any one day to me – by money order is best,
I think, or perhaps postal order, I'm not sure which. Also, I have my
post office book with me, together with my savings stamp book and 2
certificates which I will send by registered post. Oh, it is all such a rush!

Mary Dugdale came down yesterday … and we had a very merry
evening. Everyone has been sweet to me, and I am terribly sorry to
have to leave them.

This must only be a short note, as I must scribble 2 more whilst on
the track to Bert and Paul …

Heaps of love

Sheila

Please send me 1/4*d* for the scissors. They are in one of the cases and I do apologise for not sending them before. S.

———•———

In the Bank
13/2/42

Dear Mama,

I am sending my P.O. savings book, 2 certificates, and 3 2/6 stamps, all by registered post – also a Book token, because I won't have time to change it, I'm afraid. Please change it for anything you think would be nice, it's for 12/6*d* and I can read it when I return (or them, as the case may be!) Am having a lot of bother re extra cash, but am surmounting the difficulties by travellers cheques, which are being prepared now – there's no time for any other method. No cash shortage though – everything grand.

It was nice to hear you last night – I hope all my things arrive safely. I've just seen Sybil off. Wasn't it sweet of her to come over, it made such a difference as it would have been horrid spending the evening alone. A lovely day here – am getting quite excited about it all.

Must rush now

Heaps of love

Sheila

Sheila was not allowed to tell anyone apart from her parents where or how she was going, so the few letters written from on board give nothing away. However, she kept a copy of her joining instructions, which contain some rather intimidating 'notes':

Every member of the party is to remember that the reputation of the WRNS in Alexandria will depend largely upon the impression which they make. It is hoped that everyone will both in their conduct and appearance, maintain the traditions of the service.

On board, ratings may wear 'bluette overalls in warm weather to save the washing of white dresses … gloves are not worn with white uniform'. Civilian clothing was not to be worn throughout the voyage save for 'sports kit or fancy dress' but could be worn on arrival in Alexandria on leave of '24 hours or longer, for recreation, for private dances outside any Naval, Military or RAF establishment'.

Like a school uniform list, the WRNS kitting list is extremely detailed and specifies approved suppliers. The rules of underwear were very strict:

> For Alexandria a slightly larger quantity of underwear will be required than is necessary in England owing to the frequent need for frequent changes in a hot climate.

> White knickers, closed at the knee, must be worn with white uniform. White petticoats will be required.

> Anything tight or 'scratchy' is very uncomfortable in a hot climate.

Wrens were also advised not to drink the tap water, not go about in bare feet as 'many unpleasant germs lurk in the dust', and warned not to go to sleep inadequately covered for fear of catching 'severe cold, stomach and back ache'.

Nevertheless life on board the three-month journey on HMST *Nea Holland* was not all bad. Sheila managed to post a couple of short letters in February before they left for Africa, where she reports that 'nothing seems to have happened. We have plenty to eat, but at odd hours'.

Rather blighted by the rules of censorship, 'there seem to be orders everywhere telling you what you mustn't say … I'm absolutely certain my other letters won't have got through the censor all right, as though I thought I was being most discreet, I gather I said quite the wrong things!'

24 February

… However, here I am, quite well, and feel I'm getting fatter every moment – because all we seem to do is eat – hundreds of other people seem to be writing terrific letters at great length. 2 and 4 pages, but I cannot think of anything to tell you. Oh yes I can – we have started classes today learning the language – a dear old boy is teaching us – so far we have collected reams of words, but I find it very difficult to remember them all, as yesterday – I can't imagine why – I started to learn Turkish, but have given it up, temporarily anyway.

We've had 2 P.T. classes which have been rather fun, but most strenuous – but no doubt very good for us. One dance, and one cinema show have also been arranged, but for some reason both have been cancelled.

Sheila was to make some good friends on the long voyage, among them Diana Chard, later Booth, and a longstanding boyfriend, Robin Chater, described on first meeting as 'quite nice, musical and theatrical and may prove quite fun'.

In March they make their first landfall in, I believe, Sierra Leone and she writes a more detailed letter, which gives a good idea of the daily routine on board ship – mainly a lot of eating and drinking:

13th March 1942

My dear Mummy and Daddy –

You won't have got my last effort yet, I know, but here is another note to add to the collection – the 4th I've written since we started, I think. Well life is progressing according to plan, though it's still a trifle boring – rising, eating, boat drill, drinking, eating, deck games, tea, drinking, eating, drinking then a spell on the deck, and so to bed. However, we have been ashore once – very lucky too, we were. When we got ashore, we were met by 2 naval officers, who drove us off in their car, the Wrens following in a lorry. Then we drove through villages to the town and then on to bathe on a lovely beach with great waves breaking on the shore – it was very warm – about 90 degrees F I should think. The natives were interesting and also very interested – their funny clothes and houses amused us terribly, and all around were thickly wooded hills, and lovely flowers all very brightly coloured. After one bathe we had tea and returned to the Base for dinner. By that time it was dark and we were driven 6 in the car, up into the hills to see what it was like by night. So cool and refreshing and very different from the sticky heat we'd been accustomed to. Then we had to head back to the base as we were due to take the Wrens off at 2015. It was grand fun.

I have turned a marvellous brown – my legs and arms at least – I just can't imagine what it's like at home now – I suppose you are still wearing thick overcoats and not even thinking of spring clothes at all – I feel quite ashamed of the amount of food there is to eat.

… I refuse course after course every meal including breakfast. Also chocolate in profusion and I have even just bought a fountain pen, as mine has died on me temporarily!

The sea is such a marvellous blue it has to be seen to be believed. I'm told it's the salt in it which makes it so – also, we see quite a different set of stars as the time wears on – it's great fun helping to find out what they are and we gaze at them every night, after dinner, when it is cool. We even had a dance on deck one night, but it was rather hot, though great fun.

Laundry is rather bad still, but I managed to wash 2 of my white frocks the other day – but it was the ironing that floored me completely – I just couldn't get there today and in the end was so hot I felt as if someone was continuously spraying me with a hose – horrible! However we have just acquired a batman – a dear little man – and he cleans our shoes and brushes our clothes and generally makes life more pleasant. We don't even have to make our beds now, as we had a bust up with one steward, and the lazy hound was somewhat galvanised into action after that.

We've had one or two lectures lately on Naval affairs, and are having another one tomorrow on submarines at my request. Goody, it certainly makes something for us to do – and the Wrens too …

Our language classes are growing more and more muddly – don't think I shall ever be much good (which reminds me I haven't done my homework yet!) I find I took deplorably few books with me, and have to rely on other people for amusement, bar knitting. What did you get with my book token, Mummy? Something nice I hope. My rug is doing more than it's ever done before – working overtime in fact because we always sit on rugs on the deck, not in chairs. I am very annoyed, all those shampoos you bought have inadvertently been put in my case which is in the hold, and I've now to rely on Lux – or the ship's barber who is quite good really. We have a ship's sweep every day, but I've won nothing yet; also housie-housie games about once a week – Margot won twice running the other night, but it's a very poor game really!

There is an escaped monkey on board which tears about the rigging madly, and behaves in a very queer fashion. No one has been able to catch it yet, but we throw it bananas, so it does get something to eat. Somebody alas saw a rat on our deck last night – so I do hope it doesn't mean we're due for a nocturnal visitation tonight! Thank heavens I've a top bunk. I'd be terrified if I saw a rat peering at me in the dim light of morning!

I think I've exhausted my present stock of news pro tem, but I may be able to add more later on, before the mail goes.

I sent you a cable the other day, but it was impossible to send them in the end, so it was withdrawn – Pity – I'd picked a most suitable 3 groups from the list they gave us!

No air mail, I hear, so you'll probably get this in 6/8 weeks' time. Doesn't it seem ages? I'm just rushing off to my lessons, so no more.

Heaps of love

Sheila

Finally, towards the end of April – after three long months and another glorious stopover, this time in Cape Town – the *Nea Holland* docks in Port Said, and Sheila joyfully writes to her parents, scrawled with numerous PS's indicating her excitement:

Alexandria
23/4/42

HMS Nile
c/o GPO London EC1

Did you get my cable I sent in March?
Love to R what is her address?
1st two letters arrived today. Will answer later!

Dear Mummy and Daddy

Look at the address and you will realise your fears are over! They were
quite groundless too but none-the-less inevitable I suppose! We thoroughly enjoyed the journey – the second part better than the first I
think because we had made quite a lot of friends on board. I told you
about the first time we went ashore – well the second was even better;
I can't mention names, but I had a parcel of stockings sent to you,
Mummy, so you'll probably gather from that (hope they aren't too
thick – will send some more, and cosmetics and food soon). There was
plenty to see at this place and we took the girls out in two buses one
morning all around the countryside. It would have made your hearts
bleed to see the fruit – it was marvellous and so cheap. The country
was very beautiful and the sea lovely – in fact, lots of people have lost
their hearts to the place and want to live there après la guerre – (Not
me tho'). People were extraordinarily kind and dances were arranged
for us, though I think they were more interested in the men! 2 nights
running we went to an awfully nice club to dance, and of course there
were various preceding parties. On the last day there, another girl
and I, Diana, decided to spend the day on our own, so we set off
for a well-known bathing beach, munching gorgeous chocolates all
the way. The surf was wonderful, and we had such a good bathe, followed by a long walk along the beach – Then the sun set behind the
mountains, so we changed, had dinner (someone insisted on standing
us this) and then connected with some friends of her aunt, who lived

in the place. They met us in their car and drove us round the country in the dark, and then we visited Diana's two small cousins, who live here at an old school. About 10.30 we returned to the ship – presumably to bed. However, Diana met a friend of hers on board [Robin Chater] who was feeling rather browned off, so he collected his best friend. We retrieved our passes from the gangway, hired a taxi, and set off for a voyage of exploration – The lights really were LOVELY – I don't suppose we'll ever see anything so beautiful until the war's over. Eventually, after driving round for ages, we stopped at a little road-house, where you were served straight in your car; I ate and ate – But that wasn't all. When we got back to the ship, we had another feast and didn't get to bed till 4 a.m. – It was such fun – all so spontaneous. This all led to tremendous times once we got going again – there were very few nice people on the boat really. I won the ship's sweep twice, which I think was rather clever, and of course this called for tremendous celebrations – I'm afraid drinking became rather a bad habit, but not an unbreakable one! We gave a cocktail party to all our friends, and the biggest draft on board (to which Robin belonged) gave one too, and there were various private parties happening all the time. I borrowed a lilo and used to sleep on deck a lot, but it meant rising at 6 am, otherwise you got soaked by the hoses cleaning the decks! I'm afraid I never became much good at the language classes, but it does form a basis to start from – we were all very sorry to leave, really, and as a matter of fact, 5 of us nearly got left behind, but managed to get off an hour or so later – We had a hurried meal, and then were headed into a train (sleepers) and next morning we were here. Alas, tho', I felt terribly tired and retired to bed – Next day still felt tired, had the doctor who announced I had German Measles!! So I was carted off to Hospital, where I still am – quite well now and happy. But rather tired of being shut away. Another girl from my cabin has joined me, and quite a lot of people came to see us. We had O/E Troops from the ship yesterday, who is stationed near us and who promises us lots of parties when we recover. Phil's Naval brother has also been to see us and our doctor sends in his sister and cousin periodically so we are well looked after! I don't know what my work will be yet –

probably starting next week –I have had <u>NO</u> mail from you – how have you been writing? Airgraph is the quickest – you can write several in continuation, if you have lots to say, or air mail P/C is pretty quick – Letters not so good but air mail is the only way. Otherwise it takes 3 months!! The weather is very pleasant, quite cool and we are still in blues – I wish I had brought a few more warm things with me ... They're very strict about long hair – mine will have to come off, I can see!! We have to chaperone the ratings to dances and get them back by 10.30 and also sleep in the convent where they live for the night. We are living in a hotel pro tem, but our Quarters will be ready soon – I haven't seen Bert – he is quite a way away, I hear, but have seen old Kay Way, who used to share my room in Methil – What has happened

With Diana Chard in Cape Town.

about my watch? Have you heard from Mary Dugdale? I would very much like to be in England now – it must be looking lovely, with all the green trees and flowers – there are lots of flowers and trees here – I was surprised. But they are all bright and palm-like. We get one of these letter cards a week – I will write that, or an airgraph weekly, with an air mail letter thrown in occasionally for any extra news and snaps. Have not been able to send cables from here yet as have been shut up!! Tons of love – Sheila

The airgraph became the standard method of letter-writing, but space was limited, hence all Sheila's letters from here onwards appear in one long paragraph and jump from subject to subject, in a very modern stream-of-consciousness fashion; she hopes her parents won't mind the 'squashiness'. This gives them a breathless and enthusiastic tone, a true reflection of her first impressions of life in Alexandria.

Alexandria is an ancient city, built in 330BC on the orders of Alexander the Great, after whom it is named. It was the most important provincial capital of the Roman Empire and boasted the lighthouse, Pharos, one of the Seven Wonders of the World, was home to Cleopatra and was conquered briefly by Napoleon, but retaken by the British in 1801. King Farouk had a summer palace there and, in keeping with his lavish lifestyle, infuriated his people and the British by burning the lights all night during the blackout.

In the Second World War it was of great strategic importance to the British and the Allies; it was a bitter blow when it was raided by Italian submarines in 1941 and the *Valiant* and *Queen Elizabeth* were sunk and put out of action.

Because of its location, Alexandria was a Levantine city, full of Greeks, Jews, Italians, French and, of course, during the war, British. It was a city renowned for its depravity as well as its cosmopolitanism; its most famous son is the poet Cavafy, whose main themes are sensuality, homosexuality, uncertainty about the future, all in the context of the great Hellenistic tradition. E.M. Forster, T.S. Eliot and David Hockney have all paid tribute to his genius. He encapsulates Alexandria's schizophrenic character.

To get a flavour of the city that was to be Sheila's home, you can do no better than to read Lawrence Durrell's *Alexandria Quartet*, a long love-song to the city, both rich and poor:

Capitally, what is this city of ours? What is resumed in the word Alexandria? In a flash my mind's eye shows me a thousand dust-tormented streets. Flies and beggars own it today – and those who enjoy an intermediate distance between either. Five races, five languages, a dozen creeds ... Fragments of every language – Armenian, Greek, Amharic, Moroccan Arabic; Jews from Asia Minor, Pontus, Georgia: mothers born in Greek settlements on the Black Sea; communities cut down like branches of trees, lacking a parent body, dreaming of Eden. These are the poor quarters of the white city; they bear no resemblance to those lovely streets built and decorated by foreigners where the brokers sit and sip their morning papers. Even the harbour does not exist for us here. In the winter, sometimes, rarely, you can hear the thunder of a siren – but it is another country. Ah! The misery of harbours and the names they conjure when you are going nowhere. It is like a death – a death of the self uttered in every repetition of the word, Alexandria, Alexandria.[6]

For the British forces it was a very different city; although Sheila enjoyed visiting the bazaar and bargaining for goods, I am sure she never went anywhere near the notorious red light area, around the Rue des Soeurs (named after a convent; I wonder if it was one of the ones where Sheila stayed?) and the backdrop for several of Lawrence's novels.

Her second letter begins to describe her living conditions, work and the daily routine. I still have the portrait referred to in the letter, by a Polish artist she met in Methil:

6   *Justine*, in The Alexandria Quartet (Faber & Faber, 2012 edition)

27.04.42

Dear Mama and Papa –

I was so pleased to get your two letters Mummy – they both came
together the day I wrote my last letter card.

I hope you're both well – I'm quite recovered now – I came out of
hospital on Friday last, all spots now vanished and I started work for
the first time today. Naturally I can't tell you what it's all about, but I
do find it most interesting and think I'll like it very much once I get
the hang of things. We are still living in a hotel and a big Naval brake
calls for me in the morning – on the way we pick up the rest of the
office – We have a whole brake of our own; all the other people working with me are men – a great change from my last Base! Our offices
overlook the harbour [hole in letter so a guess] and all the ships, and
we have a lovely garden so I think we are very lucky. I went into town
today to have my hair done, and I bumped into old Kay Way – poor
dear, she had a cable the other day to say her mother had died, but
she has borne it very well, and is quite her cheerful self. Did you hear
from Mary Dugdale by the way? I gather my watch should be on its
way by now! Which of the crayon sketches did you like so much? The
portrait, or the one sitting down? I think the portrait was excellent
really. He was a dear little man – maybe I'll see him out here – there
seem to be plenty of his compatriots about. Diana Chard, one of the
girls who came out with me is being married on Saturday to a Padre
here who is running a club for boys under 20. They are going to do
the show together, and she was specially made a Wren and sent out
here for the purpose. She is a sweet girl and my best friend so far – it
was with her I had so much fun the 2nd time we went ashore … I
had a long letter from one of our boat companions, Robin, the other
day, and we hope he and 1 of his friends will be able to come for the
wedding. We move into Quarters on Friday – the 1st lot have already
gone in. I hope to share a room with 1 of my draft but may be shoved
in with 5 others. Not so good! My watches are very queer too. At
times I go on watch at 0400 (that's am) and also come off at 0400 on

other days – a grim prospect! I still haven't been able to send you my arrival cable – isn't it awful? We are told to send them through Naval sources and I've not been able to find out quite how to do it. Will try again tomorrow – but anyway you've probably got my 1st letter card by now. Hope so. The shops here are quite good – lovely shoes, flowers, confectionery, but otherwise things are frantically expensive. I'm thinking of sending you a parcel of things including soap and soap flakes because somebody has just told me how hard the rationing is and of course we don't come in for that racket … Yesterday evening we went to a cocktail party in one of the Naval establishments – their C/O travelled out with us and so we know him quite well. They have invited us to go there at any time for a drink, bathe, or dinner etc. The bathing here will be very good. I should think. The sea's a wonderful blue and we go into whites on Friday. I have done nothing about getting any more made – there hasn't been a moment but nobody else seems to have done so either. Still, I have 3 nice clean ones. Also I hear we may be probably allowed to wear ordinary stockings, or none at all. White are too grim. A lot of my gramophone records got bent in the heat, but we are able to buy fairly modern ones here, so I don't mind. I visited my other sick companion yesterday and she was looking very well. Our doctor was very kind to us, bringing all his relations in turn to see us, but it is all rather awkward now I am 'out' as I have so little time for going about and we aren't allowed to wander about after dark. There are 100s of cats here – all very thin and gaunt and of course donkeys and mules by the 1000s. Cars go on the right hand side, and everyone tries to rook you right and left. There seem to be so many Jews and Greeks and rather oily looking creatures about the place, almost all the women seem to wear black, very dreary. They have most queer sort of trams, rather like tubes they are (gosh the cats are squealing!) on special sort of fenced rails – The food is marvellous, I eat far too much – ice cream, fruit, lots of poultry and everything very beautifully cooked. I wonder what it will be like in Quarters? Do keep on writing, weekly and I will do the same. Try an airgraph now and again – sometimes they are surprisingly quick. I had a letter forwarded from L. Links the other day which must have come out with us, as it came by sea. I do love to hear all the news for although I think I'll like this place very much once I get to know a lot of people and get used to my work, it's such fun to hear what's going on at home. Do let me know if there's any special rationed thing you'd like or anything queer you're short of. We'd probably be able to get it here.

Heaps of love, Sheila

Diana Chard's wedding to David Booth in Alexandria on 2 May 1942.

Letters from home begin to play an important role in Sheila's life from an early stage:

> I really think I am the most fortunate of anyone … everyone seems to write to me and I do so love getting letters … I can't tell you how marvellous it is to have so much mail – everyone envies me as I seem to have much the most.

She frequently reports her letter counts, '21 letters in 21 days'; '6 p.c.s ranging from 11/9 to 15/10 and 4 letters, 2/8, 30/8, 1/9, 7/9', 'I have just written 10 airgraphs and 2 letters'; 'I've had the most tremendous mail this week, I just don't know how to answer them'; and she even compliments her mother's letter-writing skills: 'I love your letters, they make me laugh so, and I read them round to everyone in my room, and they all capsize with laughter.'

She must have had a sense of history in the making as she asks, 'Oh by the way, do you save my letters, because if you do, coupled with a diary (only a very discreet one as we aren't allowed to keep them!) I keep, you will get a very good picture of what we do out here, when I come home'. For her part she is keeping all the letters she receives, and is 'going to file them, so I shall have a sort of book of what is going on at home all the time I am away. How I love to hear all the gossip!'

She writes 'roughly' every Monday and is constantly fussing over letters going astray, 'has my mail been coming through all right? What is the datal order of my letter cards – Tell me and I will let you know if there are any missing.' Naturally, letters quite often went down when ships were lost, or they took months arriving if they went round the Cape.

Sheila is frustrated, on both these counts, in trying to keep up with both Paul and Jaap. Paul seems not to have known where she was and rang home and spoke to her father and rather implied he thought she was still at Methil. She wonders if he is still on the *Sheffield*, 'because otherwise my letters won't be reaching him, and I'd rather like them to, as he seemed a bit miserable'. A few weeks later she enquires again if they have heard from Paul, 'I would like to see him again.' She then admits to feeling homesick, despite all the gaiety of life in Alexandria: 'Much as I like all my new friends here I do like my old ones best, and get so homesick for them all and naturally, the glorious countryside which I miss most of all.'

Of Jaap, she has 'heard nothing and have an idea he hasn't my proper address as I never gave it to him. I do hope he is all right.' However, he surfaces a few weeks later, in Edinburgh, 'He had written before, but apparently they got lost', suffering from a broken heel having jumped out of a window for a dare. She has a large photograph of him on her dressing table, along with photos of 'Daddy, Rosemary and Uncle Cecil[7] ... surrounded by all my friends'. John Pritty's photo is soon to join them.

In early June, she meets John Pritty in the hotel. He is the brother of her friend Maureen from Rosyth, and is in hospital having his knee cartilage operated on: 'It's very pathetic these boys being in hospital with no one to see them. I was awfully glad I went, though it was terrifying walking down the long ward all alone.' She is soon seeing quite a lot of him:

> ... twice to the Sporting Club, once to dinner at the Beau Rivage, such a nice little place by the sea, and last night to see George and Margaret and on to dinner to Pastrondis. I ate much too much. I am having lunch with him today at the Sporting Club. He is so nice, Scotch, wears nice tartan trousers and sensible to talk to and be with – unusual out here, with all the naval fly-abouts.

By mid-June she is writing of her 'busy and hectic time these past weeks – out bathing, dining, to the flicks and so on – all with John Pritty. What a pity I left so very much of my heart way back home, isn't it?!!' All the same, John manages to steal a rather large part of it. Many decades later, my mother would occasionally sigh, 'If only I

---

7 Aunt Rose's husband in Peterborough; they were childless but he adored children. He had another family with the housemaid!

John Pritty. This
photograph was taken in
September 1940, before he
and Sheila met. He must
have given this to her when
he went to the desert.

had married John Pritty.' When I read the letters that follow, I think
she was looking back with rose-tinted spectacles.

Meanwhile the Wrens move from the hotel to a convent, 'two
most palatial houses in town – mansions, really, with beautiful par-
quet floors everywhere, grand staircases and huge rooms.' Grand it
may be but not immune from bugs; to Sheila's horror she discovers, 'I'm bitten all over my back, and after investigation from a room
mate, and told it is a BUG!! So must rush off now on a hunt for it.
UGH! There are millions of these kind of things out here.' She is,
she reports, 'covered with bites, the mosquitoes and flies are AWFUL
– all over my face, and what with these tiring watches I look rather
a mess! But you soon get used to them, I'm told.' A few weeks later
and she sounds quite blasé: 'I can't tell you how awful the flies are,
they settle on you whatever you are doing, crawl all over you, and
just won't be disturbed. I am getting quite good at hitting and killing
them whilst they run over me. Mosquitoes are far easier to kill as they
aren't nearly so active.'

So begins the happiest period of Sheila's life. It must have been thrilling for my 21-year-old Norfolk mother to find herself not only an officer, but also an independent young woman, with scores of admirers and invitations to social events of all sorts, ranging from dining, dancing, going to the races, sailing, sport – riding and hockey – all the while working godforsaken hours on watch, albeit with a jolly bunch of people. She is also surrounded by old friends from Scotland, and always bumping into friends of friends – even 'old' Bert is not far away and she hears news of him every now and again, and indeed hopes to visit him in Syria. Her letters exude a *joie de vivre* during this period:

18th May 1942

My dear Mama –

We're hoping for some mail this week so maybe there'll be something for me. How is everyone and what are you all doing? Here life runs on in the same pleasant way – a lot of work, sleep when you can get it and a little pleasure thrown in. Last Thursday I went out to visit some people living on the outskirts of the city – friends of someone I have met here. We went swimming first at the Sporting Club, and then on by tram. They seemed very charming and I can ring up and go whenever I please. A couple of days after that Victor Streatfield, who was O/C troops on board our old tub, invited Rachel [Charlesworth] and me out for lunch at his place. He is commanding a large station not far from here, and he collected us at about 1030, and drove us out. We had drinks in various messes – all in tents and hutments in the desert, such fun. I've never known anything like the flies – they were simply <u>frightful</u> in fact. They had a tame chameleon to try and keep them down. Then there was a marvellous lunch, still in a tent in the desert and after that we drove over to another mess for a drink. History mustn't relate what we did next and unfortunately we had to hurry home after that because I was on watch at 5. I would be most unpopular if I was late. After doing Dogs and Middle watches I disgraced myself by oversleeping and missed my transport for afternoon watch the next day. When I eventually arrived at the office, the D.C.O. [Deputy Cypher Officer] insisted I must have lunch. So down I tootled to the wardroom, expecting to find the place bare – to my horror I discovered the place crammed full with brass hats – at least 2 captains, six commanders and equivalent numbers of senior 2 I/Cs [2nd In Commands]. Alas, once inside the door there was no turning back so, having fearfully asked permission I sat me down to lunch. I must say everyone was terribly nice – they were having a terrific discussion on a 'bottle' [slang for a telling-off] the C/O had given us all. I was thankful that I hadn't been present as I didn't want to be embroiled. I've just been out to buy an alarm clock – twice I overslept – and there mustn't be a third time. It cost me 16/- the cheapest tinniest looking thing you could imagine and made in Italy too! That is a good specimen of the prices here … they are shocking. I was sitting in the drawing room this evening and felt a prick on my leg I looked up and found an enormous flea. There are 100s of them here and the mosquitoes are frightful. I had a P/C from Sheila Sage to say that Sybil Hoole has left the UK to join us. I hope to see Mary very soon now. That will be 4 from Methil! Tonight I am going on watch at 0400 so am having to go to bed specially early in consequence. I rushed into the town and had my hair done this afternoon … it looks quite nice. Have you had the parcel of stockings I sent you from one of our voyage ports? I enquired about cigarettes today and am hoping to send some to Papa soon. We have got some bathing huts on one of the best bathing beaches here, and soon we are going to start afternoons on the beach. I hope our watches will be changed soon and then I'll be able to participate: as it is now it's very difficult to find time for these things. I am getting quite brown, even tho' I've not been trying very hard. The weather is lovely, but I fear we're in for some hot times later on. Please tell Rosemary I've not written a lot of individual letters to her, except airgraphs because I knew she'd see these. I hope she won't mind and will keep on writing the same though …

No more now. Tons of love Sheila.

Sheila and friends from her watch at Brownie's Hut on Mustapha Beach (left to right) Sheila, Tony Field, Margot Ainscow and Frank Putt.

A recurring theme in the letters is the sending of parcels, either with gifts from the bazaar, or food that is scarce due to rationing. Sheila obviously feels intensely guilty about the quality of life – the fruit, the chocolate, the sunshine – and is constantly telling her mother off for sending her money, although she is not shy of requesting that pink frock again! All this exercise and fresh food is making her healthier; reading through the letters it is noticeable how much sickness there was amongst the forces – from jaundice to more serious illnesses, such as scarlet fever. On the whole Sheila was pretty healthy, bar the odd bout of sand-fly fever or tonsillitis, usually due to overwork:

Office of C in C Mediterranean
7/6/42

My dear Ma –

… Tomorrow I am going out to send you a parcel of sugar ready for the jam season, if I am allowed to. We can only send 5 lb at once tho'. We have now changed our watches, thank goodness and have more time off as we do more hours at once. Consequently I feel much better and have been swimming at the Sporting Club 3 times this week. I am getting thinner – hooray! … I have seen quite a lot of Mary [Dugdale] since she arrived and Sybil [Hoole, from Methil] came this week. She is a <u>dear</u> and brought me so much news of Scotland it made me quite homesick! … I have changed my watch since last I wrote and don't like my new people half as much – none of our usual hysterics! Rosemary asks if I take my tin hat about with me – well, I don't need to and we never have to take gas masks. Unheard of here! I don't know how you send parcels to me, but I would like my pink woollen frock ready for the winter, as wool is terribly expensive here and I have no winter clothes at all. Could you find out how long it would take and how much it would cost to send please … I think I have just been roped in to do some censoring – the Wrens mail has been waiting about here for quite a while and it seems such hard luck on them … I do hope you don't worry about me out here – I am very happy and like all the people here so much – tho' of course life is very artificial, and I would love to be back in the U.K. However that will come … It seems so funny to wake up each morning to a lovely day – always sun, but sometimes hotter than others. I really must stop now, no more space for one thing. I've about six other letters to get off this morning, so heaps of love and do keep writing. Sheila

Amid talk of 'busy and hectic times', concern over 'gippy tummy', shopping and the hectic social whirl it is hard to fathom how they fitted in the work. But every now and again, Sheila reminds us of her watch timetable, and that John is part of the Eighth Army and stationed in the western desert. They must have all been on tenterhooks in June, as the British army was in retreat following its defeat at the Battle of Gazala. The troops had reached as far back as Mersa Matruh, 80 miles within the Egyptian border and, at the end of June when General Auchinleck took over command of the Eighth Army from General Ritchie, they retreated even further to a railway stop called El Alamein. Working in the Cypher Office, Sheila must have been at the epicentre of the messaging, not only about the movement of ships in the Mediterranean, but also of the status quo in the desert, as the navy and the army were working in close collaboration to deliver supplies and weapons to the forces:

17th June 1942

My dear Mama – … I went to the races on Saturday, but alas, never again as it was far from profitable. The one thing is, that everywhere here is the same, and once you've been to a place, all the others are like it – and I actually heard the 1st Officer say with a sigh at lunch 'how I long to be home where you don't have to bother what to eat or what <u>NOT</u> to eat!' You see, you mustn't eat watermelons, prawns, strawberries or apricots, as they are all liable to give you severe gippy tummy – nevertheless, we do and sometimes have to bear the consequences. As I sat down to my melon and 2 eggs, butter, marmalade, and coffee with tons of milk, this morning, I wondered what you were all having at home. Often I refuse 2 eggs for breakfast as I can't eat them! I am terribly brown all over (except for the bathing costume area!) You would think me an Indian.

Tomorrow I am going bathing with Jack Roughton and then on to the Barbers where we are staying to dinner – They have specially invited 2 very musical people who are going to sing, and I am very much looking forward to it. John will be returning to the Wide Open Spaces this week and is very miserable about it. I shall be quite lost without my gallant cavalier! I never see Mary D. these days – she works in the Base on day work which doesn't seem to fit in with my watches at all. Sybil is feeling rather miserable, and as I haven't seen much of her I feel rather guilty. I think I had better wish you many happy returns of your birthday now – because I don't know how long it will take to reach you – I would love to be at home with you, but maybe in a year's time it'll be possible. I hope so, don't you?

I am having 2 frocks made – a chalk blue silk with white fleurs de lys on it and a green pin check cotton – very pretty. I am getting thinner, isn't it marvellous. Have you heard any more of Paul? I am most anxious to know where he is and whether he has left his last ship. He might be coming out here you see. This place is looking gorgeous just now – most of the streets have trees on either side and the flame trees are just one mass of colour – a glorious vivid orange red – the bougainvilia [sic] is almost over, but these flame ones are magnificent. I wish you could see them – you can scarcely believe your eyes … I love my work – it is so terribly vital and important I really feel I am doing a good job, and it counter-balances the regrets one has of not being at home – Regrets? Of course we all have them, but they don't necessarily make us unhappy – far from it! I'm now going to dash off to the Sporting Club to meet John for tea and then back to bed before night duty, which is from 1 am to 0830. Working all the time and if you get no sleep you feel AWFUL. I know – I've tried it! So heaps of love, now take care of yourself and don't think this place is making me blasé or discontented – Just the other way round. It wakes you to reality – Sheila!

The war did indeed nearly come to Alexandria. On 28 June General Auchinleck gave the order to evacuate Alexandria and Cairo, to burn all papers, for the Delta to be flooded and for more defensive positions to be built outside the two major cities. Mussolini even flew into North Africa in preparation for the taking of Egypt, while the Germans dropped leaflets on Alexandria to prepare people for their arrival. The events of the end of June were termed 'The Flap', and at home came under much criticism for undue panic.

This was unkind as, for about a week, it was very touch and go as to whether the Eighth Army could hold Rommel and his forces from a final advance on Cairo. For many Egyptians, fed up with British rule of their neutral country and also with the high cost of living which had given rise to several strikes in 1942, a German victory was to be welcomed if the propaganda was to believed, and they rather enjoyed the sight of the British queuing round the block to raid their bank accounts, and the mayhem at the railway station as women and children were sent to the safety of Palestine and Luxor.

The following letter, describing The Flap and Sheila's own evacuation, was written in September, when the censors would allow it. It also shows that despite her relative lack of education she had keen powers of observation and a writer's eye for detail and humour. It is the first of many descriptive letters that she sends from Egypt and, later, Germany:

Office of C in C Mediterranean
C/O GPO London
27th September 1942

My dear Mummy –

I haven't written you a proper long letter for ages, and ever since we came back from Ismailia I've been meaning to tell you about our 'evacuation', but thought I'd better wait a bit before I gave you a detailed account of it!

Well, we had been working normally for quite a long time at Navy House, which was rather a ramshackle old building standing in its own grounds by the side of the harbour and everything had been carrying on as usual – We'd had a Malta convoy to cope with, which meant a lot of doubling up watches, and of course we'd been told to expect a push in the desert in June, but as ever, nobody thought a great deal about it and were far more concerned with our convoy, which after all, was a Naval operation. These convoys, I may add, are one of the most exciting bits of our work, as we direct one portion from Alex, and every signal we send out is vital and terribly important. So the push came, and at first we did extremely well – everyone was very confident and pleased. Then things began to change a bit, and it became apparent that Gerry was moving in the wrong direction. Every army signal from the desert was received with great excitement and not a little trepidation, and of course everyone was discussing what they thought would happen. I personally have, and always will have, great faith in the army, as I have met a lot of grand people in the army out here and know that there must be thousands more like them. However, things came to such a pitch that plans for the precautionary removal of Naval units from Alexandria were formed, and on the 28th of June, it was decided that we should move. But we weren't told anything definite, and although we knew what was in the air, beyond packing one's vital garments etc. there was nothing to do but wait and see.

That day I was working all morning, and was supposed to do an all night. Just as Margot and I left the office we were told it was possible we were going to Port Said that evening, but were not to breathe a word to anyone. So we returned to 11, Rue Rassafah, where I found Esmé Cameron, a great friend of mine who shared my room, packing like mad for herself and Audrey Coningham, who worked with her, and off she went at half past two. Then I discovered other people had already gone, but still no word for us. We sat around all the afternoon, Mary Dugdale, Rachel and I, and others whom I can't remember. We idly packed, wrote letters home (one of which I found the other day) ate an enormous tea, and censored a huge basket full of Wrens' letters, which we thought might get left behind if we rushed off in a hurry. I can remember Mary playing and replaying a rather wizard record of Richard Tauber singing 'all the things you are' – time and time again, I thought everyone would create hell, but luckily, they didn't seem to notice it. In the middle of all the turmoil a man who had seen John Pritty in Cairo arrived with a letter for me from him – I tried not to show that we were on the move, and think I succeeded because when he saw John afterwards he said he didn't know that we had moved.

Eventually Mary and I got bored, so we took to hurrying into town, as she had to collect some laundry, and we also did a little odd shopping, bought chocolate and biscuits and so on in case we had to go. We returned for dinner at seven to discover that things really had come to pass and that we were to go at 1015 that evening on a special train to Port Said. We rang up and booked seats, but of course weren't able to get a taxi for ages, and we all had at least 3 pieces of baggage, odd tennis racquets and so on. However, we did get one, and then there was journey after journey of 2 people plus baggage, and one returning with the car in case the driver ran away. Johnny Rathbone, who was a survivor from the Malta convoy [her friend Roddy's husband, who lost everything when his ship went down] and who was staying in the officers' rest house next door was my salvation – he appeared out of the blue to say goodbye to me, as he was off to Durban the next day and seeing me plus an enormous amount of baggage still on the doorstep at 10 o'clock, found another taxi from nowhere, and off we set with about 3 minutes to catch the train in. When I and my baggage were eventually disgorged from the taxi and flung onto the crowded platform, to my horror I saw the train slowly sliding out of the station! That was such an anti-climax that I decided there and then to wait till the morning and leave at six am. However, it was not to be so. Everyone seemed to take the most kindly interest in me – a Naval Commander patted me on the back in a fatherly way and told me not to worry and various sailors and soldiers made jokes about the last train to Munich. Just as I was deciding to spend the night in the cloakroom with all the baggage, up rushed the R.T.O. [Railway Transport Officer], an army Captain, a gunner I think. Without more ado, I and my bags were tossed into a 15 cwt truck, and with about six Naval ratings, we just tore through Alex down the Aboukir Road, to Sidi Gaber, where the train was making its next stop. All speed limits were thrown to the wind (and almost my hat as well!) and do you believe we arrived there about 5 minutes before the train.

When it eventually stopped in the station, the R.T.O. made a dash for the C in C's coach (reserved specially for us) and, on finding all the doors locked, told me I'd have to be hoisted into the carriage. There are no glass windows, so it was fairly easy. So in I went, and was given quite a welcome by 3 Naval officers, 1 large wolfhound dog, and the fleet chaplain. The bags were thrown in after. When we eventually settled down, all in the dark, the dog, Jasper, made its home on me – and we proceeded to try to sleep. We could see some kind of an air raid taking place over Alex, but couldn't tell whether it was bad or not. It was a brilliant moonlit night, and about every quarter of an hour we stopped at some small village and people climbed in and out. There was no sleep for us – me, anyway!

I should tell you that the parts of my equipment I really needed – haversack with food, <u>water</u> (it was terribly warm) washing materials, and my great coat, etc. had gone on with one of the first batches, and the train was so crowded it was impossible to move out of one compartment. Eventually we stopped at Santa, and the man who was sitting next to me discovered that his wife, baby, nurse and 19 pieces of baggage were in the carriage next door. He had to leave them to come away and had no idea they had been able to make the train. I remembered later they had caught the train at Sidi Gaber as I did. Everyone was terribly thirsty and we had most amusing bargainings for melons and eggs and lemonade (all of which it is madness to eat, as water can so very easily be tainted in this country).

However, we arrived at Banha, where we were told we were to be shunted into a siding and would stay there for six hours. It was there that I remet all my friends, who were very worried about me – they had had an awful time having got into the wrong coach and had had crowds of squealing wogs [a commonly used term in the war, possibly standing for Western Oriental Gentleman] yelling at them – in the end 2 N.O.s just arrived in the country, mounted guard outside their carriage – but it was awful for them, as they were 9, plus baggage, in one small compartment.

All my carriage, except the fleet chaplain and I, removed themselves temporarily, and with great enterprise. The chaplain produced a bottle of lime, (which turned out to be far more gin) which we shared, and offered me his cassock to sleep in, as it was then about 2am and rather cold. So I slept till about 6:30. When I woke up with sun pouring in the carriage and everyone saying what a marvellous breakfast they had had at a local cafe for the forces – The Victory. So he and I got out and ordered an enormous meal of omelette, tomatoes and chips and tea. My goodness, it was marvellous, then off the chaplain sped and bought the most enormous melon I have ever seen, and a huge bunch of grapes all fresh and with the bloom still on them. On returning to the carriage, I found Pip Pritchard, another Wren Officer, installed. She hadn't been feeling well and was swathed in blankets and sheets and surrounded by pillows.

Soon we were on our way once more, but huge smuts kept blowing over me and I was filthy. We arrived at Ismailia, and Mrs King, plus baby, nurse, baggage and so on separated and on we sped to Port Said. We were now surrounded by horrid yellow sand, and the Suez

Canal on one side. The wind from the desert ride was so hot that we had to shut the windows. Occasionally we saw a ship in the canal, which was terribly calm, and much wider than I thought it would be. The melon was a godsend. We cut it in pieces with a razor blade, and I have never loved one more.

So we arrived at Port Said, the heat by this time was tremendous, and it seemed ages before we had sorted out our baggage and travelled in a huge lorry to the YWCA. This was a flat on the very top of a tall building overlooking the sea – it was so cool and peaceful and we were soon installed. That night just as I was getting to bed, someone came in to tell me Esmé Cameron was downstairs the poor girl had had rather a dreadful time, had only the clothes that she stood up in, and had lost all her possessions [she had gone down with the Medway, recorded in a later letter, when censors would allow]. I had never expected to see her again so soon.

The next day Rachel and I trooped round Port Said, which I liked. I sent you a cable, and then we went to Navy House to see about a case of mine which had vanished. By that time Wrens were arriving from everywhere, by sea as well as by land, and when we returned to the YWCA. I was detailed to go to a convent and see about setting up beds for 40 Wrens. So into a gharry I jumped, and away to the convent, where I found about 20 Wrens already installed, large numbers of nuns who spoke no English and some Gyppo sailors. Between us we managed to erect about 35 or 40 beds in a huge room right at the top of a tall building, and arranged all about lights, bathrooms, showers etc. This ended with a complete tour of the roof and the school, as all the bathrooms, showers and lavatories appeared to be stationed up there – speaking French the whole time! It really was terribly funny, and I thought how much everyone would have laughed if they had seen me.

In the midst of all this (I had asked for tea to be prepared for 20 Wrens and those who were in had eaten the lot, so more chaos ensued!) I was phoned up by Pip, who said I must go back to the YWCA immediately, and she would carry on. So off I went, once more in a gharry and arrived just in time for a well earned cup of tea. But alas, my days in Port Said were numbered, for I was told to pack immediately and drive down to Ismailia in a lorry to be there in an hour's time! This meant packing for Renee and Rachel too – the former being missing, and the latter having to rush out to a laundry to collect a bundle of filthy clothes we'd left there in the morning. In about half an hour Margot, Rachel and I were ready and boarded a huge lorry crammed with trunks, bags and N.O.s and we set off at high speed for Ismailia. The road runs by the side of the Suez Canal and it's about 40 miles. The sun was setting and it really was a grand trip. Soon we knew we were approaching Ismailia, as we saw a lot of pine trees in the distance, and in a short time we were driving through avenues of trees with some grass growing by the sides of the Sweet Water Canal and everywhere looking almost English. Ismailia is a very green town – with grass squares, trees and palms everywhere – such a pleasant change after our dreary, dusty journey. We reported to Navy House, and were then taken to the YWCA which was just grand. A modern house belonging to the Canal Company, with a green garden and the most charming people running it. Mary Dugdale and Kay Way were already there as well as a lot of other Wrens, so we had many joyful reunions.

Rachel and I tossed up for which watches we should do as one was wanted to go on at 8.30 that evening and one at 1am. In the end I did the all night, sleeping most of the time on an arm chair. I think I could have slept anywhere!

And so our life in Ismailia began; it was terribly hot, and I have never worked in such dirt and heat in all my life, nor have I even felt so tired. But I loved it all – just one main street, with tiny shops either side, and the second storey coming out over the pavement, with pillars to keep it up, so that when you went shopping you were in the shade the whole time. Of the rest of our life in Ismailia I think there remains nothing to be told. We were there till the 8th of August, when most of the C in C's staff returned to Alexandria, including the Cypher Officer.

There has been quite a lot of controversy here as to whether the Navy's lightning move was justified or not. The RAF and the army rather tease us about it all, but I personally (and a lot of other people think the same) think that it was a wise step, because, if something unforeseen had occurred and we had not been prepared, events would have taken a very critical trend. Of course, there were many things which could have been organised better, but this is to be expected in any move of this kind. I think the people in Alex were completely shattered, or they say 'so long as the Navy is here, we are all right'. All the nuns in the convent here were weeping and I really think believed Jerry was on their back doorstep! Naturally they were delighted to see us back again.

I think probably this tale will make you smile quite a bit, it did me tremendously, because all the time I couldn't feel I was taking part in a real evacuation, and that one might see a German tank pop round the corner – as some people did. (They were 90 miles away actually) Actually we had far the best time of anyone – a great many of the Wrens travelled from Alexandria to Suez in cattle trucks, stopping by the wayside at regular intervals so that they could spend pennies. On one occasion a number of Wrens plus the wife of one of the N.O.s, got left behind and the train sped on without them. Poor Diana Booth was in hospital at the time with tonsillitis, and was taken to Palestine by hospital train. When she arrived there, it turned out to be Scarlet Fever, and she had to spend 6 weeks in hospital the only woman patient among hundreds of men.

So you see, we do see life!

I don't think I have said anything in this letter which wouldn't pass the censor, and anyway, when you get it it will be very old news. However, maybe you'll treat the matter with 'some reserve' and not tell the tale at every bridge party you go to!!! Please don't throw this away, as it's one of the longest letters I've ever written and I should like to read it over again when war is over!

With heaps of love to you all. You'll gather from this that the Navy takes good care of us!

Sheila

In early July, Sheila's parents were unaware that she was part of the evacuation and that her letters until 8 August are in fact written from Ismailia, although she is careful to let nothing slip. It might explain why Sheila gets so particularly annoyed at her mother's misaddressing the letters, as it will result in them taking far longer to reach her. She realises they must be worrying about her and tries to reassure them. She is also concerned for Paul who, she assumes, must also be anxious. She must have been desperately worried for John and Robin, and countless other friends, who were all in the desert:

Office of C in C Mediterranean
c/o CPO
London
1st July

My dear Ma –

I have just sent you a cable saying that all is well and that you are not to worry. The Navy always turns up trumps and is certainly doing so at the moment!

So please do keep writing to me at the above address – as I think I asked you to before – <u>not</u> NILE, as I have never been based on them, and it takes much longer. Letters are surer to reach me if you put C-in-C on them. We are still thoroughly enjoying life – not in the same manner, maybe – but it is all great fun. Our only concern is for you all at home, who, I am sure, are imagining all kinds of silly things which are quite untrue. I have kept writing as usual, and sent 2 cables just lately, so I hope you realise that all is quite well. I am so sorry for those poor boys in the desert – it must be hell for them.

I had a long letter from R. 2 days ago, a p.c. from you, and also a letter from Paul, who seemed rather miserable. I will try and write to him soon, but maybe you could send him a wee note HMS Sheffield c/o G.D.O, saying I have had his letter and am very fit and well?

Gosh, it is very hot here – I must now run along, and get this posted and censored. I hope you'll get it in 3 weeks as usual – meanwhile, you have the cables, anyway.

Heaps of love anyway,

Sheila

———

Office of C in C Mediterranean c/o G.P.O
7th July / 42

My dear Mama — I hope you got my 2 cables I sent and an air mail letter card telling you not to worry — all is well here — one can scarcely imagine that Rommel is on the back doorstep though I'm sure our poor solider boys know what it's all about! We are all working very hard, but manage to get in a lot of bathing and parties thrown in. I am going to write you a long air mail letter soon telling you about all the things we have been doing recently which I may not tell you about at the moment. It will make you laugh tremendously as it did us at the time!

At the moment it is terribly terribly hot, in fact it is unbearable to go out in the middle of the day. Mary Dugdale and Kay Way are with me, and we are all very happy, but we have heard from Sybil Hoole that she is miserable. I don't know quite why she ever came as she's never been terribly happy since she arrived … I'm afraid I am going to miss some of your mail as I have just heard quite a lot have been lost recently, I hope you kept the counterfoil of the money under our p/o (whichever it was) you sent me, as otherwise it will be down the drain …

Do please note my new address — not that it is new as I have always been C in C — I never was NILE — we are all appointed there for disposal. We are all just covered in bites and the flies nearly drive you mad. I found a flea in my bath last night, so left it to drown. Lo and behold after 5 minutes in water, it was still alive and kicking when I let the water out! I give up entirely!!

No more now.

Heaps of love

Sheila

Office of C in C Mediterranean
c/o GPO London
13/7/42

My dear Mama –

Four of your letters arrived at once, with 6 others from various people, so I am well occupied. To begin with, note and remember my address – it is my permanent one and I never have been NILE. My letters are censored by me myself, but none of yours are censored at all, why I don't quite know. You ask me if I want any papers – well, it would be fun now and again to read English papers and know exactly what import they attach to goings on out here. We all love so much to have news from home! Especially to see pictures of the countryside and so on ...

... I can't tell you how hot it is, really rather horrid and the glare is terrific, but we go to bathe in a lovely salt lake here which is really very beautiful. There are a lot of trees and green grass and it makes us all feel rather homesick. I went out sailing on Saturday which was great fun and yesterday, Sunday, we went to a cocktail party on board a hospital ship, where we met some most interesting people – unfortunately I left my sun glasses at the US Club on Saturday, so went back to fetch them and met a Brigadier and his friend a Major (they were at the cocktail party) who took us out there in their car and plied us with drinks. This Major knew Bert and had seen him only a few weeks ago. It was such fun to chat over our experiences with him. Mary Dugdale was with me – she is so lucky, a very great friend of hers is at GHQ and she is going to ring him up tonight – maybe he will come down and see her. I am rather unlucky, as all the people I know here are scattered – dear little Robin Chater is in the desert somewhere. I am rather worried as I've heard nothing of him for 2 months. I do hope he is OK. John Pritty has returned to the desert, I heard from him last week. Jack Roughton is here no more, but up North, in fact none of my old friends are about at all ...

Life in Ismailia seems to have been fun, but terribly hot: 'you have no conception of how hot it is, the sweat just pours off me when I am sitting still.' The flies are 'appalling' as are the bugs: 'I have found 2 bugs in my bed since I arrived, but cut them in half with scissors thus ending their little game.' They are living in a large YWCA, more 'like a hotel and it's all so English, informal and friendly [that] we all get awfully homesick', run by a Scots couple, and set in a big garden of trees and palms. There is a good Indian bazaar, and she has bought a pretty necklace, plus a present for her mother – a turquoise and seed pearl necklace and an elephant hair brooch, and some gazelle-skin slippers, powder, Revlon lipstick and hair grips for Rosemary. But 'everyone is so dishonest out here, it is unbelievable – and horrid people follow you in the streets trying to sell you things and like the flies they won't be shaken off either. It is most trying.'

There are very few white women, but '1000s of men, it must be awful for them', and although there are lots of army sisters, they are 'ugly and old – until we came along of course'. She, Mary and one or two of the 'less flighty ones' are 'terribly tired of a lot of these men, who are so obviously out for a good time, whoever they are with, and

The Sweet Water Canal and ferry – opposite the YWCA in Ismailia.

you have to be careful in sorting the chaff from the oats. We just can't think how some of these girls are out with different people each night and seem to enjoy it! We thoroughly enjoy life, all the same.'

Despite being terribly 'tired of being asked out by every Tom, Dick and Harry', she, Mary and Rachel Charlesworth, who was on her OTC in Greenwich, are having a very 'gay time', meeting up with old shipmates from the 'tub' and all Robin's division, apart from Robin 'stuck out in the front lines'. She hears 'consistently' from John Pritty and feels 'rather awful really, as though I did see a lot of him, I explained fully my position and hoped I wasn't leading him up the garden path'. It has never been clear to me if it is Paul or Jaap to whom she has lost her heart. To complicate matters, Maureen, John's sister, has arrived in Egypt, although Sheila hasn't yet seen her.

Sailing is a good distraction from the heat and the bugs ('found 3 bugs on my mosquito net yesterday and 1 this morning!!') and she and Mary frequently go out with two of her fellow Cypher 'boys', Tony and Putty. On the work front there has been a 'revolutionary change with the new Principal Cypher Officer changing the watches:

> 4 Wrens and 1 man on one watch, 2 Wrens and 3 men on another, 1 Wren and 4 men on the other watch. I am the latter, which means of course, that we all have to work very hard, but I feel in a way it is a teeny weeny compliment to me that I have been put on the smallest watch, but of course, it is only because I am a fast typist, and hardly anyone is much good at this art! I am on with Tony and Putty, and Lambert, my 1st D.C.O. [Deputy Cypher Officer], and we get on very well together.

Many things in Egypt are expensive, and although her gramophone is an 'absolute blessing', records cost 7s or 8s compared to 2s 10d in England. Laundry is also expensive, as is shoe whitening, but nail varnish is cheap, as are more local goods. With two guineas birthday money from her mother, she is buying some 'leopard skin slippers, a service handbag and cotton dressing gown … Yes, I think I will be able to get them all for that. Some things aren't dear!!' She is having great difficulty with the parcel home, however, as sugar is now rationed and she feels very bad about it.

Her last letter from Ismailia is very bubbly:

Office of C in C Mediterranean
c/o CPO London
3/8/42

My dear Ma –

I am so terribly happy in this new place – I just love the life. I have made new friends and remet old ones, and it is all such fun. Tomorrow I am being driven up to … to see Com. Maloney, Com. Williams is taking me, and we are starting at 7 am in order to miss the heat. We had such fun there last week, Mary and I went out to a hilarious dinner party at their house – the guests amused us by performing acrobatics and ballet dances after dinner (in all this heat!) and then 7 of us packed into a tiny 2 seater Austin 7 and went for a midnight swim. The following evening there was a dance in the YWCA – I walked in to see John Williams of the Signals, who came out with us and is Robin's best friend. We had a tremendous chat. Lo and behold, 2 days later, I was informed there was someone to see me, and who else should it be but Robin, John and another man from the Signals! How nice it was to see them all again. That evening Robin and I went out to the French Club to dine, unfortunately it was my 'Dogs' and 'Middle' watches but we went shopping the next morning and had a hilarious time buying stockings for John Williams' girl friend in England! On Saturday I was out with one of our DCO's and his Air Force friends, dining and dancing. Sunday, yesterday, I went to see 'Bitter Sweet' on board a hospital ship here – I had already seen it, but I didn't mind, except for the fact that their sound track was bad and it went a bit flat in parts! However, on the way home, the boat broke down and there we were, drifting downstream, but luckily King Farouk's uncle's yacht was at hand, and they lent us a boat to come home in. It was a perfect night, millions of stars and the wake of the boat was brilliant with phosphorescence.

…We are hoping to have a midnight picnic in the desert soon, Robin and John are going to arrange it. It all arose out of a remark of mine saying I liked tinned stew – they spend all their nights in the desert when they come over here as there is no accommodation – they take their little signals car – the Jeep – find a good spot and lie in their fleabags under the stars. It is so nice seeing them again – Robin and I hope to celebrate our birthday together as we are twins but for 3 days (I take seniority!)

…Well, as you can see, life out here isn't at all bad, but we work hard too, and the conditions here really are rather appalling. Rachel has just come bursting in like a whirlwind, so there's really not much chance of writing any more coherent paragraphs! (She is most hurt that I have said this and says she hopes you won't think her a horrid girl!!) With lots and lots of love, and don't worry, all is well and we are very happy.

Sheila

Mohammed Ali's yacht which they 'bumped into late one night when returning from the hospital ship, Maine'.

On 8 August most of the Wrens move back to Alexandria; on the return journey they stop to take turns having donkey rides. Sheila now finds herself living in a convent, 'a charming place, and the eight officers have a sweet little house of their own – the convent is enormous, and tho' not old, seems completely medieval'. The nuns wait on them at table and clean their rooms and Sheila feels:

> … most awkward … At night the nuns lock up at about 9pm and everywhere is quiet and dark. We have 2 Sudanese watchmen, and they patrol about inside the grounds with fierce Alsatians to see nobody breaks in. My 1st night watch here I went on at 0400 and they had forgotten to shut them up, so of course up they rushed growling and barking ferociously – giving me a nasty fright. However, the men dashed up soon after and hauled them off!

Of Sheila's friends, Mary remained behind in Ismailia, Diana Booth has scarlet fever and is being looked after in Haifa by Italian POWs –'doesn't it seem a funny war?' – and Sybil Hoole is in in hospital with poisoned bites. So she is feeling a little bereft.

Never downhearted for long, she is soon telling her parents of her latest 'craze', mangoes: 'they are **MARVELLOUS** – but terribly messy. You cut them round the middle and twist them open, then comes the tricky task of getting rid of the stone, which is enormous. In the end you finish up by being juice all over.'

The return to Alexandria also coincides with one of John's periods of leave (he has been promoted to commander), and he surprises her by collecting some 'glamorous undies' she was having made. She had been 'loath' to contact him 'in view of the myriads of letters he keeps writing me and his efforts to do every single thing he can to please me'. He has fallen deeply in love with her and is possessive and jealous of her other friendships. Nevertheless she is soon dating him again, going to the races, having tea at the Beau Rivage, lunches with him and his friends, and receiving notes and dozens of red roses. However the pattern of their future relationship is beginning to emerge: violent quarrels, which are then patched up and they become 'good friends' again.

On the return journey to Alexandria they take turns riding a donkey (left to right)
Geoff Field, Atkins, Sheila, Putty.

John Pritty and Sheila having tea at the Beau Rivage. This was his favourite
photograph of Sheila.

Finally she manages to send off a decent food parcel containing 'tea, sultanas, marmalade, cream, tinned peaches and cigarettes, which I hope will reach you quickly. Sugar is no good I'm afraid – you can't get it anywhere, not that there is any scarcity, but those people who control it here hoard it, so that the prices will go up and they make a profit! Dreadful, isn't it?'

Otherwise life is good. Racing is 'rather fun':

6.9.42

... you sit in an enormous and very comfortable grand stand, surrounded by hundreds of terribly smart people, mostly French Levantine or Syrian, all beautifully and most colourfully dressed – the course is oval and you can see all round. It is at the Sporting Club and in the middle is a golf course, football pitches, tennis courts, swimming pool, club house etc. The paddock is oval also, with shady trees and very cool and when they parade the horses around it's just like an American film of Kentucky or somewhere similar. You'd love it. I did. Of course the races are all prearranged and they dope the horses, but it is fun. They are mostly Arab ponies, small and nearly all grays.

Swimming is a great pastime and there are raucous beach parties with Tony, Putty, Mary, Rachel and Anne Halliday, one of her roommates and also from Scotland. Sheila arranges one such party for her 22nd birthday, which she describes in a letter written the following day, as her 'twin' Robin is back on the front and unable to make their planned desert picnic:

Office of C in C Med. 10/9

My dear Ma – thank you so much for your cable for my birthday. As I think I told you, I had a wizard birthday party. I came off night watch at 0830 and Rachel and I went into town to buy the food, sandwiches, patties, buns, rolls, cakes, beer, coffee, ovaltine, etc and we had a marvellous feast. There were 10 of us. You should have seen

Rachel and me with all the parcels. We had to have a taxi home, there were so many! We went down to the hut for lunch and bathed and played around most of the time. We took a lot of _most_ funny snaps of which I'm having copies made and will send you. John couldn't come because he was ill in bed with sandfly fever. That evening we went out with a friend of Bert's who was down here on leave – it was fun to hear about old Bert again. On the following day I committed a breach of etiquette by visiting sick John in barracks, but everyone was terribly nice – all his friends are mad and rather amusing. The next day we quarrelled (!!!) but it was made up in due course, he having had, or still having jaundice. Lots of people have it out here.

It's miles cooler here now and terribly pleasant. In the evenings it sometimes gets quite cold. You will be interested to hear that I had a nice letter from Jaap last week … I am feeling very sad because Rachel left us last Saturday. John will be going any day now, so I shall be very bereft. One of our Wren officers is being married tomorrow in Ras-el-Nin Chapel and we are all going to the wedding. Great are the preparations …

Oh, I sent off a tin of Turkish Delight to you last week. I thought it might be nice for Xmas. I have bought some silk for Rosemary and am wondering whether to send it home as it is or have it made up. If the latter, they won't arrive for some time. Oh that reminds me, we have just been talking about scissors and I have bought you a small pair of nail scissors which I hope you will like. We are all dying to know what it is like at home. What is rationed – and so on – as although we see papers, they are all Gyppo ones and not quite the same. Things are coming to a pretty pass here – we can't even get sugar at the NAAFI. So silly when there is really plenty. I haven't seen or heard from old Mary Dugdale for days – weeks rather. Wonder what has happened to her? I'm getting my birthday snaps this week and will send them on. Have you had any of the others I've sent. Heaps of love

Sheila

Sheila's 22nd birthday at Sidi Bishr beach (left to right) Mary Dugdale, Putty, Sheila, Geoff Field, Rachel Charlesworth, Tony, Ann Halliday, Lucien. This beach is mentioned by Evelyn Waugh in *Sword of Honour*.

At the end of September Sheila, Kay Way, Mary Dugdale – who has re-appeared from Ismailia – and Anne Halliday remove from the 'peace and quiet of the convent' to the Rue Rassafah, where they share a room and a history – they have all been at Methil at one time or another.

John is returning to the desert and she will 'miss him, as it is so nice to know that you never need be bored, always having someone to do things with'. His parting gift to her is an Irish terrier puppy:

> six weeks old and darling … not a bit the orthodox Irish terrier, but brown and white and so good I feel something awful will happen any moment! I took him on watch this afternoon and the first thing he did was to push his nose in an ink bottle full of red ink which was unfortunately on the deck and got us all red! Then he went to sleep. He belonged to a friend of John's who is going to Malta … Everyone adores him, I'm afraid he'll get terribly spoilt – but not if I can help it. He's rather like this sketch. You would love him.

She calls him Paddy. She is heartbroken when, later on, John's regiment who were house-training him take him to Cairo.

Sheila's letter with sketch of Paddy.

In a letter on 10 October, she ruminates on the relationship with John and her other boyfriends:

John has returned to his regiment and, although we had a marvellous time together, I'm not sorry – at the moment anyway! He is quite miserable I gather from his letters. He is so nice, but quiet and serious – with not very much sense of humour. That's bad for me, I think, as I love laughing and joking and mad things. Jaap and Paul were full of laughter and fun. I heard from the latter recently – a sea mail letter all the way from Canada, of course he is back in the UK or thereabouts now.

Riding becomes a serious hobby. Her friends, Eve and Clement Barber, have some horses, and she, Putty and Tony plan some outings with them. Sheila, ever ambitious and competitive, wants to take lessons and become proficient:

C in C Med 13/10/42

My dear Ma – Today I have had my first riding lesson and am very thrilled in consequence. I went out to Smouha where there is a Frenchman who has stables and who is a very good teacher. He learned from a Russian who taught the Tsars and he himself has taught the King of Egypt. Me and Mrs Barber were there, as arranged, and to begin with I was taught how to get on and off, then did exercises on the horse's back and <u>then</u> (me on a leading rein) we all 4 of us went, via the road to Smouha race course. There we trotted (yes me too) and it was just grand. I didn't find it a bit hard and got on very well. It's much easier when you aren't frightened. I am going to have lessons, and then I shall be able to ride the Barber's horses. Unfortunately, they live rather a long way from here, but never mind!

Riding at Smouha; Kay Way and Sheila are far right of the photograph, with the French teacher M. Delrieux wearing the hat.

The Barbers are 'charming people … very musical', and great enter-tainers and it is through them that she meets Elizabeth Vegdi, her singing teacher, 'a funny little woman, small and birdlike, and terribly nervous. She is German, but not a pro-axis I'm glad to say!' She is to provide another great escape from the rigours of wartime duty and the sadness that accompanies the impending departure of Tony and Putty to Malta: 'it will seem queer without them', the absence of John, in Cairo, and Robin 'in the desert'. This letter describes her first visit to Cairo, where she went in hope of finding John. It seems she can't keep away from him, despite saying she is not stringing him along!

Office of C in C Mediterranean
19/10/42

My dear Ma –

…Well, I have had a very full week again. Starting with dinner out last Tuesday with Mary Henie, a man I knew in Ismailia and another man who used to be in a ship that called at Methil but whom I didn't know in those days. Then, of course, I have been continuing my riding les-sons and last Thursday I arranged to go after night duty. So off I went and was allowed to trot all by myself. We went around the race course, all great fun. I had then arranged to have lunch with Tony Frank, Ian Lepraik and his fiancé, all friends of John. Well, we did have a session, and didn't finish lunch till a quarter to five! When I returned home I found an invitation from an awfully nice Naval Lieutenant asking me out to dinner that evening, I at first refused, but was persuaded into it and I did enjoy it, dancing, dinner and cabaret at the Metropolitan, a new place here.

The following day Tony Frank was going to Cairo by truck and asked me if I would like to go too. So I swapped 2 watches and went. It was an open 15 cwt truck. Cairo is four hours from here and we travelled through the Delta. Oh how filthy the Gyppos are, they live in mud huts and are the dirtiest people imaginable. We had a bit of a dust storm, so when we arrived certainly looked the worse for wear.

However, it was getting dark so Tony took me straight to John's mess, where we learned he was on an operation. The colonel was there and so invited us in for a drink, but horrors, they were all dressed up in mess kit, complete with spats, all ready to go and dance before the King. Imagine how awful we looked after our dirty ride. Luckily we soon managed to escape and I was introduced to Shepheards, the famous hotel there. The next morning Tony was going to take me to see the pyramids (we had seen them in the distance) but was unable to as he had to pack before being drafted elsewhere. So I set off on my own and ended up by visiting an information bureau where 2 A/Bs [Able Seamen] offered to take me to see the Blue Mosque. However, we ended up at the Citadel and visiting the mosque of Mohamed Ali – a beautiful, fairly modern place on top of a high hill fort like Edinburgh. They were so sweet to me, insisted on having taxis and paying for them themselves. They wouldn't hear of me doing so. Eventually I met Tony for lunch, bade him farewell, and set out on my long journey back with a tough Scot to drive me, a commando. Alas, there was the strongest wind I've ever known – I could scarcely breathe. Twice it poured with rain and I was soaked to the skin and then we had a puncture. Luckily the Gyppo army turned up trumps and produced a jack, otherwise I don't know what we would have done! And so I arrived home drenched, the colour of earth and shivering but happy! (I haven't a cold either!) I then worked till 1am the next morning.

Today I have been riding again and hope to go out tonight with 2 local people, Putty and Tony (another one, who works with me) but the latter isn't well so it may be cancelled.

Paddy, my dog, is improving in manners, but feels rather sorry for himself today as I gave him a strong dose of caster oil (good for worms) and it has given him a pain! Today it is quite cloudy, and as I said before, we've had a lot of rain. It is very early for it, they say. I have bought no winter clothes at all, but must really get down to it soon. They will always be useful when the war is over. I have had a nice pair of grey gabardine jodhpurs made which are really quite good. I do love riding and hope one day to become good (??). Am told

I shall have to have 30 lessons before I can jump and then only about 6 inches, but we shall see!

I wonder if it is time for tea?? Must go in and see as I'm in the garden on account of the dogs inside!

Tons of Love

Sheila

Oh the flies - they are <u>so</u> tame!

The Second Battle of El Alamein started on 27 October and ended on 11 November, Armistice Day. It also coincided with the beginning of Operation Torch on 8 November, when the US army began their advance eastwards from Casablanca and Oran, with the aim of joining up with the Eighth Army and routing the Axis forces. Alan Moorehead's descriptions of the final push in North Africa are brilliantly recounted in *The African Trilogy:*

> The Eighth Army had stalled the Germans after the First Battle and there had followed a period of stalemate, but General Montgomery, taking command of the Eighth Army in August 1942, knew that he had to retaliate before the Germans, who had vastly superior guns and tanks, were able to re-supply themselves from Italy. But decisive action by the Navy ensured that the Axis supply lines were not replenished, and the Eighth Army now had the US Sherman tanks for the first time and with these, together with superior intelligence work which fooled Rommel, Monty inflicted a great victory over the Axis forces. Their casualties were 2,349 killed, 5,486 wounded, and 30,121 prisoners, and the loss of 500 tanks. Montgomery's casualties were 2,350 killed, 8,950 wounded, and 2,260 missing, as well as around 200 tanks.
>
> It was to be the first major victory for the Allies since the war began in 1939 and provided a tremendous morale booster for everyone,

civilians and services alike. Churchill summed it up thus: 'This is not the end, it is not even the beginning of the end. But it is, perhaps, the end of the beginning.'

John Pritty is back in Alexandria still in hot pursuit of Sheila, prior to joining his regiment in the desert for the battle, but her other friends have left: 'There is only Geoff and I left, the 2 originals, and 2 new people who have joined us. Naturally, we are very busy just now (and a very good thing too) so have to keep our wits about us. Last night I worked every single minute of the night watch – I have slept this morning – a thing I haven't done for ages. The news is most heartening, I am glad to say and we all hope that things will be cleared up out here quite soon.'

With all the activity in the Mediterranean a lot of mail has 'gone down' and she is worried about 'two food parcels, 1 tin of Turkish Delight and a pair of scissors' that she had only just sent. Sheila has received a lot of mail herself but is in sick bay and has mixed feelings: 'It's marvellous rest really as quite honestly we've been working so hard since we returned 3 months ago. I was quite worn out. Our watch has always been one short!!'

She takes the opportunity to write a long-overdue letter to her father:

Office of C in C Mediterranean
C/O CPO London
8/11/42

My dear Daddy –

Thank you very much indeed for part one of your birthday letter to me, and part one of your present, which has mighty delighted me. Part 2 hasn't put in an appearance yet, but mails are so queer one never knows what to expect. I'm afraid this isn't going to reach you in time for your birthday and may not even arrive by Christmas, but anyway, here's all the best of wishes and luck.

You do make me laugh with 49 tomato plants! Why not 50, to make it even. I hope more have ripened off, otherwise I can see chutney will be indicated – not that that's to be scorned at. How I love it! I do envy you your apples and pears, for we don't get them here and you always want things you can't have! I've no doubt you'd willingly be in my shoes and be having bananas, oranges, grapefruit, grapes, figs, dates etc. though, I'm ashamed to say my banana for dinner tonight almost choked me! and I couldn't even look a date in the eye! They are so good, too!

Well, in spite of all your warnings, I haven't found Alexandria an unsuitable spot to live in, and I very much liked Port Said! Granted Tewfik is an unpleasant enough spot, but a great number of Wrens lived there at the time of the evacuation, and very many of them liked it a lot. They all lived in what was once a transit camp for soldiers, all wired in – they called it the Aviary. Actually, they all had a very good time socially, as every unit for miles round used to invite them to parties, some of them quite a journey into the desert. Even now there are about 50 still living in Tewfik but they are installed in a house. All this while we were living in the YWCA in Ismailia, a simply charming spot and run by some delightful Scottish people. Of course, we had a wizard time, too, and I was awfully disappointed when I was told our section of the staff was returning to Alex, for a long time we were the only Wrens in Alex, and lived in the convent, which was really ratings' quarters, but eventually almost the whole flock returned and we were cast out to Rue Rassafah, our old officers' quarters.

This was a most unpopular move, but actually now we're back again, we're quite happy. I have my dog Paddy, and share a room with 3 great friends, so all is well. At the moment, I regret to say, I'm in sick bay, but it is a marvellous rest, and if we weren't so busy I'd be completely happy. All this activity in the desert has livened our work up considerably and it doesn't do to be short these days.

I've had to forego my riding lessons lately, as really I've had too much to do and been far too tired – but I certainly intend to carry on with the good work. It is all such fun – we go on one of the race-courses here – with a golf course in the middle and it is all so green you can easily imagine you are at home. I shan't be happy till I can jump and it will take 30 lessons I'm told.

We are all very thrilled to hear about the desert news, though even tho' we are at the Mursa Matruh it doesn't mean we've driven the Germans out completely. However, since a great deal of our work is built up around these things you can guess it is very exciting for us. I am very annoyed at being away from the office at such a time (I'm in sick bay not <u>very</u> ill with a streptococci bug in my throat!) Have told you this twice owing to lapse!

We are still in whites, tho' we anticipate changing to blues any moment now. The weather here, is, as you probably know, very mild, tho' I hear wild tales of terrible cold and everyone shivering. Never does the temperature reach freezing, that's one thing certain, so I can't imagine what everyone is so worried about! They do have snow in Syria, but as the Navy never gets leave on Med station, I can't think that we shall ever get proof of this fact! Pity, because I should love to go there – mountains, green trees and grass, waterfalls and beautiful scenery, so I'm told. Not so here, the Delta reminds me of the Fens, all very flat and rather dull. Actually our life here is extremely pleasant and again I smile when I read letters from home full of imaginations as to how unpleasant our surroundings are!

…We have plenty of food and *safragis* to wait on us, plenty of friends and countless opportunities of going out, helping in canteens, sport to play, tennis, hockey, swimming – horses to ride, sailing, in fact everything anyone can want for, except beautiful country to live in – so I don't think we are too badly off, do you? We all wonder frightfully what it is like at home, but letters seem to be most reassuring, tho' of course we never know whether it is just a gallant front put up for our benefit.

Good heavens, 20 to 10 and me meant to be an invalid (I feel fighting fit except for the rotten throat, actually!) So no more.

With very much love to you and mama,

Sheila

And to her mother, also on 8 November, she says :

It makes me laugh when you say in your letters what hardships you think we are going through. Admittedly I think we'd all rather be in UK, but life out here is just a picnic – we live in comfortable houses, have tons to eat, can buy clothes and food without coupons (provided you have the money). In fact it all boils down to the fact that you can do anything. I feel sorry for the troops, because they don't get paid so much as we do, and there aren't nearly enough girls to go round, not English ones anyway, and beer is very dear here …

The desert news is excellent isn't it? I am rather annoyed I am stuck away here at such an interesting time because our work is formed to a very great extent from these activities. I hope we shall clear up Africa this time, and can then turn our attention to other fields.

Yes I did hear from Jaap – most queer, he certainly had written before, but nothing had reached me and one had even been returned to him! I've heard quite a lot from Paul, one even from Canada, but nothing much lately.

John is having a birthday party this week, but I don't know whether I shall be up for it. Maybe they will put it off! I feel fine, except for this foul throat – I sound awfully tonsilly when I speak! I am handing Paddy over to John for complete house training, as he hasn't quite got the knack yet.

With heaps of love,

Sheila.

Once back at work she concentrates on organising the Wrens' social life. A hockey match between John's regiments and the convent turns out to be embarrassing for her, following one of their famous 'disagreements', for they had decided 'not to see one another and there he was, large as life on the pitch, but however, we've managed to patch things up and all appears to be settled once more.' It didn't last long, however, as John is posted back to Cairo, with appendicitis 'all very miserable'. They had two 'tremendous bust-ups' before he left but managed to make it up and become 'firm friends' once more.

Even more annoying is a change on the work front:

> ... perhaps the most revolutionary that there will be no more Wren
> head watches, (a little blow for us, who have been here longer than
> many of the men and have seen more months of service as an officer
> – even cyphered longer!) However, we have to accept this, hard tho' is
> may seem – I have been in the office now longer than any Wren tho'
> of course haven't the long seniority several of them have. We have
> about six new O.T.C. Wrens with us – a good thing as they are all
> most conscientious and work harder than most men.

This is the first sign of dissatisfaction since Sheila has been in Egypt
and is the beginning of an unsettled period.

Of her friends, Sybil Hoole has got engaged:

> ... we are all thrilled, as she has been rather unhappy here ... Kay is
> leaving us for a more Northern place – lucky girl, but it is not far away.
> As a matter of fact I'd like to be there myself, with the kind of boats
> I'm interested in, and quite near dear old Bert, whom I haven't seen
> for ages. Diana Booth, (the one who travelled out with me and who
> married the padre) is back here recovering from a septic appendicitis.
> She is very week, poor dear. We sorted out her goods yesterday and
> she is now on a fortnight's sick leave.

Anne Halliday has left for Cairo, so only Mary Dugdale and Sheila
remain.

And so the year draws to a close with another Alexandrian
Christmas, which seems to have been the greatest of fun:

> In bed 28/12

> My dear Mama – First of all, I hope you had a very good Xmas – if
> half as enjoyable as mine, it would have been grand! Was Rosemary at
> home? Well, as space is short, I'll tell you what I did now. We began the
> week by carol singing – a huge party of us with big lanterns and a lorry.

We started off in RN Barracks, and then proceeded to the A.O.C.'s house, where we were warmly received. After that we passed on to a nearby hotel, and from there to the C in C's house, where we were all invited in, and entertained with drinks. A very exalted party with admirals galore! From there we drove on to the FSO's house, and after singing outside, were all invited in to drink a hot punch! It was all such fun, most picturesque with all the lanterns, but most unfortunately, I had a bad cold and was not allowed to sing, so I just had to be content with collecting. We made £22 – not bad! Another drawback was that I had to go on night duty afterwards, but luckily we weren't busy.

There were no more festivities for me till Thursday, when Ann Cartwright (one of the recently made cadets) and I went out to a Christmas party given by Eve Barber. It was such fun, other guests were the Delrieux family (who took us riding) and a very amusing man called Sidney, a gunner, and of course Ivan, their Hungarian friend who lives with them. We played mad games, and laughed and laughed, ate the most enormous buffet supper and greeted in Xmas with Champagne! It was poor Ann who had to go on night duty this time! Then on Xmas Day, Ann, Mary Henie and I all went to the Scottish Church. Again I wasn't able to sing! I worked all the afternoon, and when I returned found a big tea party in full swing in the quarters, with a lot of young N.O.s from the various ships that were in. Audrey Dean (a nice girl on my watch) and I tucked into an enormous tea and then I had to run away and change, as 10 of us were going in a big party of 20 to the Union Club, where there was a dance. The male members of the party were of a Scottish regiment (not John's) and were great fun. We ate the most tremendous dinner, turkey, plum pudding, flaming on the plate, fish, asparagus, mince pies etc. washed down by sherry and champagne. We had a room of our own and the most glorious sheaf of red roses on the table! We danced and danced, me with a charming man from St Andrews whom I had met previously at a cocktail party held by the same regiment. Again it was me to go on night watch and I had to leave at 12 o'clock – quite Cinderella like, but I didn't lose my shoe! Night watch was awful – luckily I was able to crack it down. On Boxing Day I promised to do an extra watch for Mary Henie, and have regretted it ever since, as I've been so terribly tired; my second extra watch this week, but all my own fault! However yesterday, when I came off duty at 1300, I went out to the Barbers again, Ann Cartwright too, for lunch and riding. We made up a big party and went to the school. Eve and Clement, Ann and I, Sydney and my St. Andrews friend, whose name is Valentine. Oh it was tremendous fun. Ann, who is an excellent rider, was given monsieur's own horse, a tremendous honour. I was given a good little gray, but jiminy, he could go! I'll continue on another card and hope they both arrive together.

Lots of love pro tem.

Sheila

Also in bed. 29/12

Dear Ma – (continued) We were all turning round onto the sand track, when suddenly my horse, Ibn el Ansi, decided to dash ahead, and my goodness there was nothing stopping him! It was a marvellous feeling to be tearing along in from of all the others, and I didn't feel a bit like falling off! After we had finished riding, Ivan took us to see his mare, Belle Aurore, which first he rode, and then Ann. She really is a beautiful beast, and needs no kicking or hard work at all. Then to my great surprise and joy, Ivan asked me if I would like to ride her! Of course, when I was up, I could tell immediately how different she was from the riding school ones, responsive to every slight touch and movement. I trotted and cantered but alas, pride did come before the fall, because while cantering a corner of the paddock, I didn't pull her round enough. We swerved and I slid to the ground with a tremendous bang. Neatly landing on my situpon! Of course, it completely served me right, and I had no business to be riding such a good horse, but the temptation was far too near! Anyway, there are no ill effects today, spare a sore backside and scraped elbow.

Today I am spending the morning in bed, going for a singing lesson and tea with Mme Vegdi, and then on to a cocktail party this evening. On Thursday I am lunching with Mrs Goldie [a family friend] and playing in a hockey match afterwards, and on Friday I go on leave to Cairo!

Yes, we have all been given <u>three</u> days leave, not very generous, but leave! John will be out of hospital and we will explore Cairo together. Then he will return to Alex with me, for the rest of his time. I am very much looking forward to seeing Ann Halliday who has now got a job there, and who likes it tremendously. I had such a nice letter from her today ... I miss her very much, but have Mary Dugdale here to keep me company. Much as I like being in Alex, and in spite of the many interests and friends I have, I do feel that as regards my job, I need a change. I have been here longer than any Wren and, of course, get no consideration for any work I may do or have done. I am in no better a position than I was when I arrived and am on equal par with all the new cadets and raw recruits we have to train. I feel it is not good enough - but I don't get on at all with the P.C.O. [Principal Cypher Officer] and he makes good use of a willing horse! I don't want to leave all my friends, of which there are many, or my singing or riding, but I must move soon, where to, I can't imagine. Maybe it would have been better for me to have gone to Cairo, too. We shall see!

I don't know what's happened to our mail, but I've had no <u>letter</u> from you since 29/11. Granted I've had a few P.C.'s and airgraphs, but they aren't the same. I wonder how you have been faring? I have been thinking about you all and what you have been doing and wishing I could send you some of our food. I am heartily sick of tangerines and oranges and grapefruit. Doesn't it seem awful when you can't buy them?

No more now. Tons of love and many happy new years to you both.

Sheila

The unresolved matters of 1942 – her affair with John Pritty and her discontent with her status and role in Alexandria – are to dominate events in 1943.

1943

'I am bursting with pride'

In July 1942, General Montgomery had taken over from Auchinleck and the tide began to turn. The Anglo-American First Army had landed in North Africa in November 1942 (Operation Torch), and met up with Montgomery's Eighth Army in Tunisia, finally capturing Tunis on 10 May. The three-year battle for the Western Desert and North Africa was finally won. This paved the way for the Second Front that Churchill and Roosevelt had agreed in January 1943 in Casablanca: an attack on Europe through Italy, perceived to be its soft underbelly, leading to an unconditional surrender.

As a result the focus of the war shifted back to Europe, and Sheila was sent from Alexandria to Cairo to help Admiral Ramsay and his team plan Operation Husky, the invasion of Sicily, the precursor to landing in Italy itself. She was assigned to the important work of monitoring, via cyphers and signals, both enemy and British fleets in the Mediterranean. The work she did with Ramsay remained her proudest achievement and she was rewarded with the coveted 'second stripe'.

When looking through her papers, I found a letter she sent to *The Times* on the fiftieth anniversary of D-Day, singing the admiral's praises, which elicited a response from his son, David Ramsay. In her reply she says:

For myself, I knew little about your father when I was plucked from the C-in-C's cypher office in Alex to join his staff at Cairo, save that he masterminded the evacuation of Dunkirk. Only 22, I was to be in charge of the speedy circulation of signals which came up from Alex each day ... we were a motley crew to join the cream of Navy in a dusty old house in the backstreets of the road to the Pyramids, crammed into a tiny room with nothing but functional furniture – no detailed maps on the walls, and wastepaper baskets which had to cleared and the contents burned only by responsible personnel ... security was minimal, although first class. No Wren in those days ever signed the Official Secrets Act, Egypt was bursting with spies, and we all lived ashore in various YWCAs in the city. It goes without saying that we were entirely trusted.

As for the Admiral, his calm and friendly manner belied the importance of the task he was undertaking. He had time to entertain even most junior officers such as me, and I was enormously impressed to hear from a Wren friend who had been on his staff at Dover in the days of Dunkirk that he had recognised her walking down the street in Cairo and had stopped to greet her by name.

It may seem strange to you, but in after years when faced with problems of integrity it was the memory of your father's example which guided me to stick to my guns.

Her scrapbooks contain an admission ticket and a copy of the memorial sheet from his service in Westminster Abbey (he was killed in a plane crash in France in 1945, not long after the D-Day landings, when he was Naval Commander-in-Chief). She writes vehemently in his defence to her mother, who must have been critical of him.

While the letters reveal a seemingly never-ending social whirl of dining, dancing, sightseeing, yachting, the races, all jockeying for position with her hobbies of singing and riding, there are frequent mentions of the long hours and the rigours of office life – including an obsession with hair length – and her desperation to rejoin the war on a more active front after the thrill of working with Admiral Ramsay on the invasion of Sicily. As she herself says, 'Our shadow is diminishing instead of increasing. Soon I feel we will fade out altogether and then what?'

North Door

𝕎estminster 𝔸bbey

ADMIT ONE

MEMORIAL SERVICE

for the late

Admiral
SIR BERTRAM H. RAMSAY,
K.C.B., K.B.E., M.V.O.

at 12.30 hours.

Monday, 8th January, 1945.

2/0. g. mills. W.R.N.S.

Admission ticket to Admiral Ramsay's memorial service.

Cairo in the middle of the war was a vibrant place, despite all the political upheavals of the time and a profound anti-British sentiment felt by some sectors of Egyptian society. Things were not only expensive for the forces (Sheila complains about the price of various necessities), but for the poor fellahin, or peasant, the wartime inflation and shortages of cereals, sugar and paraffin represented an enormous hardship. Anti-British propaganda – for Cairo was a hotbed of spies – would have fuelled such feelings; and with the king openly at loggerheads with the British ambassador, as well as with his own Prime Minster, the state of Egypt was far from calm.

Nevertheless for the officers, whether stationed in Cairo or when on leave, life was to be enjoyed at all costs. The military working day began at 9 a.m. and then broke for lunch at 1 p.m., when one retired to either the Gezira or Turf Club to swim and play tennis, with lunch being a sumptuous buffet. Then back to work from 4 p.m. until 9 p.m., when it was out to a restaurant followed by dancing. Other ranks were not admitted to the clubs, nor to the more upmarket nightclubs, such as the Continental and Shepheards, where Sheila danced the night away with her beaux. Groppi's, on the other hand, was open to all, but was prohibitively expensive. This is where old Cairo society met for gossip and coffee on a daily basis.

The ratio of women to men meant that women were, according to Artemis Cooper, a 'privileged minority'. She continues, 'it was open season for husband hunting … young women in Cairo knew they would never have such choice again, certainly not in post-war Britain … the war provided not only the first real romantic opportunity for these young women, but also the most powerful argument for giving in to male supplication. That the man in question might be killed next week lent not only a poignant intensity but also a noble, generous element to the affair.'

In 1943, Sheila is tiring of the endless rows with John Pritty, although I imagine she felt torn, as he must have endured privations in the desert, weeks on end in terrible conditions – either stranded by sandstorms, or bogged down in mud (yes, mud) depending on the season – and mindful of the extremely high casualty levels suffered at the front due to the Germans' superior air power, tanks and guns.

She has all this time retained a friendship with Robin Chater, whom she met on the boat coming out and, now in Cairo, meets a much more stable suitor in the form of Bruce Booth-Mason, a major in the Indian Cavalry, although he, too, is also drafted to the Eighth Army. She still writes fondly of her 'childhood' sweetheart, Paul, and of Jaap, her dashing Dutch officer, whom she met in Scotland. I suspect it was a case of rather hedging one's bets, as the chances were that one or more boyfriends would not survive.

I only discovered the answer to the obvious question of whether she slept with any or all of her boyfriends when I, quite by chance, found a bundle of love letters from my father to her, written in 1946, during their engagement. Despite Olivia Manning's loose living or, as my mother would have said, 'fast' ladies in *The Levant Trilogy*, the rule seemed to be that ratings did, while officers didn't! I will return to these letters in a later chapter.

The New Year gets off to a rocky start with a row with John Pritty, her current boyfriend:

C in C Mediterranean
10/1/43

My dear Ma and Pa –

First, a happy New Year, second, thank you for your cables, letters, pc's and aircards which have just started coming in again. I've had no airmail letters, tho', since the beginning of December, and fear they may be lost. I do hope not.

Well, I wrote and told you of my Christmas so now of my new year. New Years Eve and I had to spend on duty unfortunately, but Audrey Dean (a new girl and so nice) and I danced round singing Auld Lang Syne, and we drank to the New Year in ginger beer and munched bananas! Then the next day (New Year Day) I had 3 days leave and went up to Cairo. I had arranged it all beautifully, to fit in with John coming out of hospital, but he suddenly took umbrage and we only met once. However, I stayed with Ann Halliday at the YWCA and was determined to enjoy myself. So on my 2nd day, 3 of us took a gharry and went to the Musky, which is the native market and bazaar. There you really see Egypt as it has been for thousands of years. Narrow narrow streets with little shops open to the street, and inside men and boys sorting cotton, beating copper into pans, making minute and intricate silver bracelets in filigree. It's full of shrieking children, beggars, guides, merchants and people buying. We suddenly found ourselves by the Blue Mosque which is a place I've wanted to visit for ages. It's the oldest mosque in Cairo and is 900 years old. We went inside and soon found an awfully nice little man who became our guide. It was small, really, inside, with very high ceilings and a dome 40 or 60 feet high. Pillars of granite and marble which had been brought by goat from Aswan, taking 3 months. The tops of the pillars and the ceilings were inlaid with gold and lapis lazuli, and the windows were filled with the most gorgeous coloured glass you've ever seen. In the centre was the tomb of the man who built it, a king from Turkey: this was plain and made of sandalwood, and there was a short pole at the head with a monk showing how tall the king was. Actually, he was a hunchback and therefore very small. Then a fortune teller came along with a little bag of sand which he laid on the floor, drew a circle in the sand, and told our fortunes. Apparently I am destined for 3 children, the 1st being a boy with red hair and green eyes! So! While coming out of the Blue Mosque, an old old man came in in rags, bearing on his back a water bag made from goat carcass. It was just like the Bible. Then we went on to see a very old home, now protected by the Egyptian government, which is the only one of its kind left in Cairo. It is 600 years old, and perfect. You go down a narrow street and through a gate and find yourself in a courtyard with a palm in the middle, and then house all round. There are rooms for reading the Koran during Ramadan, and balconies for the women to sit and listen too. Coffee rooms, with fountains in the middle, and old old carpets on the floor. Bathrooms with hot and cold water and the harem where the Sheikh lived with his 3 wives. Little mosques and large garden behind with vines and orange trees growing and lastly, a water wheel and wheel used for grinding corn. All exactly as they had been 600 years ago. I was just thrilled. There was a dear old boab or ghaffer in charge who had been a sergeant in the last war and who had won a medal. Well, our little guide then took us to a silver factory, where we saw little boys of 5 and 6 making beautiful filigree brooches and bracelets. I bought one which I am sending to Rosemary. I didn't think you'd wear bracelets, mummy. After drinking coffee with the owner, a young man who was most helpful, we then proceeded on to a silk shop, because the Egyptian brocade is heavenly and I have an evening gown made of it. Well, I bought a glorious bit – a deep royal blue, with gold flowers all down it, and shot so that it shines gold when worn. Already I have given it to the dressmaker and she is making an evening dress for me. By this time we had been exploring for about 2 hours, and really thought we had better go back to lunch, but no, the little man insisted on taking us to the perfume shop which we found in the spice market. The smell here was simply marvellous. Great sacks of cloves, chilies, cinnamon, corn of all kinds were displayed in front of the shops. When we found the perfume shop, the man immediately produced chairs and we proceeded to smell, and have dabbed all over us, all the perfumes of Arabia. It really was most amusing! Ann eventually bought the secret of the desert (!) (it smelt like citronella to me!) and I, Camabon (which I have since lost). Then we really had to go, so having tipped our guide (who was most fair about it) we rushed off to find a tram – which was so full that we had to stand on the step and cling on for dear life! How we all laughed and everyone was so kind to us, gave us seats, told us where to go! I did enjoy it so. I know you would have adored it mummy. I think I'll do as last time and continue this on another card. I hope they both arrive at the same time …

Well, that afternoon Ann and I decided we would go and visit the Pyramids. Unfortunately we left it rather late but set off on a tram, as usual, it was terribly crowded and we found we had to travel 2nd class as there was no room. It was absolutely packed with fat old women with baskets, people who looked like Bedouins with all their earthly possessions with them. English, Arabs, Greeks – just everyone. Eventually we got out at Giza, and took a taxi. We arrived at the Pyramids at about 4:30 and the sun was almost setting. However, we hurried on, and saw 2 horses which we decided to hire. Here we did strike a patch of unpleasantness as the 2 syces kept saying 'give me tip now', but we were firm. We chartered a guide and off we sped. I wasn't in the least bit disappointed, as most people are, and wanted awfully to climb up and go inside, but there wasn't time. The sun sets so fast here. So we rode round to the Sphinx which I adored, but I am very annoyed with Napoleon for knocking off his nose. We also saw an old granite temple nearby, and a lot of tombs cut into the rock. Unfortunately it really was growing dark, so we had to turn back. What we want to do next time is to start out early, thoroughly explore the Giza pyramids, and then take horses and ride over to Sakara, where there are some more far older pyramids, tombs of the kings and the ancient city of Memphis. But I'll have to get more leave before we can do this. It was now quite dark, for we rushed off and caught a tram and landed up in

Cairo about 3/4 hr later. The blackout there is negligible, and all the shops were open and ablaze with light. We really were terribly tired by now, and so had dinner and went back to bed.

The next day I had to return to Alex, but I visited Ann's new office which I liked tremendously, and we had coffee in the famous Groppi's.

Since I have been back here, John has been staying here on convalescent leave, and eventually, after seeing him around the place, we did meet. The trouble is, in a nutshell, that he wants to become engaged to me now, and I feel it would be a silly thing to do, we have been engaged, on and off, several times now, and at the moment I'm not at all sure how things stand, but he really is so temperamental it rather frightens me. I really feel the best thing to do is to wait till the end of the war and see how we feel. Another thing is that he's probably leaving this country and going miles away, which wouldn't entirely help matters would it? Anyway, at the moment, we are the best of friends.

I was told this week by the P.P.O. [Principal Personnel Officer] that he had recommended me for a 2nd stripe but not to bank on it as all promotions have to come from home. Well, I just know that I won't get it, or really deserve it, in view of the far senior people there are out here, and anyway, feel it must just have been a matter of routine as you have to give an assessment of everyone's ability at the end of the year. So I never expect or even want to rise and think of the jealousy it would cause. All I feel pleased about is that I have been recommended, so please don't breathe a word to anyone – and will wait and see. You see, to get 2 stripes restricts you terribly. You can only do jobs which are worthy of your rank!

… I suppose you haven't heard or seen any more of Paul! He is still in your waters, I know, and I have had no mail from him for some time. We have lost a tremendous amount of mail lately, and I just hate to think of all the letters of mine which will have gone missing.

So no more, with tons of love to you both and many happy new years,

Sheila

In the Musky.

The next few letters describe the ups and downs of her relationship with John, and she is still hankering for news of her old boyfriends, Jaap and Paul. It must have been hard for Sheila with so many of her friends getting married or engaged and seemingly settling down. Nevertheless she is determined to make the most of life, seeing the sights of Cairo and Alexandra, while shopping and having fun – riding, singing dancing – just like any normal 22-year-old. She finds time to send parcels home as well, and voices her disapproval – again – of her sister's activities:

C in C Med 19/1

My dear Ma – ... Well, this week I have sent off a parcel containing 2lb sugar, 2lb marmalade and 1lb butter, which I hope you will get all right. We have at last found a shop which can send sugar, and I will send you some as often as I can. I have also packed up very carefully a necklace which I bought ages ago for you, but didn't know quite how to send it and a bracelet I bought for R. Today I found some Velouty [perfume] which I know you like and am wondering how I'll send it. I think it is better to send things separately, as if they get lost, it's only one article … Yes, I think it would be a very good thing if R could get her commission quickly, as I thoroughly disapprove of going about with this and that just for the sake of a 'good time' (if you call it such). We never did when we were Wrens but then of course I always had Jaap in the background which completely kept me going. What is all this about promotion after being commissioned a year? We've heard nothing of it out here – if it's true, then nearly all of us automatically jump up.

I have been busy this last week, as John has been spending the last week of his leave here. He has gone away now, and really I think it's quite a good thing as he was getting more and more worked up and we seemed to do nothing but argue and argue each time we went out. Pity, as he can be so nice. In all fairness to us both I couldn't prom-ise to marry him, as he is such a jealous person I should have been expected to immediately retire labelled 'property of J.F.C.P. keep off'. Every time I went out with anyone he at once imagined I was vio-lently keen on them and it wore me out having to account for my every harmless action. When one is at home and there's no war, it's slightly different, but out here with everyone away from home natu-rally a bit more lonely. It's too much to expect one to stay in the whole time. And I'm not an awful gadabout. I had an awful fright because he calmly told me one evening he had announced our engagement in the Egyptian mail – all without having told me. Sure, at one point I had agreed to marry him, but not till after the war and I saw no point in making it public with him going away as it wouldn't be a good thing for either of us. This was too much for me, as I felt it was all a way for keeping me safe so I rang up the paper and cancelled it. We had a frightful row, and then were terrified that it would appear, because he'd entered it in the Cairo office and I'd cancelled it at Alex. However, it hasn't appeared yet so I presume all is well. I suppose it may have seemed queer but I don't think you should announce your engagement unless you're quite certain it'll come off and with him going away for perhaps years, anything might occur to either party. So he said he'd see me no more, or write even. It seemed a pity after all the good times and fun we've had, but what could I do but agree? However, the day he left, my favourite pink roses appeared with a note saying we couldn't part thus, which means, I presume, we will be writing as usual. Oh the trouble one has! Diana [Booth] and Mary [Henie] have been advising me all the time and we've come to the conclusion it's better this way. Somehow having fallen hard once, it's difficult to fall again in a hurry.

Mail has been shockingly bad and I know we have lost a lot. Promised letters from other people haven't arrived as well as yours. It is so disappointing. I am going riding this afternoon, then on duty. But to dinner on Thursday and Saturday, singing on Thursday and Friday and riding again on Thursday. My singing is apparently progressing very well. I certainly enjoy it and am now allowed to practice by myself. I do hope you get all the parcels I have sent off. If you don't reply that you've had the food one in nine weeks, the dealer with send another free!

Sheila

With heaps of love (please keep my story QUIET. I should hate all the family to discuss this).

———•——

C in C Med 20/1

My dear Ma – ... It is really awfully cold (not freezing but bitter in comparison to Summer) and we are all in greatcoats, have extra blankets and hot water bottles and just shiver. These houses are so vast and airy, with no central heating and we only have one fire – you can't imagine how chilly it is. I am thankful for my winter dressing gown and wish I had brought more warm clothes. I am a lucky girl – a big bunch of roses and asters has just arrived from John, asking why I haven't written. I didn't know I was expected to! Anne Halliday has just become engaged to a marine. She is still in Cairo and another girl we need to work with has also announced her engagement. Seems to be the fashion. I have just been to a singing lesson which I enjoyed tremendously. Mme Vegdi is a dear and strange as it may seem, is very pleased with my voice. Unfortunately it takes 2 or 3 years to fully produce it, and I'm sure we won't be here for that length of time! As for riding – well, I am still very much in love with it, but I went on Sunday and had a typical riding school horse, which wanted to walk the whole time and always tried to take the short cut home. He was terribly obstinate and we kept going round in circles – in the end he fell down a water hole and I was terrified that he'd break his legs, but he was alright. I had to jump off and pacify him, but found it awfully hard to get on again as he was so tall. One really needs spurs for such an obstinate brute … Did I tell you I had a contretemps with the C/O. resulting in my having my hair cut. It wasn't frightfully long (some of the others are far longer and haven't been told) but she was with a Rear Admiral, who remarked on it, so poor old Mills got a bottle! Within 15 minutes I was in a gharry and off to the hairdressers, where I had it cut and permed. Actually it really looks quite nice, tho' it felt a bit strange at first. I haven't sent off the necklace yet, but will do so soon, and you should get it within a month, anyway I <u>love</u> it and have one like it.

With heaps of love

Sheila

———•———

C in C Med
9th February 1943

My dear Ma – I haven't heard from you for some time but mails have been awfully bad lately. I sent off another food parcel last week with 2lbs sugar, 2lbs butter and 1lb marmalade. I do hope it reaches you all right. Unfortunately we are only allowed to send 2lbs of sugar at a time or I would send more. I have just returned from a couple of days in Cairo. I went up on Saturday morning and returned last night Sunday. I met John, and we spent all the time together, on very good terms. I have told him definitely I won't be engaged now, and he accepts the fact and we seem to get on very well in spite of the fact. We ate an enormous lunch where we gazed at Cairo from above – a wonderful sight, mosques, domes and minarets rising above the houses, the pyramids in the distance and the sun shining on it all. It is very much like being in Edinburgh castle and looking over the city. Well, we then drove through the Dead City, which is nearby and out of bounds really. There is a part of Cairo which had plague very badly 600 years ago and which was closed. People were buried just where they were and consequently there are tombs in houses, tombs everywhere. I longed to get out and look at some of the mosques, all is old and interesting but of course couldn't. Then we went to have tea at Shepheards, the very famous hotel everyone goes to when in Cairo … After a prolonged tea, John went to have a bath (being in more or less desert, baths are scarce) and I to change and then we went back to Shepheards to dance, me in my new blue brocade evening dress which was quite a success. The following day we were only able to have lunch together and I had to catch the 4.30 train back. … Our pay isn't bad at all, and tho' things are terribly expensive it's easy to manage if one's careful. For instance I spend most of my money on singing and riding, 2 things which are structurally beneficial and I try and buy as many useful clothes as I can, as I know <u>how</u> hard they must be to come by at home. Just to show you the prices out here, my short time in Cairo cost John £10 – do you know that 2 Pimms No.1 cost 40 piastres, or 8/- isn't it fantastic? The weather is so pleasant here now. Warm and Spring-like, and not too sunny. It was lovely in Cairo yesterday afternoon. We walked to the Nile and looked over one of the bridges near Kasr el Nil Barracks, with Gezira Island to the right of us, all trees and green. Today was a rest day because the King has been here. Great arches were erected in Rue Fuad and banners, flags were flown from all windows. Soldiers lined the streets and there were bands making an awful din. On top of all this, tho' I was out and I missed the King. Apparently, in Cairo he drives about in an enormous car escorted by 90 motor cycles, fore and aft all going very fast at about 40 mph. We are enjoying the strawberry season now – oh they are heavenly. Oranges, tangerines and bananas are at their best. I'm even rather tired of them! I think probably your Xmas present to me has gone down, as it hasn't arrived yet.

With very much love to you both. Sheila

17/2/43

My dear Mama – I've at last had some mail – 10 letters in all, including 3 of yours It was a lovely surprise … I have had John down for the weekend, but he has gone back now and I know not when we'll meet again. I asked Eve and Clement [Barber, Alexandria residents and riding friends] to meet him and their opinion afterwards and one was that I'd be a fool to marry him as they think he is too serious and old for his years for me. However, I've told him definitely no for the moment, but what will happen in the future I can't tell. He won't change, that's the one thing certain. We went to the Union Club dance on Saturday night, and I wore my new blue brocade dress. It's a deep deep blue with gold flowers on it in shot gold, and is made plain with low neck, short sleeves and a split back. … No, I didn't hear the broadcast from the Wren who has been to Casablanca. But did you hear Anne Halliday broadcasting home to her mother from the M.E. the other day. Just before the end she squeezed in 'John Pritty of Prestwick sends his regards to his people.' Quite illicitly for John, and we are wondering what it sounded like. They get all the luck working in Cairo! No, I am still in the same job and still a 3/O. There are dozens of others of greater seniority then me in the same boat. I certainly won't get promotion. I am going to ask for a move tho' so that I can get more into the war. It's getting rather backward here and I'm tired of the people I have to work with … I had a letter from Dundee who mentioned Jaap is now a Lieut. Commander. With all this loss of mail I feel very discouraged!!! But I haven't written either, for ages. And still no news of Paul too … I've got so used to being out here that I often wonder what it will be like returning to UK. Tho' I often long to be back among the green fields, trees, hills, and sea, especially when we have weather like this mild and sunny, not too warm – rather like May at home and everywhere rather misty and dewy in the early morning. Naturally I want to come back and see you and Daddy but having come this far, I want to go on and see more though of course with a war you can't do everything you want to. I don't feel for a moment that we shall return before the end of the war and I don't think that given the chance I would accept it! I am going to learn to ride from a new master, who is going to teach me to do exercises on the horse, lie down while it is trotting and all sorts of tricks to make one feel confident on the horse whatever he may do. I have my first lesson tomorrow with Eve. I must get up now. My clock gets fast and so I found myself up and about at 0700 instead of 0720, hence writing this now.

Tons of love to you both. Sheila

Having been the longest-serving Wren officer in Alexandria, she is devastated when the office is demoted from C-in-C Med to C-in-C Levant – and so feels more than ready to move on:

C in C Levant
C/O CPO London
27/2/43

My dear Daddy –

… As you will see, we have now changed our address and are now C in C Levant – a very great come down! I have been in the office longer than any Wren and more than most of the men, so now I'm agitating for a move. I have 2/3 definite places in view, which I can't of course mention here. The C/O says I am selected for accelerated promotion, but whether that will even come to anything I can't say. <u>No</u> I should guess, really. However, as promotion is NIL in the service and I'm happy as a 3/O, I don't mind a bit. It's really rather difficult working with men, as they get the promotion automatically and after 6 months you'll find a sub/lieut. you know and trained as a raw recruit from King Alfred is then a Lieut and your boss. It makes me rather cross!

However, life is really quite pleasant. Alexandria, unlike Cairo, is a quiet spot. Everything closes at midnight, and it's more like a provincial town – like Bournemouth or similar places. I should say, I simply adore Cairo, and try and get up there as much as I can – once a month if possible at the moment. John is stationed there and it is great fun going up. I've explored the Musky, Citadel, Blue Mosque, Dead City and Pyramids, but I want to go to Sakara and see the Pyramids there as they are meant to be much older and more interesting. Whenever I shall have time to do all this I can't say, as I only have one day off at a time, and it's rather a wangle going anyway. It's really rather a blight working in C in C's office, as we're the only people who haven't had leave. All the other Wrens have had a week and been up to Palestine and even Syria – places I long to visit! I want very very much to go to Luxor and Aswan – one member of my watch has been and I've seen his photographs – the Egyptian remains there are wonderful, only have to be seen to be believed, and you know how I love old buildings and tombs!

There is very little of that kind of thing in Alex – we have some catacombs, which I'm afraid I've never yet seen, but will do so some day. Alexander the Great is reputed to have been buried in Rue Nebi David, but as it's under the street, nobody seems quite to know. We also have a big pillar attributed to Pompey (!!) [the name of their cat] but nothing is left of the Pharos as its foundations are now under the sea beyond Ras el Jin.

In spite of all those interesting things, I feel a move on is indicated – one gets stale in one's work and I'm just a little tired of the men I'm working with! When it will come is debatable, but I hope it will be quite soon.

… It's terribly English to talk about weather, but really it is heavenly just now – very cool, yet sunny and perfect for all sports, even swimming, tho' I haven't swum since last October!

… So au revoir, camera films are almost nil here, otherwise I would have sent you some.

With much love,

Sheila

———————

C in C Levant
5/3

My dear Mama – I've had your airgraph in which you ask if my tale of woe re evacuation [The Flap] can go in the school magazine. I don't think it can, actually, as we aren't allowed to publish anything about the service without it being vetted first. On Monday I went round the Catacombs with Miles, one of the men from our office. It really was awfully interesting – you go down a long spiral staircase deep into the solid rock until you come to a series of corridors and rooms, all with holes cut in the walls where bodies need to be put.

There are layers, 2 of which you can explore, and the 3rd which is filled with sand. After thoroughly exploring these (we went with a special guide and about 50 other people in a fleet of yellow Alex taxis) we then went to Pompey's Pillar which is a very tall pillar erected to commemorate something that I can't remember. All around are earthworks and a couple of sphinxes and other statues – mostly of Roman time and origin. I was awfully glad that I'd done this, because 2 days ago, when I went on watch at 1300 I was told I was to go off to Cairo and work as soon as possible! This was a tremendous shock. So off I rushed, packed all my things, saw my dressmaker bade farewell to Mme. Vegdi and Eve and all my friends, and caught the midday train from Alex yesterday …

Heaps of love,

Sheila

She has in fact been summoned to work with Admiral Ramsay on Operation Husky, but of course cannot mention it. She must have been thrilled.

Operation Husky was the result of the Casablanca Conference held on 14 January 1943, where Roosevelt and Churchill met to discuss the next step in the Allied strategy, following on from the successes of the north-west African landings in November 1942, and Montgomery's victory at El Ālamein. At this stage the Allies were split in their views: Stalin desperately wanted an Allied offensive to relieve his forces from the relentless German attacks on the Russian front, while the British and the Americans wanted to make safe the Mediterranean sea-routes, reduce Axis air power and eliminate Italy from the war.

By the end of the successful and extremely short campaign – Husky only lasted from 10 July until 16 August – both sides could claim that their objectives had been met. The Italians had surrendered, their fleet captured; the Germans were diverted away from the Russian front and, of foremost importance, the Allies had shown they could attack the Axis on its home territory and win. It was a demonstration of grand strategy at its best; the whole of Operation Husky took only six months from inception to delivery:

C/O RNGHQ, Cairo
16/3/43

My dear Mama – …Well, here I am in Cairo – quite settled down in my new job (not cyphering this time) and living in the YMCA. These are very good places, not a bit full of tents or grim, but quite charming, well furnished, good food and altogether pleasant. I share a room with Mary Henie, who came up with me, Maureen Brennan, who has been in Malta since the beginning of the war, and a Polish girl who doesn't speak English. I'm working quite hard for me – 08/30 till 1300, then 1500/2000, but at the moment I don't have to go till 1700. When it gets hot and we have to go in at 1500 I don't know what I'll do! John is in Transjordan, on a course, and won't be back till 30 March. HOWEVER, I have been having quite a good time, mainly due to the fact that an awfully nice person called Ronnie Croker, Major, Skinner's Horse, is on leave in Cairo, and we have been hitting the high spots. I knew him vaguely in the summer – he is a friend of Pam Boyne, who was in our draft, and also knows Robin Chater very well. We have been dancing these last three nights, twice at Shepheards, and the other time at a nightclub here; today we are lunching at Gezira Club and I expect we'll watch the polo. Tho' it's not supposed to be very good. Ronnie is a crack player, I believe – I'm afraid John'll disapprove frightfully as he hates me going out with anyone but him, but as we aren't engaged I can't see any thing against harmlessly enjoying ourselves … Life in Cairo is very gay; dancing at Shepheards every night, full evening dress, lots of cinemas and good places to dine, but the food is really better in Alex. I <u>like</u> Cairo, but oh it is awfully expensive. I had to pay 3/6 for a bottle of Swan ink which I'm sure is only 1/- at home – and everything else in comparison … About the photos, I told you I sent you 2 of which I had taken in Alex in the Autumn – by sea – so they should be arriving soon. They aren't too bad – John likes them anyway. You say you think he sounds a dear – well he is and he isn't. Awfully temperamental and hard to get on with, and oh so jealous. It quite frightens me, and I find it makes me rather deceitful against my will, as I never like hiding any of my activities from anyone. He really is very good looking, not that that's terrifically in his favour, tho' … By the way, you never need worry if you don't hear from me, if anything happened to me the admiralty would wire you at once! Have you had the necklace yet – I sent it a month or so ago. I'm very pleased with my new work, as I'm the only Wren officer on the staff and everyone is so nice. Long may it last! I had something so important to tell you but I can't remember it. Oh dear. Tons of love, Sheila.

Despite having to work gruelling hours, Cairo was obviously fun and, with John away, Sheila loses no time in finding a new admirer to take her to Shepheards, dancing – she obviously loves dressing up – and to the Gezira Club (her temporary membership card is stuck in the scrapbook). Rosemary is still firmly in her sights now that she is on a roll, yet it doesn't prevent her from sending her lovely gifts:

RNGHQ MEF 27/3/43

My dear Ma – I've just had your airgraph of 2nd March – very quick. Did you ever get the necklace? I did send it and you should have had it by now … I've just had an airgraph from Paul, who is in UK again, doing a course at Portsmouth. Very browned off he isn't out here! He'll be ashore till the end of the year. Funny, isn't it, I've not seen him for nearly 2 years now, and he still seems keen to meet me again and keep up contacts. I like him. When I write I'll tell him to look you up if he's ever up your way. As regards life out here – I'm still very pleased with it. Ronnie Croker went back to Iraq last Saturday. We had several good evenings together before he left. I like him too! Very tall, rather thoughtful, and very much the soldier, dances well and is altogether rather after my own heart. John, alas, won't be coming back here, this I rather feared, but the regiment has moved and he'll have to join them. He may, however, manage to get down here on Monday for the night.

… I've had several airgraphs from Rosemary lately. I think it's a great pity she can't get her commission quicker, as I really do think her activities sound rather 'cheapening'. Actually, I know this sounds awful, but she really sounds as if she'd go out with anyone in trousers, whatever he's like, from what I can gather in her letters. Have you felt the same? … I wish Rosemary would get married, much more fitting of her to do so and then perhaps I could (not that I'm thinking of it at the moment!). One of the people on our staff is just like Jaap – same laugh and smile – it's most disquieting! Tomorrow's my half day, I do hope it's fine, as last Sunday a horrible dust storm arose, blotted out all the sun, made us all filthy, and was, to all intents and purposes, exactly like a pea soup fog in London. It made us so depressed! With heaps of love, Sheila.

My last letter, unnumbered, was 41.

RNGHQ MEF 4/4

My dear Ma – … Well, life in Cairo is still very happy for me – most days I work 10 hours and when you come to think that it's now pretty hot over 80 degrees in the shade and getting warmer. I don't think this is at all bad! But I love my work and everyone is so nice – it's a pleasure to be able to work under such conditions. I'm waiting for the bump, as usually one doesn't get a lucky break without a snag or two. I work with 2 Pay Lieuts. (1 RN and 1 RNVR) and we laugh and joke all the time. Tho' I work flat out without stopping from the time I start to the time I go home. The snag is, I suppose, that I'm terrified of the secretary but that keeps me up to the mark, so I suppose it's a good thing. The dust is appalling, and we have plagues of ants, but I've a tin of Keatings handy and that soon kills them off. The day I wrote my last letter, which was delivered I hope, by an officer returning to the UK, I had been to the Musky with Flags and two other officers. First of all we had lunch at Gezira with another of the staff and then off we set in a taxi, Flags bought a grand pair of slippers, and we spent a minute or so in a perfume shop, but otherwise we didn't buy much. The smell in this latter shop was heavenly. It costs £1 an ounce – undiluted. We did have fun, all smelling different perfumes till we didn't know where we were. In the end we walked out without having bought any. You would love the amber shops, mummy, I go crazy about necklaces and have seen a natural turquoise one I've just got to have, tho heaven knows how much it is.

… Tonight and tomorrow I am going out with Ronnie Croker who was here on a course. He's nice. John will be down on a course soon. He sent me a message from his mother. I quote 'I am happy to hear of S.M. and always welcome your confidence (!!!) Maureen (his sister I knew as a Wren) says she remembers Sheila and thought a lot of her. Give her my best thanks for being so good to you' !!! So I am approved of – but what a terrifying message! He goes on to say 'it's such a pity you are looking for someone with more than me!' However, whatever happens we are still the best of friends, though if I don't marry him, I feel awfully sorry for him as it must be dreadful to feel as he does and

BY AIR MAIL LETTER CARD

IF ANYTHING IS ENCLOSED THIS CARD
WILL BE SENT BY ORDINARY MAIL

POSTAGE REVENUE 3D

No: mountain

42 A

Mrs. P. Findlay Mills
8 The Grove
Durham City
ENGLAND

FROM H·M·SHIP
SIGN.BEL:MAG:ADMR:M.
PASSED BY CENSOR
SIGNATURE DATE

WHEN FOLDED THE LETTER CARD MUST CONFORM IN SIZE AND SHAPE WITH
THE BLUE BORDER WITHIN WHICH THE ADDRESS ONLY MAY BE WRITTEN

give her my best thanks for being so good
to you"!!! L. Jam approved of - but what
a twisting of message! He goes on to say
"It's such a pity you are looking for someone
with more than me! However, whatever happens
we are still the best of friends. Though if I
don't marry him, I feel awfully sorry for him
as it must be dreadful to feel as he does
+ not attain his desires. He is now a Captain.
We had a tea party here this afternoon.
Maureen, Mary + I, 2 N/o's from RNOSQ +
Mr. Padley (Maureen's boss - + had Sort's Malta
representative in Cairo) all quite here. Ronnie
has just been on the phone to say the Continental
again tonight, + so what shall I wear?
Yhat I've just told him (No, mummy, not
shorts) I shall wear a new Nile blue-green
one I've just had made ←like this. So
you like it? And some   new deep
burgundy shoes like   this
rather smart. I think (!!!)   I suppose you'll
think I spend too much   on clothes (John
does says I should save more) but I have
saved £5 which is in a new P.O. Book + I do
feel clothes are an investment. Tuesday 6/4
Here I am again feeling rather tired having
been on the razzle 3 nights running. I did enjoy
Sunday at the Continental, + yesterday I had
tea at Gezira with Ronnie to meet of his friends.
all very pleasant - a very nice girl who is
married + lives here. In the evening we went
to see 'Nazi Spy' a film with Conrad Veidt
which I didn't like very much - It turned so
cold - I was frozen in the frocks - We'll
be in whites in 10 days! I had a sea mail
letter yesterday from Scotland written on 8th
March - I'm sure it was put in the wrong bag!
With tons of love to you all - Sheila

not attain his desires. He is now a captain … Ronnie has just been on the phone to say the Continental again tonight, and so what would I wear?

Short, I've just told him, (no, mummy not shorts) I shall wear a new nice blue-green one I've just had made (like this). Do you like it? And some new deep burgundy shoes like this, rather smart I think (!!!). I suppose you'll think I spend too much on clothes (John does and says I should save more) but I have saved £5 which is in a new P/O Book and I <u>do</u> feel clothes are an investment. With lots of love to you all …

Sheila.

The sinking of the *Medway*, referred to in the next letter, in fact took place in early July 1942, just off Port Said. She was sunk by two torpedoes fired from a German submarine. Sheila's two great friends, Audrey Coningham and Esmé Cameron, were on board as signals officers. As Alexandria was preparing to evacuate for The Flap at the end of June 1942, they had been ordered to join the *Medway*:

RNGHQ, M.E.F.   14th April

My dear Ma – Many thanks for your card of the 1st received today (55) No. 52, and an airgraph … Every time you write R. seems to have or just going to have, leave. I'm so jealous, as I heard yesterday all C in C's Cypher officers are having a week – as I'm out of that racket, I stand little as no chance of getting any at all. I feel I never shall see Palestine or Syria. At the moment I've got tonsillitis (of the walking variety) nothing at all serious tho'.

I went with Maureen to the Musky on Monday and have bought you some slippers, tho' I'm now wondering whether they will be big enough. They are bright royal blue leather. I also got some leopard skin ones for Rosemary and will pack them up and despatch when I can find a box to put them in. We had more fun there – I also treated myself to a gazelle skin (all hairy – like the beast itself) handbag. <u>Would you like one</u>. Do <u>please</u> let me know <u>at once</u> and I will buy you one. I think I shall get you one anyway. They are most unusual at home, and I love them. I also bought for 12 piastres (about 2/4d) a native bangle of very heavy metal which I'm rather pleased with. In silver they are much more expensive about £1/4/-.

On Sunday morning I rose at the crack of dawn and went riding with one of the chaps I work with. I've had rather bad horses and I'm now so stiff I can hardly walk! In the evening I went out with Myrette Acfield, another Wren officer, who is public relations officer here and we went afterwards to a houseboat called 'Puritan' which is run on the profits of Gezira club for servicemen on leave. There we met some of the repatriated P.O.W.'s back from Italy. Most of the ones I met had been taken at Tobruk, what tales they had to tell!

I see the paper today mentions the loss at the 'Medway'. Well now we can reveal more – there were 3 Wren officers on board. Esmé Cameron, Audrey Coningham and one other. The day we left Alex, Esmé came rushing into our room and packed up everything she had, down to her fur coat, and all Audrey's things as well, as they were sailing that night. Off she went and off we went to Port Said. The following night just as I was getting into bed very very tired, a girl came to my room to tell me Esmé was downstairs and wanted to see me. The 'Medway' had been sunk!! I just <u>couldn't</u> believe it – our most valuable ship with all s/m [submarine] torpedoes, spares and equipment for the E. Med on board. Frightful. However, I dashed downstairs to see Esmé looking bright sun burnt pink all over, absolutely filthy and without one thing in the world – everything having been lost. She'd been on watch when the ship was hit at 0830, had locked all the C.B.s [Citizen Bands – radios] in the chests, and with the 2 other girls, had clambered down the side of the ship, already heeling over, and had had to swim for it. They were in the water about half an hour, by which time the ship had sunk – a terrible sight they said – a very calm sea and the ship taking it's last plunge. Audrey (she was always the cat that walked by itself – she came out with us) swam with the other 2 to a nearby destroyer, decided she didn't like the look of it much, so turned round and made for another one. En route she met two sailors, one without a life belt and very exhausted, so she took hers off and helped them both to the ship. She was recommended for an immediate award of life saving medal – I noticed it in Levant orders last week. What times we live in! You see, Wrens do go to sea. Yes I shall miss the sea now I'm in Cairo, but I still like being here. Ronnie reappeared last Friday, his course having been put back a bit and we went to Gezira Club dancing ...

With tons of love to you both,

Sheila

The film *Desert Victory,* referred to in the following letter, was a documentary charting the Battle of El Alamein, considered by many to be the turning point in the war, when the Allies eventually routed Rommel and his Afrika Korps. As well as explaining tactics, it contained footage of the battle itself, including some captured from the Germans, and of Churchill, Montgomery and other leaders. It also paid tribute to the men and women who played their part by working in factories at home, which made it extremely popular. King Farouk himself attended the premiere in Cairo, a rare occasion, as he was avowedly and openly anti-British. Indeed, most people believed that even though Egypt was nominally self-ruling, Sir Miles Lampson, later Lord Killearn, Ambassador to Egypt, was really in charge:

RNGHQ, M.E.F.   20 April

My dear Ma – as usual I'm completely adrift with numbering – I know I wrote roughly a week ago – 14th I think, when I'd a bad throat, well, as I couldn't go sick, I celebrated by going gay and have recovered. I went to see an amateur rendering of 'The Shine and the Rain' with Maureen and some of her friends, but it wasn't awfully good. The following evening we went to Gezira club and danced and the next evening Ronnie came back from his course and we made up a party of 4 and went to Shepheards to dance. It was great fun. Unfortunately he has departed for Persia indefinitely. Funny he knows Robin Chater isn't it? I have had 2 letters from Robin this week who is still up there but hopes to be down sometime. I should like very much to see him again. On Sunday, Mary and I had arranged to go to the Pyramids and Idwal Humphrey (yes Welsh) who works in the same office as I do, (a Pay/Lieut. RN) wanted to come too, so we made up a three and went. The journey was made via tram, incredibly crowded – and when we got there we at once hired camels and proceeded up the hill in traditional style. They do lurch terribly, you have to cling on to a sort of pole on the saddle to stick on at all. Eventually we dismounted (the guide, too from a little donkey we had hired for him) and were conducted to a tomb belonging to some Prime Minister or other (who we were never quite sure, but possibly it was to do with King Cheops, because it was near the Cheops Pyramid).

Eventually we came to the tomb itself and of course had to clamber down doubled up – as it was a very narrow hole. The guide took us to the coffin which was a huge stone affair terribly tall, and then we climbed up and looked inside and there, according to the guide, was a 'skellyton'. How we laughed! There was too! After this, crouching in the corner of the tomb by the light of two fluttering candles, he told our fortunes in the sand. I have 61 1/2 more years to live! More laughter! We then proceeded forth on camel past the Sphinx, did a bit of trotting (very bumpy) and took some snaps and then back to the Great Pyramid itself, which we'd promised ourselves we'd climb. It is 450 feet high, and the blocks are as big, and sometimes bigger, than a man. However, up we went. Mary gave up half way, but Idwal and I pushed on and eventually reached the top in under 20 mins, which is quite good. It really was an amazing sight.

You could see so clearly where desert ended and Delta began and of course you could see all Cairo, the Citadel, the Pyramids of Sakara, some 8 miles away, and so on. I was quite frightened of falling off, but the top is a flat surface of about 15–20 square feet. There were also on top an American and English RAF officer, and a funny little Syrian who climbed to the top of the flag post (much to my terror!) and insisted afterwards in taking lots of photos of us with my camera, for which I was very grateful as I discovered afterwards he was a professional photographer. Once down again, we had a large tea at the Mena House hotel, which I am sure had never seen such tramps, all in shorts, beneath its portals on a Sunday afternoon. Now, of course, we are all terribly stiff, but it was certainly worth it! ... Tomorrow 4 of us are going to see 'Desert Victory' – I am longing to see it. Actually, I have also been invited to go by some more people tonight, but of course, can't see it twice. It is showing in 3 cinemas at once here. Tomorrow, also, I am having lunch with my Big White Chief [Admiral Ramsay], rather awe-inspiring, but he is a dear and in the afternoon we have been asked (Wrens I mean) to take part in a quiz over the wireless, but as I'm working don't expect I'll be able to go! Oh yes, life is very pleasant.

I have had 2 airgraphs from you lately Mummy. I feel such a pig writing and telling you all the lovely things I do when you all at home aren't having such a good time. You would love it out here, I think, in Alex anyway. I am in whites again, much to everyone's amazement, but I am not cold and enjoy the sun – will send photos when printed. Tons of love Sheila.

In Cairo, Sheila meets Bruce Booth-Mason for the first time, then a major, and later a captain, in the Indian Cavalry. He is destined to become one of Sheila's serious boyfriends, competing for her affections with John Pritty. He was a completely different character to John: considerate and kind and, above all, calm. We can only guess at how the romance blossomed, but taking a girl dancing in the moonlight at the Mena House Hotel with the pyramids as backdrop is a sure way to a girl's heart. John is predictably possessive and jealous. Meanwhile Sheila is working hard with Admiral Ramsay on 'Operation Husky', the Sicily invasion:

RNGHQ 5/5/43

My dear Mama –

... Cairo is getting very hot and you can now go out in the evenings without a coat at the risk of gippy tummy! I have been working abnormally hard and have had to ask for someone to help me – the superintendent excelled himself by sending us a 2nd officer who, luckily, I know and I like very much. However, she is only temporary as the situation might have been rather awkward. What a time I had last week – again I felt ashamed at enjoying myself so much – On Tuesday I went to Shepheards with Idwal Humphreys the A/Sec I work with, Maureen Brennan and another Paymaster who works with us – on Wednesday the film and the following evening found me at Shepheards again – this time with Ula Bowing (the 2/O) and 2 friends of hers, one very tall and one very short. We had also played tennis all the afternoon till 5. The following day Idwal and I went sailing at the Yacht Club, and there we were entered for a race! Of course, this terrified me, as I'm no experienced crew. However, Idwal showed me the ropes and off we set! It was such fun and we were getting on really well, when on rounding the first buoy, we hooked on to somebody else, and had to withdraw! We were annoyed. However, we had a good sail on our own and went back to work at 5. In the evening Ula and I had arranged to go to Mena House Hotel (near the Pyramids) to dance, with Bruce Booth Mason (a vague relation of Diana Booth's) and an unknown quantity whom we'd specified had to be tall, dark and handsome. Well he turned out to be a Major in the Indian Cavalry regiment, and the party turned out to be the most hilarious one I've ever been to. We drove out there in a taxi, it's about 10 miles and as soon as we got there started dinner. The dance was held in a huge Moorish style ballroom with tables all round – well, I've never laughed so much in all my life, they were the funniest pair, in fact quite disgraced myself with ribald laughter! We are planning to go again when there is a moon so that we can go and scan the Pyramids in traditional style. On Monday I had arranged to go sailing with Bruce, but our plans fell by the wayside and I came back here to Connaught House champing at the bit. A minute or so later a knock came at my door, and was told someone was waiting to see me outside. That someone turned out to be John! What an afternoon we had, nothing but arguments and disputes as to my behaviour since I have been in Cairo ending up by a most unfond farewell – to my intense amusement 10 minutes after he had taken his leave, a parcel containing a sheaf of four huge lilies on one stalk appeared for me – stating that lilies were usually given at funerals! How we laughed. However, the great high and mighty reappeared the next day full of apologies for his behaviour!

Yesterday afternoon Ula and I had lunch at the club and then I went on to the Yacht Club and sailed with Bruce and another man and we all got <u>soaking!</u> No races this time, tho! Tonight and tomorrow and the next night I shall be out with John and tomorrow afternoon I am having lunch and a sunbathe session at Gezira with one of our staff and Friday I am duty secretary which entails working the best part of 12 hours at a stretch!

… My scrapbook I am keeping is getting on so well and is nearly full. It's filled with snaps and cuttings and everything under the sun. Oh yes, I have had my hair cut yet again. Really I shall look like a convict any minute now, but those things must be done! Now I have got to rush out and get tickets for a thing called Polish Parade, which is an all Polish revue on this week, John and I hope to go this week. So no more – with very much love,

from Sheila

RNGHQ MEF
11/5

My dear Mama – I've just had your airgraph of the 10th April, but have had no mail from you for ages.

How nice the garden must be and I wish I was there to see it – you would love the flowers here – Just now the shops and street corners are banked with roses, carnations, arums, delphiniums, stocks and all sorts of gorgeously coloured flowers – men pester you in the streets to buy them late at night even. But we get no green – no grass or fields – just blazing colours and sand. Last Monday John suddenly appeared from out of the blue – on a course till Friday. I'm afraid we didn't have a hilariously happy time, because all the time he was attacking me because I have been having such a gay time in Cairo. I'm afraid he expected me never to go out at all and to sit at home waiting for him! I tried to explain that I couldn't do this after all, working as I do sometimes ten hours a day and with very little free time – I must enjoy myself while I can and get away from work and the YWCA. However, nothing seemed to be any good, and it all ended up in what one might call a free fight – him struggling with me to pull off my scarab ring which he gave me and which he succeeded in doing – nearly breaking my little finger into the bargain and me giving him a sound slap on the face for his pains. We did <u>not</u> part friends I can assure you. It all seems such a pity, but I couldn't end my days married to someone so impassioned with jealousy so maybe it's just as well. I have many regrets, now, especially when I look back on the tremendously happy times we had in Alex which are now a closed book. I often wonder if I shall ever go back there. Now I am away and it is so hot here (has been over 100 degrees in the shade last week) I remember our lovely bathing parties, riding, and visits to Eve Barber all so well. She is coming up here to stay next week, I hope. I have been sailing again this week, twice with Idwal Humphrey, whom I work with, and once with Bruce Booth Mason, in the army and a vague relation of Diana's. He is the most amusing boy – Ula and I, and he and another person called Waddylove (yes, it's true) all went to see a Polish Revue on Saturday – very good. Ending up at Shepheards with champagne and sandwiches at midnight. It had been the hottest day of the year so far and all I'd had to eat since breakfast was an ice cream, punctuated by glasses of lemon and orange! We'd had dinner, but that mostly consisted of fruit cup, you just can't eat in the heat. We all laughed so – I have been working hard under not so ideal conditions, rather at loggerheads with my sec, and to laugh makes all the difference. Please apologise to R. that I haven't written – and explain that as well as having been out a lot, I have been working sometimes 10 hours a day which makes one rather dead beat in the heat! …

With very much love to you all,

Sheila

RNGHQ MEF
19/5

My dear Mama – … I'm delighted you've had the 2nd parcel and there should be another on the way if I remember rightly. We have all laughed and laughed at having to cut the sugar in half with a saw! How did you like Desert Victory. I thought it was just wonderful – and relived it all once more – though, of course, we weren't there, we were all so very near and I remember well on the night of the 21st October (the night it began) hearing the guns roaring away in the distance. For some days we'd known in the Cypher Office 'something' was in the air, and that was what it was! The same thing applied to the landing in N. Africa. Even way back in July we'd known of the mysterious 'thing' all very hush, and so it had grown bigger and bigger till we knew what to expect. Of course I had to be ill at the crucial moment, so that I wasn't on watch when all the exciting signals came through. I remember well the VAD coming in and announcing with glee what had happened, and I, with boredom and a feeling of being very much in the background, answering 'Yes, I know!'

… I have heard no more from John so expect he really <u>has</u> cut me off with it this time. Well, maybe it's for the best – we were temperamentally <u>very</u> ill suited. It seems a pity though! … Tons of love S.

June 1943 marked the transition of Operation Husky from planning to action. Admiral Ramsay, in charge of the British Eastern Naval Task Force, was himself transferred to Malta, where the landings were being co-ordinated, and where the Admiral of the Fleet, Sir Andrew Cunningham, had already shifted. Sheila's promotion and mooted move to Kilindini are therefore unsurprising in this context:

RNGHQ MEF 2/6

My dear Ma – many thanks for No 63 which has just arrived. I'm glad you got the snaps and that you liked them. Well, I have got rather a surprise for you, I am now a second officer! Isn't it amazing? I will tell you all about it, ages ago, last February or so the PCO [Principal Cypher Officer] had told me I was being recommended but naturally I rather pooh poohed the idea as ridiculous. When I was just off to Cairo, the Superintendent told me I had had a very good report and that they would try for my 2nd stripe – however after being here for some little while I quite gave up hope, as I am working for an over efficient man who gives me a complete inferiority complex and makes me feel an absolute boob! Well one day I was looking through a batch of signals and read one saying that I was to be promoted + immediately transferred to Kilindini – relief being sent from there. What a fright – as I'm not particularly keen to go anywhere much hotter than this. However, a signal was sent saying they wished to retain me here, but as recommendation had already been sent for promotion to 2/O, it was requested I should become 2/O and reappointed – and Admiralty agreed!! I really am rather pleased as there are only 2 other 2/O Cypherers out here, and one of them is a P.C.O. – I do feel, though, that although I have worked hard (and dammnably so) I'm not the most efficient person there is, but I <u>can</u> do things awfully fast – hoping hard I haven't made a mistake. It is really a very good thing working for someone as efficient as I do, I just can't afford to be slack – every little point is noticed – <u>BUT</u> I never get any encouragement, which would go an enormous long way in the middle of all the toil. But I don't care <u>how</u> hard I work so long as I can help. What does worry me terribly is that there are others (or only one, really) who do deserve promotion – Anne Halliday (now Bamber) being THE one. She is most terribly efficient and conscientious – better than I am I know – and my senior, too, she has been rather done out of promotion by moving around a bit, and I know she will feel it dearly. Mary Henie will, too – but she isn't really as good, or conscientious as Anne and I am very sorry about it. Others in Alex will be furious – but I don't care about them.

… With very much love to you and Pa (who promised to write and hasn't!) Sheila.

Sheila: 'the planning' (quote from scrapbook).

The following letter was received on 20 June. Scribbled on it in my grandmother's writing are the words 'Brought by Gen Montgomery'. Montgomery worked closely with Ramsay in planning the Sicily invasions: Ramsay was in charge of the naval strategy and Montgomery of the deployment of the Eighth Army once landed. Initially he had rejected the American plan, which 'breaks every commonsense rule of practical battlefighting ... and has no hope of success and it should be completely re-cast'. Indeed, the eventual plan for the invasion was changed and followed Montgomery's suggestion to concentrate the attack on the south-east area only, to avoid dispersing the troops. A rather fitting way to learn of her daughter's promotion:

6/6/ 43

My dear Mummy –

... I don't suppose you have had my air letter card yet, but I am now Second Officer Mills, much to my amusement – because it wasn't exactly anticipated. I have told you fully about it in my letter card posted 2 days ago, no 3 ... Really, this is such a surprise – I can't believe it.

I have made up the quarrel with John, and he has given me my scarab ring back. He came up all unexpectedly last night, and though we started off badly, ended up all right. So that is a good thing. I can't bear these often quarrels. Life is too short. I am on the scout for your lipstick, and hope to be able to get it and send it on this week.

It must be very lovely at home now – here strange to say it is still beautifully cool. We have started dancing in the open air, though and everything is as summery as it possibly could be. My only regret is I have so little time to wear cotton dresses and for swimming etc. We do miss Sidi Bishr beach very much, as you can guess – but still, Cairo has its advantages.

With very much love to you and Daddy,

Sheila

xx (one each)

RNGHQ MEF 21/6

My dear Ma and Pa – it is now the longest day of the year and I am Duty Secretary, but as I've no key (Idwal having promised to come in early, but hasn't) I'm not working awfully hard as everything is locked up! Did you get the parcel, by the way – It should have reached you by now, and also a letter written a bit earlier on, which I sent by someone [General Montgomery] travelling home by air ... – I've thought quite a bit about what I should do if the war suddenly ended (I don't think it will yet – but still!). If I get the chance of staying on in the WRNS I certainly would, as if I wasn't married, I'd far rather be in the service than in a civilian job. I always did hate offices anyway – and as a Wren I'd have a fairly good chance of seeing the world. However, it's really too far ahead to speculate <u>what</u> we'll all do! … On Friday I went to Ula's birthday party, which was held at a new place between Giza and Mena called Auberge des Pyramides – a very good band, quite large floor too, but rotten food. It's all in the open, and with a bright full moon above, it was really rather fun – but without the moon I don't know what it would be like – as there were very few lights. The following evening, Saturday, I went out to dinner with Bruce to the Mena House Hotel (I sent you a snap of it). It was just perfect, dining and dancing in the moonlight by the side of a swimming pool, all very gay – at about midnight we decided to walk up the hill and see the Pyramids – it was rather glorious – you walk out of the hotel garden and up a hill which slopes round to the foot of the Big Pyramid that I climbed – and all in the bright moonlight – beautifully cool. Yesterday I was frightfully tired tho' after all this gaiety, but this afternoon Idwal and I are both working early and if there is not much work to do, we are going to leave at about six and go for a sail – It's really not awfully hot yet, tho' last year at this time it was boiling, and we were just preparing for the flap! I told you I made it up with John, didn't I, and that I am now in possession of the ring once more? Robin writes from Iraq that he may be on a short course in these parts fairly soon – in the meantime I have to set about buying him a new signals side cap, and a pair of sunglasses – I should like to see him again very much. Mails from UK have been generally very bad. Well here comes Idwal so it's work for me now. He's just had his hair cut and looks quite different – it was curling round his cap at lunchtime! Heaps of love, Sheila.

The following letter was written the day after Admiral Ramsay sailed from Malta on the headquarters ship, *Antwerp*, to witness the convergence of the convoys of big ships from both Europe and the Middle East, and landing craft from Sfax (Tunisia), Tripoli and Malta as they headed for landfall on the south-east coast of Sicily on 10 July, when Syracuse fell to British forces. On 19 July after the success of the Sicily landings, Admiral Ramsay's appointment came to an end and he returned to England, where he became pivotal in planning the D-Day landings. Mussolini was to fall only a few days later on 25 July.

As for the campaign itself, it was led by the two most able Allied commanders – General Patten of the Seventh Army and General Montgomery in charge of the Eighth. It is remembered as a shining example of the value of sea and air power working together, something that had been rather lacking in the previous North African campaigns, mainly due to Italian and German dominance of the Mediterranean. It was, from a naval perspective, the greatest assembly of ships ever massed at one time, and it took the Italians completely by surprise.

It was not all plain sailing, however. The weather deteriorated very suddenly just before the primary assault and there was much debate around postponing the attack. In the event it was decided to continue, a decision that was vindicated despite the atrocious conditions suffered by the landing forces, often waist- and shoulder-deep in treacherous, choppy water. The success was due in no small part to the meticulous planning of the assault, mainly carried out by Admiral Ramsay and his team, including Second Officer Mills, in a dingy house in Cairo.

With Ramsay's departure, Sheila's role in Husky is over – she is still not able to talk about it – and she finds herself back in Alexandria, and it's rather an anticlimax:

C in C Levant 10/7

My dear Ma – I wonder if you got my EFM saying I had changed my address once more, and am now back in Alex again. I knew I should have to leave Cairo fairly soon, but I did hope very much I wouldn't have to return to Alex. However, here I am, back in C in C's Cypher Office, this time as a duty Cypher Officer with a watch of my own – and again I am living in a convent. Not Notre Dame de Sion, but Sacré Coeur, which is nearly on the sea front and quite a long way away from the town and shops. I am thankful not to be at the Rue Rassafah – 50 Wren officers is too much for me, and we are only 7 here! I have just discovered that my promotion dates back from 29 April, and that it is a permanent one, unlike so many 2/O's out here. There has been mass promotion on account of a new order saying that all heads of watches are to be 2/O's but mine came through before that and for an entirely different reason – which will be divulged later …

On my return from Cairo I was promised some leave, but just as I had decided to go to Beirut and had been vaccinated, a phone call from the fleet signal office bade me go on duty at 1300 that day! And I've been working ever since. However, the secretary has been most kind and has promised I may go off exactly when I like for 10 days. I think he was rather terrified I should fall by the wayside after my strenuous time in Cairo, but I seem to have survived so far. I'm afraid I find this rather slow and would like to be out of it – but one mustn't grumble I suppose.

Bruce came down to see me this week – we didn't have time to do much as he had to be away again quickly. I haven't seen John for a month or 6 weeks – I'm afraid he'll never be quite normal. I've had a couple of letters from him but on the same old lines – his sister Maureen whom I knew at Rosyth is terribly ill with high blood pressure and may not recover. It really is awfully sad. She is very young and awfully attractive.

… I am hoping to go on leave in 10 day's time – to Beirut. Unfortunately nobody can come with me as it's rather difficult to arrange and I don't want to let it slide too long.

With heaps of love,

Sheila

Sheila did manage to go on leave, but unaccompanied. As she writes elliptically to her mother in a series of letters written on 13, 14 and 27 July:

Of course, I've never even told you where I am going, and why. Well, it is quite a long story, but it all evolves from the fact that I have been working very hard in Cairo on the staff of Admiral Ramsay, which should convey quite a lot to you, and now I have been given four days' leave in return for my labours … I am very thrilled at the idea of going to another country – I shall really see two, because Beirut is in

Syria and I have to go through Palestine to get there. It is extremely beautiful up there – high mountains and hills, and I hope very much to be able to go into the Lebanon to see the cedars.

She set off from Alexandria towards the end of July, following the same route as when they were evacuated during The Flap, enjoying a plate of egg and chips in Sidi Gabr en route. The journey involved going by train to Port Said and thence to Palestine. She had interesting travelling companions: first a gunner officer, who had been at Sfax, in Tunisia, and the scene of heavy fighting, who had interesting things to tell:

Apparently there are quite a lot of French people who had olive farms there before the war where they used to spend the odd weekend over from France. When things got a bit hot in France, they decided to go and live in Tunisia and there they have been ever since. They are terribly snobbish, funny as it may seem and hate the Jews more than the enemy, in fact, they attribute all the trouble in France to the Jews. They have very few clothes, their shoes are rough ones made by the natives, but funnily enough, they had quite a bit of makeup. I can't think where they got it from, though. Contrary to my imaginations, it is hot desert up there, and the most beautiful flowers grow there in Spring time, two and three feet high and they smell marvellous.

Then there was Miss Roberts, an ancient missionary who 'seemed far too old to hold such a job, but she was very alert and alive ... just wouldn't stop talking!' And, finally, a nursing sister, who had been working in a mobile unit in the forward areas, 'even as far as Tunisia – so thrilling it sounded, I was quite jealous'.

Train travel was not luxurious, and Sheila ended up sleeping on the floor 'lying on half my rug and with my shoes, handbag and towel as an assortment of pillows'. The 'cloakroom' was 'a frightful place ... but I had a quick wash, and returned to the compartment cleaner, but a little sick inside'.

On arriving in Lydda, she disembarks:

... to have a cup of tea at the NAAFI buffet across the line – This was a very primitive place, but we managed to buy some tea which we drank from cut down beer bottles and bought the morning paper. I was most annoyed to see that they'd left out Admiral Ramsay from among the pictures of the force commanders who have been taking part in the invasion of Sicily. I was glad, though, to read that all has been going so well, particularly in our sector.

Sheila would have been relieved that the naval losses were small compared to the army's, with under 1,000 dead and wounded respectively from the US and British navies. The Seventh Army took 12,000 casualties, and the Eighth 9,000, out of a total of over 250,000 men. The navy, in particular, performed superbly – several types of new landing craft were used for the first time – and deployed vessels on dummy runs to divert the enemy's attention to the real battle plan. Tactics such as a decoy dead body with top-secret papers were used to mislead the enemy further, with the result that the attack on Sicily was an outstanding success. Although the Italians did not surrender immediately – the Germans would not allow them – they did finally surrender the fleet on 10 September, the sight that Sheila describes in her letter of 18 September, below.

From Lydda to Haifa via the Sinai desert but, approaching Haifa:

... now the countryside was completely different, there were hills in the distance, the immediate surroundings were undulating, and there were groves and groves of orange trees, all a delightfully vivid green, with shiny glossy leaves. The ground was covered in grass, rather parched, and thick green weeds, and now and again we passed a village, on a hill, or in a valley, but looking far cleaner and less dusty than any Arab settlement in Egypt – where they really are the lowest, filthiest dwellings you ever could find. It was delightful – such a change from the Delta, which is as flat as the Fens and very dull ... And so to Haifa, it very much reminded me of Cape Town – with hills in the background, an enormous bay, and behind that, in the mist, more hills.

After a late breakfast in the Officers' Club, she managed to get a lift in a courier's car to Beirut, where her great friends Esmé Cameron (who had escaped from the sinking *Medway*) and Kay Way, stationed there, had not received her telegram and were not expecting her. No matter – she was soon installed in WRNS officers' mess.

Nevertheless she had a high old time seeing her old friends from Scotland days: 'lunch and tea with Bert, bathed again when most unfortunately my bathing dress collapsed and Bert had to come to the rescue in public, with no towels!'; moonlight barbeques; swimming in mountain streams; canoeing; dinner up the mountain in Aley, 'good hotel and excellent food. The fruit was so heavenly, cherries, plums, peaches, pears. The hills by moonlight were really magnificent and it was so cool up there.' It was 'topped by a visit to the Patisserie Suisse for a chocolate mud (a glorious cream - ice and chocolate affair) … the next day I came back to Alex. Short but it was a grand leave and such a change.'

On her return at the end of July, she was 'greeted with 10 letters including … one from Sicily written 3 days after the invasion – saying they were still leading the lives of gentlemen and even playing cards every evening!' This must have been from John as she refers to it later.

The next letter refers to the jubilant return of the ships involved in ferrying Montgomery's Eighth Army to Sicily, including John and Bruce. A select few were invited by Rear Admiral Troutbridge to celebrate aboard HMS *Bulolo* – under the invitation Sheila has written 'A grand party – Bulolo had just come back from the Sicily invasion'. No wonder they were all in party mood!

C in C Levant
5/8/43

My dear Ma – …Yes I am back in Alex once more and in a way quite glad now I have settled down. I have been having a very gay week starting off with a cocktail party given in one of the ships here, as you know, we are usually not allowed in them at all out here – but this time the Superintendent let us all go (and went myself as well!) It was so absolutely grand for me as I knew nearly everyone there – because most of them had worked with me in Cairo. Oh it was marvellous to see them all again and what a lot we had to talk about. It was a real peacetime affair. On one of the starboard upper decks, bunting and coloured fairy lamps hanging everywhere and plenty to drink and eat, music playing softly over the amplifier – everything just marvellous! I had to be just dragged away to catch the boat ashore, there was so much to see and hear about. The following day I went out to tea and dinner with the Vegdi's and we bathed from their hut at Cleopatra, after which we ate the most enormous dinner of chicken and then I returned to my convent, for night duty. Sunday, the following day, was most eventful. To begin with, previously I'd been to visit the SPCA with Ivan [the Barbers' Hungarian friend, who lived with them], for his dog had been poisoned and wanted to choose another – there I saw an adorable wee scrap of a white dog, very miserable and decided to have it. Lenna Hardy who is in charge of these Quarters was away leaving me in charge so I took the plunge. Well, they sent him on the wrong day and he arrived just as I was going to bed. When I examined him I discovered he was one <u>mass</u> of fleas and ticks, and even tho' I bathed him and smothered him in everything under the sun, I couldn't get rid of the beastly clinging creatures, so in the end I had to return him for further cleaning, poor wee fellow. (I have him now, and has bucked up no end – calls himself James). Well, after this there was no time for bed, so I dressed and met Audrey and Idwal Humphrey and we went to the Yacht Club for lunch to be joined by one 'Guns' a really delightful person, who is a great dear … The next day, Tuesday, Barbara and Marion and I went out to the Carlton cabaret with Idwal and Guns (one man short unfortunately) where we wined, dined and danced. They are both so nice we did enjoy it so, and yesterday the three of us had lunch with Capt. McCrum, Warren Tute [a rather well-known writer], and Idwal at the Beau Rivage. They are the proud possessors of 2 Jeeps, in which we roared up and down the Corniche at umpteen miles an hour – hats flying, hair blowing. It's all so friendly, we meet at Unica's for coffee in the morning, then do a bit of shopping – a drink in Maxim's bar maybe, and then lunch at the Yacht Club, all whizzing around in Jeeps – 8 of us yesterday, of course we work in between times but it's such a rest cure after Cairo …

Tons of love, S

The next letter contains the first specific mention of 'the assault' in any of the letters. As it was in the *Illustrated London News* – no doubt hailed as a great victory – Sheila would be more at liberty to mention it. Despite enjoying Alexandria, she is hoping to rejoin her naval colleagues back in Cairo:

C in C Levant
13/8/43

My dear Ma –

I haven't had any mail from you this week – and I've certainly had very little time for writing letters, but now all our friends have gone away again. So I can get down to it. Oh every possible occasion we've been down on the beach bathing – Captain McCrum, Warren Tute and Idwal used to call for us in the jeep, and away we'd fly along the Corniche at breakneck speed – On Sunday we drove out to Aboukir – or just beyond – we were tearing along at about 60 mph when there was a howl from Captain McCrum who'd lost a pound note from his pocket in the wind. Eventually we pulled up and backed to where it had fallen in the middle of a canal! Out they all jumped and threw sticks in to the water to try and rescue it but alas it sank – much to Capt. McCrum's chagrin, and everyone got awfully dirty and muddy. Warren nearly fell in and it is very dangerous to do that in muddy water as you can catch a dreadful disease called 'bilharzia'.

The following day, Monday, Barbara, Marion and I gave a cocktail party for remaining members of our Cairo staff left in Alex – this we held on a large balcony overlooking the sea and the setting sun – about 20 people came including the C in C's secretary. When it

'A fruitless quest – by Warren Tute and Idwal – for Captain McCrum's £1 note, lost from a jeep.'

eventually got dark, we decided to go on to dinner and dance at the Carlton, and ten of us piled into one jeep and away we flew. It was so crowded I had to stand up and when we got there I don't think I've ever been so hot in my life. I was just in a bath of sweat! But my goodness, it was fun. The following day, Capt. McCrum, Warren and Guns all departed to Cairo – leaving Idwal here. We've bathed with him a lot and 2 nights ago Marion, + he + I and I all went to see the 'The Young Mr Pitt' but now he's gone, so we are on our own again. It has been just grand having them all here. It's so difficult to explain, but they are all real people, friendly, amusing in the extreme and just grand fun to have about the place. A great tragedy of my life was that James, my dog, disappeared and no one could find him anywhere, even after ringing up the municipality, seeing the local police, etc. I gave up hope – only to be rung up by Lenna 2 days ago to say he had been found and was being looked after by a civilian cyphering at Ras el Din, about 10 miles from here and he was returned to us this morning, terribly pleased to see us again and looking much fitter. Apparently the women had given him 3 baths in 4 days!

... Tonight I am having supper with Eve and Clement – a terrible thing has happened. Ivan's beautiful mare, Belle Aurore, has died. As his dog has just died of poisoning, I feel sure there must be foul play somewhere, but will hear all about it tonight.

I am hoping to get a draft from C in C's to join all my Cairo people again. So if you get a cable with a new address, don't be surprised. It is very difficult to work these changes, and it's quite on the cards it won't come off, but we are doing all we can. I have had a long descriptive letter of life in Sicily from John, and also (but not so recent) some from Bruce in the same lines. Most interesting it is to get first hand knowledge from the army and then to talk to the Navy who have actually been there at the assault and see all their photos. Please could you either tell me the date or forward me a copy of the Sphere or Illustrated London news which tells of the assault? Heaps of love S.

———•———

C in C Levant 18/8/43

My dear Mummy – ...Well, we are still pretty busy here and life is good here. Yesterday I went on a picnic with Eve and Ivan, another Wren officer and 2 Poles. We drove past Aboukir in Ivan's caravan and then stopped by the side of the road for lunch under the shade of a palm. Scores of small Arab children came up, and watched with solemn eyes. Eventually, we encouraged Eve to speak to them in Arabic, she didn't want to encourage them too much and they are very charming. When asked, they said that Eve was 12 years old, Diana 10 and me 8! They guessed in the right order anyway. We asked one of them if she would like to come home with us, and she said no, she didn't want to be a slave. When told she wouldn't be she said well, her mother would beat her if she went! This particular child looked very European, with longish fair plaits, and a face of great character. She said she wanted a gold watch and some nail varnish like Diana's! After we'd had lunch, Ivan, I and the 2 Poles went in for a bathe – the sea was very rough and we had a strenuous time jumping the enormous rollers. When eventually we had to go home, there was a great send off from them all! Although only about 10 or 12 on average these Arab children are terribly grownup for their age and their philosophy most sound. They told Eve that if she wanted to take one of them away, she must take a baby because they'd all formed their minds and were settled. But why, they said, didn't she take one of the nice gentlemen with her for a husband and then she could have children of her own! Apparently when Ivan was washing up, they asked him which was his wife and when he said he wasn't married they wouldn't believe him until he said 'Do you think I'd be doing the washing up myself if I had a wife?' To which they all said 'that is true'. In the evening Captain McCrum and Warren Tute who had come down from Cairo, came to take Lenna and Barbara out (I was Duty Officer so couldn't go!) it was grand to see them again we met them again this morning at Unica's for iced coffee and now they are jeeping their way to Palestine for a quick call. I'm so jealous! This morning I was at the dressmakers and am having my beautiful flame coloured Damascus brocade made into an evening frock. It is a wonderful colour, shot with gold, and small birds and flowers all over it.

'On the beach near Aboukir: Eve Barber, Diana Stokes and Edward something, a Polish captain. With Arab children.'

I went to a shop and bought you a length of blue green woollen material for a winter frock which I want you to make up. I think you will like the colour and I'm sure it will suit you, now please don't give it away to Rosemary. It is for <u>you</u>. It is lying on the end of my bed now, together with a large carton of French Fern powder, Velouty, 2 lbs of icing sugar, and a large wad of wire wool which I'm told is very hard to get. All these will be sent off as soon as I can find a suitable box to put them in and they are ALL for <u>you</u>. The last parcel I sent you was taken home by one of our staff, together with all our planning orders for the invasion of Sicily, rather funny. Capt. McCrum did up special bags marked most secret, etc. and sent them as official mail. Old Moore, the secretary, disapproved and sent his by the hand of the officer, and his were the only ones seized by customs! How we laughed. It's a great shame really. The letter I wrote to you on June 7th (I think) was taken by General Montgomery himself, as he worked in close cooperation with our staff, and was flying home to London for a conference or something. I saw him once in our buildings – small and unprepossessing, but with an iron look, the whole show has gone so wonderfully well, it makes one wonder what next? With very much love. Sheila.

Robin Chater seems to be making a late run on the outside in the race to win Sheila's affections. Of all three men, she has known him the longest as they came out on the ship together, but he is also the youngest. Sheila, meanwhile, is bored with the downgraded job in Alexandria, despite having a 'plum' role and is champing at the bit to get a transfer. She never lost this characteristic of always feeling that she was missing out on something better, and that the grass is always greener elsewhere. I think it emanates from her deep insecurity as a child:

C in C Med Levant!!
28/8

My dear Ma – No home mail this week. Life is quiet again here, but quite pleasant … 2 days ago Ivan drove Clement, Eve and I, plus James out to Amriya – this is fairly far west, the most I had ever been and not far from the battlefields. James and I sat in the dicky and nearly fell out the road was so bumpy. Eventually we turned down by the edge of the salt lake, crossed a rocky ridge, and then ran parallel to the sea along a road bordered with fig plantations. We turned right through an Army Camp and over an incredibly sandy road, until we could go no further. Ivan, Eve and I then walked the last 100 yards to the sea. What a lovely sight it was – the sand all white, the sky deep violet, and the sea a glorious transluscent turquoise shade, deepening towards the horizon. Eve and I didn't bathe as we hadn't our costumes, but Ivan went in in his pants! Eventually we drove back to Mex where we had a magnificent fish lunch at about 3 o'clock! My arms were terribly tanned after it all and I considered myself pretty brown before that! … I have just received the most lovely bracelet from Robin as my birthday present. It is Persian – minute pictures painted on bone squares with rounded tops which are set in frames of silver. All is done by hand, and the pictures themselves aren't more than an inch square – all country scenes, men riding horses, bathing, threshing, hunting, milking cows etc. I love it. It arrived beautifully packed in a rose wooden box, sealed in black and wrapped in a piece of khaki turban! He hopes to get a move from Iraq, the staff college hasn't materialised, but I think it is a good thing really, as he is far too young to sit on the staff in Cairo or elsewhere boring. Bruce and John wrote a lot from Sicily – the former enjoys life terrifically. He is a very cheerful, jolly type and never lets anything get him down. I've never met anyone so patient and kind. For I used to keep him waiting hours some evenings in Cairo when we were going out, and then when I was ready, often I was too tired to go out dancing or do what we had arranged and never once did he grumble. John, as ever, is still a wee bit difficult.

I don't think he'd ever be different. He says he will still wait for me to marry me, but I haven't held out any hope for him at all, as he really is so childish, and fiendishly jealous. There is a terrific buzz at the moment that we will all be home by the time our 2 years is up. I personally don't see how they can possibly work this – what I feel as regards myself is, that I'd hate to return to a Methil kind of job, as a 2/O and a D.C.O. [Deputy Cypher Officer]. I'd probably be sent to Greenock or Liverpool as head of a watch, but I'd hate that. Naturally I would like to stay in combined ops but it might be difficult to get in. Alternatively, I could return home, have leave and then agitate for further service abroad, India or somewhere. I can't bear vegetating. C in C Levant Cypher Office is an appalling place to be stuck in – as a D.C.O. it is imagined and quite rightly so, the plum of cyphering jobs on the station – but if I could get out to a more interesting job elsewhere, I'd go like a shot. I saw the C in C's secretary last week and he has promised to put me first on the list of officers transferring to India. There may not ever arise the opportunity but if it does turn up, I wouldn't hesitate to go. I have had my hair cut again and look far better. It was so thick before. This afternoon, Barbara and I are bound for the beach. Some friends of hers are picking us up at four. We do night watch tonight. I rarely find them tiring these days. It's far quieter doing watch than working days like we did in Cairo. A very self centred letter. I'm sorry!
Lots of love,
Sheila

They are completely up to date with news of the Italy landings, which is hardly surprising; as a Cypher Officer, Sheila would see all the messages that were going through and of course be involved in co-ordinating the landings themselves. She kept the original cable dated 11 June, marking the first success in the Sicily campaign, from the Italian Admiral Pareas, 'Beg to surrender through lack of water' and the reply from the British, 'Surrender of Lampedusa accepted from second-in-command who fully agreed with terms. Governor not yet contacted, soldiers landed':

C in C Levant 3/9

My dear Ma and Pa –

… This morning we went to a service at Ras el Jin (HMS Nile Naval
Base and HQ of Rear Admiral Alex). It was to celebrate – if you can
say such a thing – 4 years anniversary of the outbreak of war, and was
held in the open. Lots of Wrens were there, naval ratings, marines,
Navy and Army officers. Unfortunately the man who played the piano
played all the wrong tunes so we all got in a dreadful muddle … Today
we have heard that the Eighth Army have landed in Italy – good old
Monty and well done the Eighth Army. That will be all the people we
know in Cairo once more, Bruce and John I expect … No, I have not
had the parcel yet, Ma. I do hope you did it up well as they get terribly buffeted about. I packed most carefully and sent to Robin a pair
of Polaroid glasses he asked me to get him and he now writes and says
they arrived almost falling to bits and that if I hadn't wrapped them in
cotton wool they would have broken to bits and that only to Persia! …

Lots of love to you both

Sheila

Italy surrendered on 8 September; Mussolini had been deposed
and the new government had made peace with the Allies, although
the Nazis were still entrenched despite Hitler ordering Rommel to
concentrate on defending northern France. Nevertheless Germany's
defensive positions, the weather and the mountainous terrain proved
too difficult for the Allies to overcome, and it was not until the Battles
for Monte Cassino between January and May, 1944, that the Allies
began to make headway further north.

In Alexandria, the vanquished Italian fleet arrived from Malta,
accompanied by the British warships HMS *Warspite*, HMS *Valiant*,
HMS *Faulkner*, HMS *Fury*, HMS *Echo*, HMS *Intrepid*, HMS *Raider*
and the Greek naval vessel RHNS *Vassilisa Olga* [*Queen Olga*], the
French FLN *Le Terrible*, all commanded by Admiral Cunningham.

'Surrendered Italian Fleet Arrives at Alexandria – One Year After Alamein' screams the *Egyptian Mail* headline, faithfully recorded in the scrapbook:

C in C Levt 18/9/43

My dear Mama –

… Oh isn't the news marvellous? I had just come in in the evening when a Wren rushed out to say that Italy had surrendered and we dashed upstairs and immediately there were drinks all round to celebrate the occasion. We have been frantically busy and as you can guess it's all been most terribly interesting. I've done so many extra watches it's almost been like Cairo again. Perhaps the most exciting event of the week has been the Italian warships which arrived here 3 or 4 days ago.

Barbara and I decided we just had to go and see them come in – so although we had been on watch till one, we got up early and took the Wrens transport down to Ras el Jin where Rear Admiral Alex has his offices. Barbara used to be a coder there, so we went to the coding office which is right on the edge of the sea and climbed onto the flat roof. It really was a most wonderful sight, on the horizon slowly drawing nearer seemed to be a toy fleet, headed by 2 of our biggest battleships one ahead of the other, the first one dark and the second camouflaged pale gray and blue – destroyers followed and then in the rear the Italian ships. I counted 15 ships in the horizon at one point and it seemed so funny that Alex which has been so denuded of the fleet ever since we've been here, should be graced with the pride of both the British and Italian Navies at the same time. These were the ships that we had been receiving photo recce reports about for months. Taranto! Cavour! Littorio etc. I just couldn't believe my eyes to see them all spread out in front of me. It was a perfect day too, not too hot, the sea calm and a cloudless sky and as we stood on the roof watching, our planes circled round over the convoy. Some of the other girls stayed in bed but I wouldn't have missed that sight for anything – it was history. We have now gone into 3 watches which means we don't do extra watches but are on more, if you can see! Yesterday we moved into our new officer quarters. I have the most lovely room on the top floor with a balcony overlooking the sea. Unfortunately it wasn't finished and so we had no lights but had to creep about with candles and this morning there has been a frightful rumpus because some people found bugs in their beds, so we have all had to move out again till it is fumigated. Personally I think it's silly to make such a fuss, Egypt is alive with bugs. I am so used to them and so blasé about them you would be shocked! Anyhow, I am still lucky as my bed is on a balcony on the sea side of the house and gets the fresh air. I have heard no more of my move east and fear I won't be allowed to go as we are now so busy. Absolutely no news of Bruce and John. They must be in Italy. I hope nothing has happened to them …

Heaps of love to you all.

Sheila

PS the sun has just set and I have seen the green flash!

It is hard to know from this distance whether Sheila's mother's snub in failing to acknowledge her daughter's role in the war was deliberate or not. Sheila is justifiably nettled and, as ever, gets her own back by belittling her older sister's morality. It is rather priceless that she is allowed to date as many men as she likes, but Rosemary is not: the crucial difference was that Rosemary tended to go for 'sergeants' i.e. other ranks, and not officers. Rosemary continued in the WAAF after the war, where she never married but seemed to have a number of affairs. She finally married a widower, after her retirement, at the ripe old age of 60:

C in C Levant
23/9

My dear Mama –

… I am enclosing some snaps which were taken on leave in Beirut from which you will get an idea of what the country looks like. It is really very beautiful. Also enclosed are some taken from George Buildings Cairo, where I was working and you can now see what aspects I viewed all the time we were planning Sicily. I am rather amused because you have made no comment on that show at all. For myself, I was, and still am, just bursting with pride and having a hand in the show, and working with such wonderful people as Admiral Ramsay and also have the feeling that I have just a wee, wee spoke in the success of the show for all the hard work which I, and all the others, put in in those 4 months in Cairo. If I never do another thing in this war, that will be behind me. It's funny, because coupled with the marvellous job, I had the most tremendous fun in Cairo, far better than any I've ever had out here before or since, except perhaps last August when they all came back from Malta. I am still rampant to get back to them, but fear it's no good, as we are terribly short of old hands and are even now in 3 watches to try and keep the work under. Not that I think I'm a cut above the rest, but experience is bound to tell and so many of the people are new and do the most incredibly silly things.

All my boyfriends have deserted me – even James my puppy has disappeared!! Mails have been shocking lately, none from Sicily for a month, nor from Robin in Iraq and yours from home have been pretty elusive. I had an airmail letter card from Rosemary yesterday who seems keen on a New Zealander this time. Well, I hope it comes off, tho' I must say to add yet another Bert to the family seems deplorable. Maybe he could change it (is it Albert, Bertram or what?) Soon I shall be the only unattached female in the family! That'll never do!

The news re coming home at the moment is that we have to do 2 1/2 years abroad, so I shall definitely try for a change, if not now, in a few months time. No more Levant for me, thank you.

Our new quarters which we have moved into on Friday had to be hastily evacuated on the Saturday as they were found to be full of bugs! Personally, I was neither bitten, nor ever even aware of <u>one</u>, but judging by the fuss everyone made – there couldn't have been less than a million! I now sleep open to the sky and sea, on a balcony, which is very pleasant, back in our Sacré Coeur Convent …

Well no more, my 5th and last letter for this morning!

With heaps of love

Sheila xx

I am sending this by sea, let me know how long it takes. S.

———————

C in C Levant 29/9

My dear Ma, Thank you for 85, 86 which arrived within 2 days of each other. How I envy you blackberrying. I miss the country and everything pertaining to it terribly - when I see pictures of fields, trees, woods, and mountains, I can't imagine what they are <u>really</u> like. I'm sure I shall go mad with excitement when I actually do see these things again – everything is so barren out here. Well, as regards my coming home in the New Year, I'm afraid it's no go, because we have just signed a paper to say whether we want to go home after 2 1/2 years out here and then only if the service can permit. Of course I said yes, however, since signing, I hear from the secretary that he thinks he will be able to send me to India – and he is seeing the Superintendent about it. I am really very pleased about this because I don't think I should like to spend another year in the Levant. I have worked in the most exciting office (with exception of S/M's maybe) and any other place like Suez or Port Said would be rather deadly. Of course this is all taking work as the primary factor, maybe I would do better to think of the social side for a change, but I don't think I could. I also think it might possibly mean coming home even sooner than from here – but that of course is pure guesswork. Anyway, if I do go it will mean being with all my old friends which I shall like. At the moment we are in 3 watches and I am really ashamed of the girls on my watch for the way they grumble. I don't like it much either, but it's the least one can do to carry on without a perpetual moan. It's funny, but it seems just to be the people who were commissioned out here who are so trying. Those who were officers at home have far more guts ... – I am still all packed up as we haven't moved into our new house yet. The grumblings then will be even worse as no one wants to go in. These are times when I HATE these women (or girls!) who are my fellow Wren officers – they are so spoilt and self-ish. I'm certainly not looking forward to living with them. The ones at home were so different. Oh – there is no chance of bringing James home with me, because I now have lost him for over a week and fear there is no chance of his returning now. Poor wee thing – still I am quite confident he is perfectly OK as he is so terribly independent. I am not really in a very good mood to be writing letters, I feel too scratchy with the outside world to be pleasant. There are times when it is no asset to be conscientious, one gets so terribly disheartened at the behaviour of others – to go to India would be a blessed relief. Still no news from Sicily or <u>Italy</u>, but a long long and very funny letter from Robin this week – it really did cheer me up quite a bit. We are in the middle of the mango season, they really are marvellous things, but I never fail to get into an awful mess – they have huge stones in the middle and I always end up with the stone in both hands – gnawing away! Dates have begun too, but I ate so many last year, I can scarcely entertain the idea of one this year! I must now get up properly and go to the laundry. Then have an early lunch and go to work. Sorry for this moan.

Lots of Love

Sheila

Sheila finds herself back in Cairo 'three weeks only this time' as she notes in her scrapbook, changing roles. There is definitely a sense of the theatre of war having moved on, and those left are scrabbling around to find interesting jobs to do. Hence her great angst about trying to get a challenging new role. I think she must have dreaded the inevitable posting back to Britain, as the war at this stage was far from over, and her love life was still in a muddle:

RNGHQ MEF
10/10

My dear Mummy –

… As you already know, I am in Cairo again. This time working for Admiral Waller who has come to Cairo as Director of Combined Operations in place of Admiral Maund. This time I have switched to secretarial work and am secretary to his Chief of Staff who actually hasn't arrived yet, but we expect him minutely. Admiral Waller is a dear old boy but rather terrifying in that he's so vague and never knows where he puts anything or what he has seen, etc. His secretary went down to Alex the other day and I was left to cope with the Admiral, I love it but it nearly sent me grey! However, we went out to lunch together to Shepheards and became good friends …

All the boyfriends are well, and Bruce is now a Major! He seems to be having a marvellous time in Italy, even John is cheery. He sent me £4 for my birthday. I felt quite embarrassed! I've also heard from Idwal Humphrey on the way to India – not since he arrived – I think my chances of going there are about nil now – but I still hope!

… The first few days we were here I nearly passed out with the heat – never known anything like it – thank heavens it is quite cool now, hardly anyone I knew in Cairo before is up here now. One of the first people I met was an ex Commodore from Methil who has been pressing me to go out with him ever since. I'm not a bit keen, for when I said I'd have to work he said did I know any other Wren officers etc. I said no. What cheek these men have! I wonder what he thinks we are? I hope you are all well and enjoying life. We are still in whites whereas I expect you're all in wool and wearing stockings (what a problem the latter are – even here!)

No more now,

Heaps of love,

Sheila

———————

c/o Fleet Mail Office Alexandria
17/10/43

My dear Ma – I was delighted yesterday to have 3 letters from you
87/89 (wrongly numbered for I have had 87) since I have been in
Cairo my mail has been held up. I don't think I shall be here very
much longer alas and alack, as the man I was to work for has gone
home – so I shall be in the drafting pool once more. I shall do everything I possibly can to avoid going back to C in C Levant as far as
I can see, there is <u>no</u> job on this station for me – a confirmed 2/O
unless they check out and demote one of the ailing 2/O's and so,
as I always say, it is no advantage being promoted as you always get
stuck. However, this time, if I possibly can, I am going to hang out for
India, if not with my old people. I know they will want lots of Cypher
people in Delhi. The only alternative to India is, as far as I can see, to
go to Suez as a P.C.O. [Principal Cypher Officer] – they will need a
Wren one in due course – I wouldn't mind going there at all actually.
The work of course wouldn't be very thrilling, except that everything
through the canal goes there and there is quite a good traffic these
days and also you have a very gay time there. But to be in charge of
a whole Cypher office is not up my tree, I hate doling out bottles (of
which there are always thousands) and I dislike being in charge of
Wrens. I really want a job more on my own. However, I am lying
low to see how much longer they will let me stay here undetected, for
I have already written a letter to Idwal in Delhi to say if he can use
me to send a signal now. I do so hope I shall be allowed to go. I really
don't want to have to stay in the Levant. We have a new C in C and
new secretary, so that may help.

... I am glad R will be going to her Octu [Officer Cadet Training Unit] at last. I hate the sound of all those people she mixes with. There are 2 WAAF officers in my room here, both of whom are extremely nice. There are a lot of them out here, but very few O.R.s. [other ranks]. What has happened to this N.Z. bloke she was so keen on? I have been having a very quiet but most enjoyable time here ... But it is such a marvellous change to be away from all the Alex crowd. I have grown extremely unsociable – dislike more people than I like – and hate communal life. What shakes me is that several of my old friends turned me down flat on my promotion – which shows that they couldn't have been very true friends, could they? One of them is reputed to have said I was too high and mighty to have anything to do with her, but as I immediately rang her up on my return to Alex, was certainly not met half way. NOR was I ever told how nice it was for me to be promoted. I rather gathered jealousy had crept in. So I washed my hands of all of them save those I knew were true friends, and consequently there was a lot of discussion – But I feel sure I did right – why be hypocritical and pretend to be friendly with people when you aren't especially when they say rather horrid things behind one's back. So you can guess to return to Alex and to turn an acting 2/O out of her job would be a bad thing!

Yes, all are well in Italy, and Robin in Persia. Idwal wrote last from Bombay and said that as he was jobless he didn't think he could fix me up. Do you know that Warren Tute wangled a jeep for his personal use out of GHQ here, took it to Malta, plus its driver, L/Cpl Askew and they have taken them both on to India without any reference to GHQ. I think it is a scream – Warren is the person who had tea with me at the Goldie's, he used to be in Alex ... He is very arty, writes plays, is terribly witty and amusing, knows all the stage and screen stars and really rather a dear. Anyway he did his damnedest to get me to India – I think I will write to him and see if he can pull a string or 2 to get me there in another capacity! Apparently he disliked the 2/O in charge at Gib, wrote to Admiralty and said so, and she was removed! And he's only a Pay Lieut. R.N.! ... With much love, Sheila,

Your Xmas present is on its way – I have one just like it. From John.

Please address me to the above for the time being. Exactly 3 years ago today that I went to Dundee!

Sadly all her plans come to naught and she finds herself back in Alexandria again, but is undeterred in her efforts to move elsewhere, as we shall see over the next few months:

C in C Levant 23/10

My dear Ma – as you can see I am back in Alex once more – and in my old job as DCO [Duty Cypher Officer] in the Cypher Office! And you can guess how annoyed I was – so much so that I went straight to the secretary, who is new and awfully nice, and poured out my tale of woe – he was really very funny and agreed that I had been tossed about a bit in the last six months … The next day I had an enormous letter from Idwal in Delhi to say he'd not done an honest day's work since he left Malta 3/4 months ago, so I know now that there's no chance of going there at all!

… I am getting very involved with 'les hommes'. Safety in numbers they say, but I'm not so sure – Bruce nearly had a fit when he heard I was in Cairo, and Robin in Turkey – no Iran – is going to try and do a course in this direction and come and see me. John, of course, is always John. I, having been bitten once or twice already, am much reserved, but the boot seems to be on the other leg, this time! Oh dear. Bruce says he is sending me some silk stockings from Italy – apparently they make them very well there and my latest shopping down here is to buy Robin a Signals side cap – which should be arriving today. We spend our time sending postal orders and cheques to each other asking for different purchases – and so life goes on!

… Yesterday I went to the Anglo-Swiss hospital and visited the merchant seamen, officers and men who are ill. They are very much neglected here and Audrey and I went with an old English governess and did enjoy it. We felt so sorry for them and they were all so cheery. I am going to take my canteen cigarette ration to them each week. Then I went to Eve's for dinner and an N.O. was also there, played the piano. Today I am having my 1st singing lesson, visiting the dressmaker, and riding this afternoon, a jump I hope. Oh, Bruce's stockings have arrived and are too short in the leg so I will send them to you. Tons of love, Sheila.

———•———

C in C Levant 5/11/43

My dear Daddy – One birthday letter deserves another – and I feel very guilty at not writing you a letter of your own before – I've calculated this should reach you on about the 16th – Many happy returns of the day! How is the garden – and the Jeep? When I come back home you must teach me to drive it – Riding I've learnt out here, but not driving.

As you know I am back in Alex and still working for C in C Levant. Our shadow is diminishing instead of increasing. Soon I feel we will fade out altogether and then what? It is awfully disappointing to see our fame lessening, operations moving further away and not even a Jerry on the door step! I hope to move on – somewhere – to a more operational job soon. I did hope very much to go to India to join my Cairo people, but I'm afraid there's no hope of that now. Maybe we will all go to Italy, we shall see. Meanwhile, it is getting colder and colder here and last night I wore blues for the first time – we go into them finally on Sunday. It has been pouring with rain and yesterday I went into town only to find that my shoes leaked terribly! As they are the only white pair I have left, I was forced into blues for the night watch!

… John Pritty, whom I have known ever since I came out here, has just returned from Italy with the rest of his regiment. They are in Cairo, which would be the case just as I am transferred here. I am longing to hear all about Italy as from all the letters I have had it really sounds rather fun, though of course they tell us the dreadful things like typhoid disease which is raging in Sicily. I believe all the towns are out of bounds, I hear. I feel awfully disappointed at being stuck here, as having had a hand in <u>perhaps</u> the biggest allied invasion of the war to date, I simply long to follow up the good work and in amongst the people I have worked with before. Still, if I do nothing else in the war, I shall have had one very worth while job. I am terrified of being sent to a non operation base. As for coming home, it is difficult to say when that will be. After 2 1/2 years, they say, but then that's dependent on relief and you know what that means. I long to see more of the world before finally returning to UK, but maybe, if I am a Wren after the war as I want to be, I'll have plenty of chances for that! In month or so I hope to take a long weekend and go down to Luxor with Diana Booth, for we both want to see Tutankhamun's tomb and all the ancient remains down there – and if I have more leave I really want to go to Jerusalem – It would be criminal not to go to such places when they are so comparably near. We are meant to have 7 days every six months, but I don't know how it will work out. Very much love, Sheila.

To her mother she is more frank about her affairs of the heart:

C in C Levant 9/11

My dear Ma – ... I really am pleased R has gone to OCTU, per-haps she will forget all these queer sounding friends she seems to have made! ... Life goes on the same out here – John and all his crowd are back again and he wants me to go up to Cairo this weekend to see him as he is not allowed to come to Alex. I want to see him and hear all about what has been happening but I am not a little nervous as to what he will be like. If he is still persistent and difficult I shall have to put an end to courting as it will do neither of us any good. Another surprise yesterday: a letter from Robin to say he is going to do a mountain war-fare course in Syria and has been given 2 weeks' leave in Egypt. So he is coming down here at the end of the month! It only needs Bruce to fix a liaison visit to M.E. to make the picture complete (and complex!) It will be rather fun to see him again as although I knew him very well on the way out these boat friendships are very difficult on dry land! So far I have been to the Anglo-Swiss hospital with Miss Decks to visit the merchant seamen. They are so nice, afterwards I went back with her for tea. She is a governess in one of the richest families in Alex – Syrian millionaires and live in a magnificent house in Rue Fouad. The daughter of the house sings with Elizabeth and that is how I met them. She is 20 and is seldom allowed out by herself. She is sent out of the room when others wish to talk of things she is not allowed to hear, and her brother has been given a special villa in which to entertain his friends, as some of them aren't considered suitable for May to meet. Did you realise such feudalism could possibly exist today? I didn't. I have had, for the past six weeks, ringworm on my arm! Yes, you will be horrified (as I was!) but you can catch anything out here. To make matters worse I dosed it with extra strong iodine and produced the most frightful burn on top of it! It hurt like hell, but I really believe both ailments are better now. The Superintendent and dear Admiral Alex are inspecting quarters tomorrow. I think I shall pin a notice with 'sleeping' on the door and hope for the best. Otherwise it means tidying up and as I've no room for anything it'll be a hard job. I'm so sorry this is rather dull. I'm not wearing my 'writing pants'.

With lots of love

Sheila

—•—

C in C Levant 15/11/43

My dear Ma –

… I have just come back from a very hurried weekend in Cairo. John was up there, and as he isn't allowed to spend his leave in Alex, he asked me if I'd go up there. So in fear and trembling, I went. I must say he was awfully nice – no awful rows (that was what I was afraid of) and we both enjoyed it very much … John met me at the station, and I immediately went back, bathed and changed, we had lunch in a quiet restaurant off Kasr el Nil, and then rushed off to Gezira for the races. It was quite a lucky day for me – I backed a place every time except once and so kept fairly square. John didn't do so well, and as he backed fairly heavily must have lost quite a bit. We then went off to Groppis for tea – I had to have my usual ice cream there, a Maytime – they are marvellous. In the evening we dressed up – me in my new flame brocade – and went out to Mena House for dinner. The hotel is being closed as GHQ are taking it over. I think it is a great shame as it must be one of the most famous hotels in the M.E. and certainly the favourite honeymoon haunt. It was warm and there was a moon, so of course we visited the Pyramids – they really are very beautiful at night and never fail to give me a thrill, they are so enormous – I had to leave at 12:30 on Sunday, so we drove up to the Citadel because I love standing so high up and looking at the whole of Cairo lying at one's feet – you can see both groups of Pyramids – the Dead City, and the whole dishevelled mass which is Cairo, higgledy piggledy below – swarming with civilisation and strange noises. It fascinates me. John was awfully disappointed at returning here. He loved Italy, and I must say it does sound rather marvellous. He really has entirely changed. I like him far better … I am so glad R. has at last gone to OCTU. Maybe her sergeant friends will fade a bit now.

With heaps of love, Sheila.

—–•—–

C in C Levant 25/11

No 84

My dear Ma –

… Last week I sent you two parcels – one with 2lb icing sugar, and the other with 4 yards of rather nice thick woollen material which I think should make a very pretty winter dress. I loved the colour. Did you ever get the parcel full of odds and ends I sent off at the end of September and also a food parcel posted at the beginning of the same month – I do hope so.

I am rather disappointed because Robin, who was coming down here this week on leave has just written to say that the course he was going on has been cancelled and that anyway he has moved further away than ever. We are both rather cross about this as it would have been rather fun to meet again after over a year. Other news is rather scarce. I've not heard from John since I was up there for the week-end and think he must have moved. I am so pleased to have got that straight at last – Bruce is still in Italy, but I have been rather naughty in not writing lately – I just haven't felt like it.

… I am touched that granddad thinks I am winning the war. I suppose I am in a way, but so is everyone else, wherever they may be – I really must write to him again. I have the periodical fit of writing to out-of-the-way people and granddad is usually included in the round – Oh yes – I was on watch the other evening when the phone rang and a voice said 'is that you Sheila' and it was Idwal Humphrey ringing up from Cairo. He hadn't been doing any work at all in Delhi and old Pongo Moore, Admiral Ramsay's secretary, sent a signal asking for his immediate return to UK. So he went back by air priority A! … Heaps of love to you and Pa.

Sheila

C in C Levant
6.12.43

No. 96

My dear Ma, Sorry this is being typed, but I can't find my pen anywhere. I'm doing it on my knee with Esmé's portable, so don't mind any mistakes. Your Christmas parcel with the lovely handkerchiefs arrived after only one month, which I think was rather good going – they really are marvellous and I am so short of handkerchiefs – the dhobies [laundry] are frightful here. The Almanack has been read through, but we've come to the conclusion we were all born on the wrong day, as nothing seems to work out all right! And the calendar reminds me of Cromer, and the Christmas card of being in Scotland, so you can see I have been thrilled with the whole thing ... I had a real field day on Saturday, and felt awful after having spent so much money when you at home aren't able to do so! I collected my beautiful nightie I have had made in pale gray blue crepe de chine with natural coloured lace trimming it (it really is so lovely I don't think I shall ever dare wear it!) Then Mollie Rendell and I did a grand tour of the shops, when I fell for some very dark gray flannel to have a skirt made, and two lengths of Chinese silk in scarlet and a bright purple-gentian blue for blouses. Somehow, if you are clever, you can buy almost anything you want in the shops here, and I simply love pottering about the quaint little streets. Some of the shops are really tiny, just little square holes in the wall, with shelves and shelves packed with bales and bales of materials. If you are clever, you can bargain for your stuff, but it takes time and endless patience, as well as plenty of good temper and humour. The shopkeeper will like you if you laugh and joke, but won't move an inch if you get cross. I have just had your newspapers and picture posts – thank you very much for sending them. I had, actually, seen the one with the article on Admiral Ramsay in it, but hadn't a copy of my own, which naturally I wanted. Having worked for him, and also knowing him socially in a small way, I think the writer's criticism of him is very hard. He is said to be a bad mixer; well, as mere Third Officer, and the lowest of the low, I found him simply charming. He never failed to forget a name once he had been introduced to a person, and always gave one the impression he really was interested in you. For instance, once he invited me to his flat for lunch, together with several other members of our staff. I was the only girl there (and, in fact, the only women they had ever had to a meal in their flat), and there was no talking of shop with the other members of the staff, everything was brought down to my level, even to the point that I was the centre of all conversation. When he talks to you, he really looks straight at you, his eyes seeming to pass straight through you, and he gives you the impression that you are the only person that really matters. When my promotion came through, I remember we were all working feverishly in one of the halls, with pages of operation orders in piles all round the room, and I was sitting at a table pushing the orders complete into huge envelopes. The Admiral came through the hall with flags, and seeing me, came straight up to me and congratulated me on being promoted, and asked me why I hadn't got my stripe up. I really do think that if I found him like this, the criticism of him as a bad mixer is wrong. One is given the impression that he is hard on his staff, who dislikes him, but that he gets the results from them the same. I think this is wrong, too, for everyone on our staff had not only extreme respect for the man, but great liking for him, and most of the staff officers had worked for him planning the North African campaign. When I met Commodore Douglas-Pennant on his return from Malta at a cocktail party on one of the ships, I congratulated him on an apparent 'leg-up' in the Naval world. But he told me he was lost without Admiral Ramsay, as he had worked with him so long a Chief Staff Officer. And I could well believe it. I will admit that he doesn't suffer fools gladly, but then who but a fool himself would, and anyway, it doesn't win the war to be weak in that respect. Having read this criticism, I really feel justly proud for having worked for him, and for being personally thanked by the Admiral in Cairo railway station just before everyone left for Malta, via Alex. And I felt such a fool too, for being thanked for what after all, was only my job, which I felt I'd scraped through anyhow because there'd been so much work to do I couldn't possibly make it as efficient as I'd have liked. I'd give anything to work for him again. I am having a week's leave in January, and plan to go to Jerusalem – have I told you this before? Our watches are very favourable for Christmas and New Year, but at the moment the prospects seem very dull, as everyone is away, and it's so much more fun to spend Christmas with your friends. Oh dear, this seems to be all – a very happy Christmas to you, and a wonderful New Year. Heaps of love, Sheila.

This is the article to which I think she was referring; it was stuck in her scrapbook and is of an English newsprint quality.

C in C Levant
16/12/43

No. 86

My dear Ma – Thank you very much indeed for your Xmas present
to me – I always feel rather awful when you send me things as I am so
well off – I now make £19 – and all found – so do please think twice
before sending me things. You will make me very self indulgent if
you keep telling me not to send you things … John is up in Palestine
instructing at the M.E. OCTU – he likes it rather – for which I am
glad, as he hates a staff job. Bruce wrote to me yesterday (or at least I
got the letter yesterday) and says he is sending me a tin of chestnuts.
I am very thrilled at the idea of this, as we don't get them here. I
have sent both him and Robin Chater a parcel of Turkish Delight and
crystallised fruit, but don't know what to send John as he is able to get
these things …

Last night I went to a dance given by the Australian forces for the
Greek Red Cross – who were very good to them whilst in Greece.
Prince Paul of Greece was there, tall and very distinguished, with
a monocle, in Naval uniform. I'm afraid when I got there I wished
I hadn't gone, as I was the only Wren officer there, with quite a lot
of ratings and there was a frightful crowd of people there. Luckily I
wasn't in uniform. However, one mustn't be snobbish. Today is the
first day of Winter – terrific winds, huge seas. I nearly lost my hat
when I was in town this morning and it has been pouring with rain
– oh thank you for your letter enclosing granddad's Xmas present, it
was very sweet of him – and I must write to him. With all good wishes,
and lots of love to you all. Sheila.
Have you had any of my parcels?

C in C Levant
25/12/43

Dear all of you – It's Christmas Day, so I must just stop a minute and wish you all a happy one! It's just 1105 and I expect you are all in church singing the first carol – as for myself, I have been unromantic enough to have to pay a visit to the laundry and have just returned laden with shirts and collars. I went to church at 0800 and as we go on watch at 1300 and have to have an enormous dinner before we go, haven't been able to go to Matins. The weather is just perfect and I am sitting on the balcony with the dark blue sea all round, bright blue sky and clumps of heavy white clouds making deeper blue patches on the sea. It's breezy and sunny, but warm. It seems very funny to think that you probably have snow at home – when we went on watch last evening our driver told me he had spoken to someone who was in England 5 days ago, when everything was white. We've all been hopefully singing and wishing for a white Christmas, but nothing's happened so far. It's hard to work up a Christmas spirit out here – but we decorated the house with red pepper branches, beautiful roses and chrysanthemums, and we even have a Christmas tree all lit up in the little niche in the front hall – and of course we are having a huge Xmas dinner at 12 before we go on watch. I started my Christmas on Thursday when I went to a party at Eve's. She had a Russian tenor there who was one of the 'Chauve Souris' people – and he nearly sang the roof off. I really do think that if he hadn't have had laryngitis, the ceiling would have cracked. There was much drinking and merriment, and at 1030 we proceeded to Pastrondis, a nearby restaurant, for dinner, sherry, wine, whisky, it all flowed like water – and so did our conversation, as you can guess!

… Next day I was up at the crack of dawn and into town for I wanted to buy flowers for several people, we went to the shop where I had ordered them, and were told that they were 5/- a dozen when I had been told 3/-. This amazed me considerably and I was arguing strongly when in came 2 American Sergeants who at once said we must buy the girls some roses and immediately clapped down

Bruce's Christmas
card from Italy .

oh 6 have leave for X'mas

To Sheila

WISHING YOU A
VERY HAPPY
CHRISTMAS

and here's to a bumper
reunion party of all the
"Georgics" in the New Year

Bruce

← still with memories
of Mena!

15/- and 3 dozen roses were mine. Great remonstrations from me
as I wanted to give them to Elizabeth and naturally intended to buy
them myself. However, they would hear nothing of it, they were pickled as coots, a bottle in each hand, and a beautiful blue and white
pre-frill round each of their necks. <u>How</u> we laughed! Eventually we
went to the Vedgis for lunch, and then they drove me back here. I
washed and dyed my hair in 1 1/2 hours and then we went on watch.
Well! If we hadn't got the Christmas spirit, others certainly had! Even
at 1830 the S.D.O. [Sub Duty Officer] and marine messengers were
well away − in fact one of them had to be sent home early as he was
rather incapable! They were so funny − coming into ask questions
and not able to talk properly, and then, having got what they wanted,

weaving a tortuous path out of the office, missing the door by inches! Work came in, and we worked steadily. I drew a Christmas card for Alex, Cypher office, and sent it down to them with the rest of the signals – and midnight came – suddenly we heard strains of Good King Wenceslas – Hooray we cried – carol singers at last! However, as the sounds came nearer, we realised it was tinged with gin and whisky – and the complete W/T [wireless/telegraphy] watch arrived to take over – merry as kings. Then before you could say knife, a long straggling line of sailors appeared all wearing paper hats, singing happy Xmas to you, and brandishing bottles of brandy. The first one rushed up to me with a tin mug and open bottle and insisted I drank some – and then we all shook hands in turn. They completely settled themselves down staggering all round the office – drinking, laughing, and smoking <u>enormous</u> cigars. To crown it all, the little marine messenger who was so pickled stuck his head through a window connecting his office and ours, and started lassoing his pals with a long rope – laugh – I nearly collapsed! All this time one of my watch was being rung up by her boyfriend from Mursa Matrouh and she couldn't hear a word – in the end she had to give it up as a bad job. Then to wind it all up, the youngest of all the W/T crowd rushed up to me and said 'Merry Christmas old bean – I'll say it now because I daren't say it in the morning!' and shook me wildly by the hand. This was the end! I was nearly speechless with laughter by that time. Then of course, I didn't know how to get rid of them, there they were, packed all over my office, and nothing would budge them, and of course I didn't want to tell them to go. However, their leading hand, who is a good sort, came in and shepherded them out, and the last I saw of him was with his arm entwined round a very drunk sparker's waist, staggering on uncertain course into his office! After that you can be sure we had the right spirit too – I just dread to think what might happen if anything emergency had cropped up – I shouldn't think there was more than one sparker capable of taking down a message correctly – but I must say their P.O. [Petty Officer] seemed O.K. The whole affair was priceless and I wouldn't mind betting that in every part and establishment in the British Fleet – exactly the same thing was going on!

We are going on watch this afternoon armed with Christmas cake. I rather dread to think what the W/T will be like – there will be some very sore heads, I know! …

So now it's 1145 and I must rush down for a drink before lunch. I can't tell you what a lovely smell I can smell – this balcony is over the galley!

With tons of love to you all

Sheila,

P.S. Am now on watch after an enormous dinner – the pudding came in aflame! It's now 1320 and we are listening to carols. The poor W/T people look the worst for wear, but are bearing up! S.

'Christmas 1943 – we had the "Afternoon" – but after a huge Christmas dinner – who cares?' Sheila top of steps, left.

1944

'How are the mighty fallen'

Between 1942 and 1944 there were no land battles on the Western Front, and the threat of invasion by the Nazis had receded with the victory in the Battle of Britain. Of course there were air raids and smaller raids, like that on Sark, and operations by the SOE in occupied France. The Allies instead took the war to Germany, instigating bombing raids on their towns and cities, while the German army was battling away in North Africa, the Balkans, and on its Eastern Front, finally lifting the siege of Stalingrad in January 1944. The war was beginning to turn in the Allies' favour.

Admiral Ramsay, now safely back in England, was in charge of planning the naval element of Operation Overlord, which finally took place in June of that year, and became known as the D-Day landings. He was to be killed in an air crash in January 1945.

Sheila, meanwhile, is stuck in Alexandria and extremely frustrated. When she hears that one of her junior officers, who was sent back home, has managed to get on Ramsay's staff as a 2nd Officer, she is quite beside herself. Like Bruce, she is an 'invasion addict' and feels useless now that the action has moved back to Europe, and her office and work has been significantly downgraded.

Her boyfriends, on the other hand, are still involved in the fighting, as the battle to take Italy is in full swing. In January the Allies landed at Anzio and by June they had taken Rome. All of them were to be there at some stage during the year: Bruce at the turn of the year, John and Robin in August. The latter has left Iraq and she is expecting to see him in Alexandria on his way to Italy, via Algiers. She has even heard from Paul, who is now in Gibraltar as a flotilla officer, 'not at all bad for an RNVR'. She intends to visit him on her return to England, as she was 'always rather keen on him'.

Thus 1944 is the year that she tries desperately to get a transfer – India, Ceylon, Algiers or, as a last resort, back to England to apply for a final posting. Her scrapbook contains copies of all the cables she sent in her efforts to go to India and Ceylon and bear witness to this. She has not seen her family for two years and she is bored with Egypt now the battle is over. You get a real sense of disappointment and frustration as the year unfolds, although she never loses her sense of humour or capacity for enjoyment.

In January, there is 'very little news'. She doesn't even recount her New Year's Eve, normally a big fixture in her life. She is pleased to report that she is to receive the Africa Star for her services in the Middle East. However, in the same letter, she sadly notes, 'Please note my new address – there no longer exists a C in C Levant – we now form part of the Med Command Flag office, Levant and Eastern Med we are. What a comedown, how are the mighty fallen.'

She is worried that Ann Halliday, no longer a 'great friend of mine', stationed in Haifa with John Pritty, has been 'putting him off me', as she has not heard from him for over a month. Adding to her feelings of isolation are the departures of many of her close friends – Esmé to Cairo, Idwal and Dick from her watches, both to London, yet she seems to be stuck despite having been in Egypt longer than anyone, although she writes hopefully, 'we are liable for service anywhere in the Med now, so don't be surprised if I suddenly change my address.'

She has been filling her time sending parcels home, 'jellies, cream, peel and so on', and to Bruce in Italy who is finding it hard to get things like 'blades, soap, boot polish, hair cream etc. He is a very great dear.' This expression is Sheila's highest accolade of affection and she applies it rather liberally to various men, and sometimes to girlfriends too. In the next letter Robin Chater is described as 'a great dear but terribly shy.'

Her mood changes when Robin arrives, as promised, in Alexandria and they have a great few days together. She 'immediately removed … bag and baggage to Le Mediterranean Hotel nearby, and lived in luxury for 2 days. It really is the most comfortable spot I've struck in Egypt – remarkably soft beds, beautifully furnished (the place has only been opened about 4 months and is brand new) and it was so heavenly to have a private bathroom of one's own – I spent my time popping in and out of the bath!'

He is very musical and they go to hear Pouishnoff play and then to a concert by Sheila's teacher, Elizabeth Vegdi. No sooner has Robin left than she goes on to Port Said, where she was evacuated during The Flap before going to Ismailia, to the very same YWCA, and into the arms of yet another boyfriend:

In bed 29/1/44

… Sybil Hoole and Barbara Banks are stationed here and it has been grand to see them again, and Jaap van Hooff is here at the moment, and it has been very interesting to see what we think of each other after two years. He has changed a lot in my sight, but funnily enough he doesn't think I have altered much at all, so now you have first hand knowledge, from someone who should know, of what I am like at the moment! I feel very calm about the whole thing, quite different from two years ago and really we are having a very gay time. I like Port Said, it's small and friendly – a lovely flat hard beach to walk along – yesterday Barbara and I walked about 5 miles, and I even paddled the weather was so marvellous – eventually we picked up a truck and drove back – Today Jaap and I are going to hire bicycles and cycle along the beach as far as we feel inclined – and this evening we are going to dance at the Officers' Club. Tomorrow we may go down to Ismailia – it depends on duties, really. I am staying here till Wednesday. It would have been fun to have gone to Palestine, but alone would have been a bad thing I think. Anyway, the rest here is doing me tons of good – not that I've had a very hectic time in Alex these last six months! I am very much hoping my days there are numbered. I am determined to get out at all costs, wherever I go – Algiers, Gib, home, Colombo – anywhere – I can hear you saying 'I wish Sheila hadn't met that Dutchman again'! Don't worry, I'm emotionally stable these days – too much so, I think. It has been grand for 2 such good and old friends as Jaap and I to meet. By the way I sent you 8 jellies, and 2 tins of cream last week – I hope they arrive safely. I am going to look for my grandfather's grave when I have a minute. Heaps of love to you and Pa – Sheila.

It is fascinating to read that she has been looking for her grandfather's grave in Port Said. As mentioned in the introduction, her grandfather, Findlay's father, died at sea en route to China with his regiment. It was believed he was buried in Port Said where his body was off-loaded. According to the Nautical Report of 1895:

January 23rd [1895] 3.00 am Sgt Major W. Mills departed this life
10.15 am Arrived Port Said
0. 05 pm Sent Remains of Sgt Mills on shore for burial
1.42 pm proceeded

My mother was always fascinated by her father's forebears and, after her death, I found a whole series of files and correspondence with various genealogists; she was quite determined to reveal the secrets of her grandfather's illegitimacy. Sadly she never did. However, in a letter dated September 2000 to one of the researchers, she wrote:

I was in the WRNS during the war and one of the jobs that fell to me whilst serving in the C in C Med in Alexandria in 1942 was to help prepare accommodation for the Wren ratings at a convent in Port Said. When I told my father about this some time later he said Oh that must be the one to which my mother and I were taken on my father's death at sea. Stupidly, I never followed this up, and he certainly didn't tell my mother with whom he had rather an unsatisfactory relationship! The convent was on the sea front; I don't remember its name but doubtless could find it. Subsequent enquiries in Port Said, which I have visited several times since, have revealed nothing as to where he was buried.

Her letters now frequently refer to her agitation over her future and her growing discontent over her treatment by her superiors. She seems convinced that she is headed East, all the same:

Office of FOLEM
7/2/44

My dear Ma – As you see, here I am back again in Alexandria, the same old office! I really had a marvellous leave in Port Said with Jaap van Hooff – dancing, eating, drinking, laughing, and being altogether very gay. Leave's much more fun with old friends. When I arrived back in Alex I found to my fury that I had been removed from my own watch, whom I was very fond of, and in charge of one with none of my old friends on – This made me very cross, as I always seem to hold the baby for someone, so I determined not to sit down under it, added to this was the fact that we may not be sent home for at least 2 1/2 years, so I have written a request to the Signal Office for further service abroad in India or Ceylon, and he has said he will do his best to get me there, quickly – I don't know where it will be – I rather hanker for Ceylon – and don't want to go to Bombay much, but will certainly go anywhere I am sent (I'll have to anyway!) I have been medically examined and am fit, so all is well! I do realise that this may be rather disappointing to you, but as far as I can see I wouldn't be home immediately, and as you know, I am longing to see a bit more of the world having gone this far. I was very keen to take a signal course in Haslemere, but there again, I would have to wait for it and I feel I must leave this place soon –

9/2 Yesterday I went off to see the 1/O, and have got things straight with her. As a Cypher Officer I stand little chance of returning to UK until July or later, and so I really do hope to be away from here in 2 months. Anyway, she said she would do her best to expedite my draft – though I do realise she has very little to say in the matter. She suggests I might like to go to Kilindini – my goodness, I soon said <u>no</u>!

… I am having my hair permed this week, and am gathering together cottons for the East, including a red check cotton evening dress, which I know that you would love. Please give my love to Pa and Rosemary, and say a prayer for my quick draft! Heaps of love, Sheila,

Perhaps it will be Delhi, I know lots of people there.

Sheila always likes to have a dig at her sister when she's feeling depressed and frustrated! It seems as though no-one expected the war to end quickly as she talks about being posted for 18 months. Again she acknowledges her 'wanderlust' and desire to see more of the world:

FOLEM. 19/2/44

My dear Mummy – … I hear Rosemary has gone to Air Ministry which I think is a great pity, as I think it would be a good thing if she could break off from all her London friends and start afresh in a new place. However, the job sounds quite good. So we shall see!

I can't think how Aunty Rose got hold of the idea that I was coming home in February! All I can guess is that I probably told her I was <u>due</u> home in February, and she jumped to conclusions – as a matter of fact I am very surprised to hear the wheels have been set in motion for drafting home the Levant Wrens and I believe the first set of officers are due to relieve us next month. However, as they are all 3/O's, it wouldn't affect me, and anyway, as I have already told you, I have applied for, and am very much looking forward to going to Eastern Fleet. I do hope my draft will come through soon. I must make enquiries about when it went in, and see if I can make out how much longer I shall be here – it seems very funny to be gathering together one's whites while still wearing greatcoats, but that is what I am doing! Molly Rendell, my stable mate, fell out of the brake and broke a bone in her foot a week ago, so I have been kept very busy visiting her in hospital – we have been out to tea together for the first time today, to the Sporting Club, where we met some 'local' friends of mine, wealthy Jews, who are very kind and awfully nice – I believe I told you how a month or so ago, I went out to dinner with them, and we sat down 15 – all but 2 of us being family! They ran into swarms of brothers, sisters, wives and mothers, so that you never know <u>where</u> you are – and you have to be solemnly introduced to everyone – One amazing thing is that the children are so polite – always shake hands and are not in the slightest bit self conscious. <u>Everyone</u> shakes hands on every possible occasion out here. It was very strange to me at first, but now I shake hand like the rest and you will laugh at me terribly when I come home and start my tricks in your household!

Robin has arrived in Algiers, and has pronounced it a poor place – not advisable for me, he says. I wonder where he will land up – I don't expect we shall meet again till after the war – even he says this, not knowing I am off for the East – but we shall see! I don't expect to be there more than 18 months at the least, inclusive of going there and coming back – it seems too good an opportunity to miss – as you know I am a very restless person with a horrible wanderlust! I am going to make enquiries about WRNS after the war, as, if I'm not married (you never know – tho' don't expect any telegrams!) I think it is the only life for me!

Heaps of love,

Sheila

As ever, things do not go to plan and she is 'rather wild' when her transfer request still had not been forwarded to the Admiralty four weeks later. She tries to 'set the ball rolling and made the powers-that-be send a signal about it – but I don't know yet whether they will play. A very mean trick I call it – when they knew I was rampant to get away, and had promised to speed things up a bit.'

She is so grumpy that, even though John is in Cairo for a few days, she refuses to go and see him, as she doesn't 'feel it a good thing. He must come down here if he wants to see me!' Her room-mate Molly, not content with having broken one foot, immediately on having the plaster off, fell over and 'cracked the other one' and is 'worse damaged this time'. Life is 'boring' and consists of 'nothing but work'.

To add insult to injury the mails are disrupted –'not one blood-stained letter (as the saying goes)' – for three weeks. This is set to continue for the next few months, until after May, as there was a lot of naval activity around Italy to support the Allied push culminating in the battles of Monte Cassino. The navy lost several vessels off Anzio, including the destroyer *Janus* and HMS *Penelope*.

But a week later her dogged pursuance of her transfer is rewarded and she is 'on the move again, tho' I'm not sure where I'll end up':

6/3/44

… last Friday, I arrived in at midnight to find a message telling me to stand by to dash off to the place where I last spent leave [Port Said] in order to catch a ship – The next day it was decided that I should go off to this place anyway, ready to pop on to the ship should occasion arise – not bad on the Navy's part – as they had said in the signal to the ship they would take either 2nd or 3rd officer in exchange – so I dashed from dressmaker to dressmaker, packed my bags in an evening (how on earth I got everything in I don't know – but I did) and I caught the 9 o'clock train here arriving at 5 last evening. So this morning I betook myself to Navy House to fill out the form, and was promised a phone call when they knew – at lunch time it came – from the O/C Naval draft, asking me was my wish to transfer on compassionate grounds (husband, fiancé or family) as no one wished to change, but a swap could be arranged if I had a very good reason. I'm afraid I hadn't the pluck (or heart) to tell a lie, and so he said he was very sorry, but it couldn't be arranged! Alas, this was terrible, so

I rushed off to Navy House again and rang up the SSO in Alex and told him the story. Well, he said, would I like to go down to Suez, relieve a Paymaster there temporarily, and he would go and see the 1/O about sending a signal – so for the minute I am staying put. If I go to Suez it will be much easier for me eventually to catch my ship – and I won't have to rush all the way back to Alex with my luggage to the office which I loathe. So I really hope that I go there. It will be a new place anyway, and I know several of the people there. What adventures we do have! It shows, anyway, that if you don't shout for yourself you don't get anywhere (not that I've got very far to date, but I'm on the way). I have bought you a nice hot water bottle, and have packed it up with a nightie for Rosemary, and 2 pairs of Italian silk stockings which Bruce sent to me, but which were too small. The parcel isn't posted yet, but I've asked Molly to do so when she comes out of hospital – I've also sent you a photo I had taken before Xmas, which I think is rather awful, but which everyone seems to like rather. I hope you'll like it too. I must now rush off to the dhobie because I asked them to do some things in a hurry – thinking I'd be away tomorrow! Heaps of love,

Sheila

When Sheila arrived at Suez she was told that she was to be made Principal Cypher Officer and Confidential Book Officer:

… which fact didn't please me at all, as what's the use of taking over a lot of complicated stuff when you've got to turn it over to someone else within a matter of weeks. Needless to say nobody here has heard anything about the reason for my coming here – and as the present PCO is going it all fitted in very well for them. However, I have firmly told everyone I'm not here to stay so I hope they'll realise it in time.

Worse still, there is 'absolutely no work to be done at all. I come and go exactly as I please – a thing unheard of in Alex where we were so busy we nearly killed ourselves. I hate having no work to do.'

As for Suez itself, it is a 'frightful spot, dirty, filthy and anyway out of bounds as they have had plague there! It is dying out now, I believe.' However, there are several people she knows there and social life seems good: she goes to a cocktail party in her first week and on 'to dance at the French Club', which seems to be the meeting point for the officers stationed at Port Tewfik, where they actually live, a 'pleasant little spot, built by the Canal Company … with modern houses, trees and grass'.

She takes to her new job, like the true professional she is:

HMS STAG (Suez)
C/O CPO
24/3/44

My dear Ma – …I'm afraid I've not written for 12 days, but believe me I've been busy! To begin with, I have now taken over my new job entirely, we have moved shop, and my reign has begun – I work from 0800–1230, and from 1800–2000 daily, so you see I don't do too badly – Later on I am going to take the odd day off to Cairo or a half day's bathing etc. but at the minute I like to be at the office to see that everything starts OK. I do believe in kicking off as you mean to go on, and I have naturally made quite a lot of changes in the office – added to all this I have been paying visits to the Navy all round – 2 lunch parties and one tea on board HM Ships this week, the first lunch party was a scream – we'd given up all hope of going as NOIC [Naval Officer in Charge] has to give permission and hadn't done so, so we'd gone off and had lunch. Then permission came through and a special boat laid on from the ship, so off we went, 3 of us, and had another lush meal, topped with Drambuie. The Captain was R.C.N. [Royal Canadian Navy], and a charming man. Afterwards we did a ton of inspection, and ended up by sending a signal to a ship just passing in from one of the Wren officers who knew someone aboard. Quite a precedent! We came back in a motorboat and got absolutely soaked! 2 days after that I went aboard this same ship to tea with 2 other Wren officers and some ratings. It was such fun – everyone was young and full of fun.

We went off at 2 o'clock and didn't return till six! There is a rule on the station that you can only visit ships on an instructional tone – however, we usually manage to swing that – I get so bored climbing in and out of sea turrets – I do like to visit the bridge, tho', and the galley is always rather fun. Today I had lunch on a small vessel in dock here – I was horrid enough to be frightfully bored – one of the officers took the letter of the law very much to heart, and insisted on showing us everything in the ship – despite the fact she was 34 years old! Katherine Piddocke … is living in nearby. She is going home to have a baby, and it was marvellous to see her again. What a chat we had! She tells me grim tales of Eastern Fleet, so that I'm <u>almost</u> beginning to wonder whether I have barked up the wrong tree, but there's no turning back now! I hope to go up to Cairo next week – It only takes 2 hours by road and it is very difficult to get things here – in fact, I think we have 3 or 4 shops only. Mail has been putrid lately, absolutely none. Mollie Rendell is going to Aden, they asked me if I'd like to go but I refused. It's only a 9 months' station anyway. Damn cheek after two years here, <u>I</u> think! … Heaps of love, Sheila

She is still maintaining that this is a temporary posting and is pleading with Alexandria to be allowed to go on the next convoy; by applying for an Eastern transfer she is barred from returning to England, so she really is stuck! Despite her work being a great come-down after her previous responsibilities, she throws herself into activities such as arranging hockey matches and going to the club, even if the company is less than scintillating. Her mother obviously thinks her new job is 'very good', and Sheila is more than happy to disabuse her of this notion in several of her letters:

HMS STAG (Suez)
C/O CPO
24/3/44

My dear Mama – … As for the 'job' – it probably sounds better than it is – I have 8 Cypherers working for me (I had <u>one</u> watch of 15 in

Alex!) 5 of which are 3/O's, and the other 3 are W.T.S. (F.A.N.Y's [First Aid Nursing Yeomanry] from East Africa) all are very nice – I spend my time checking up on office details, placating people who say they are meant to have had such and such a signal, but haven't, granting leave, signing movement orders, phoning Alex, and even 'seeing' the maintenance Commander about giving Wren personnel a proper cloakroom and lavatory, which we haven't got here! Such are the trials of a P.C.O. [Principal Cyphering Offcier] – issuing orders and messages to ships and going gray when one sails without her last minute instructions – as for being C.B.O. [Confidential Book Officer] – that is rather a nightmare as it is up to me to change all the signal books in force whenever they have to be, see that they are destroyed on the right day, and get court martialed if any go astray. Pray for me! It's not a very terrific job, but quite fun for a change. Nothing is very urgent down here – unlike Alex when all our work was top line and had to be attended to straight away. At the minute I am sitting under the dryer at the hairdressers – thank heavens the place rises to one – (sorry – pen's run out) it is half men and half women, but the one who does us is awfully good – I played hockey yesterday – <u>never</u> again – It was a sandy pitch – a hot day, and I hadn't played for over a year. Today I have blisters all over my feet, and am terribly stiff – We played the Shell Refinery people – The umpire, one of them, was very anti-Navy and kept on giving free hits against us, explaining in detail what we did wrong – eventually he told somebody off for standing and blocking the way 'like the rock of Gibraltar', he said. I was mooching past, so I acidly said 'well, that's what we are!' Damn cheek – we won, however, by about 5 goals to nil! My swan song in the hockey world I think! I went out to the French Club to dine and dance on Saturday, and the local sub-area are having a dance in their mess on Thursday – I am going with an elderly 2/O her boyfriend a Lt. Col (medical) whom I'm not very keen on (I strongly suspect him as a dirty old man) and the P.M.O. [Principal Medical Officer] at the Naval base here, Cdr RNVR, who has one eye! However, he seems quite nice, so I am putting on my best dress, and will see what I can do!! Everyone down here seems to be either over 40, or else very wet

– the worst of a backwater! Still, we do have our fun! I hope to go to
Cairo this week – do a bit of shopping and see Esmé – I'll send you a
cable when I do a move – when …
Lots of love
Sheila

Nevertheless life is quite pleasant in the 'backwater'. Sheila goes to visit
Esmé in Cairo, enjoys bathing – 'we are all quite brown' – and partici-
pates in several expeditions to the Attaka mountains, where there are
two chalets which belong to the friends of the mountain club:

17.4.44

We were rather an ill-assorted crowd, Monica Powell, Dorothy Peck
and I – 3 Wrens – M. and Mme Daumas, a French couple who live
here (he is in the Canal Company) Mac, (Dorothy's boyfriend - a
rather colourless but very kind Captain in the RASC [Royal Army
Service Corps]), Major Roe, O/C Signals down here, and another
Frenchman who was a friend of the Daumas – the climb wasn't
too bad – but I got terribly puffed – It's no good – I always revert to
pencil, having no ink! The chalet was a small white 3 roomed affair
on the top of a hill – with a rather lovely view over Suez Bay and the
surrounding country. We took up plenty of drink and tons of food
all ending up very merry on the flat roof of the chalet, singing lustily
to the surrounding hills – The lights of Suez, Tewfik and the ships
were marvellous – they made me think of Cape Town. Of course
there is no blackout here – even tho' we did have a siren here last
week. The next morning Major Roe and I were very energetic, and
ran over the hills down to a valley known as the Garden of Eden and
back before breakfast – I got more puffed than ever! When we arrived
back at Tewfik, he was told that one of his tents had been burnt to the
ground, and he'd got the Brigadier coming to inspect that day!

That evening a party of us went to the French Club to dance –
all very gay – On Sunday we had another boating picnic, but it was
so cold, I didn't enjoy it a bit, and ended up by hearing Mac's part

in 'French Without Tears' in one of the cabins – terrific love scenes which made me quite embarrassed and everyone else laugh!

Another expedition takes her to Abu Zenima, to carry out reconnaissance for a rest camp with three other officers. Again we see the writer in Sheila beginning to emerge with these descriptive passages of the terrain:

c/o Fleet Mail Office
Suez
24.5.44

My dear Ma – If you look on the map of Africa or Arabia you will find one mid of the way down the west coast of Sinai, a small place called Abu Zenima – that is where I am writing to you from now – There is a manganese ore mine here or nearby and this is where the ore is brought down to the ships – But to tell you how I came to be here – One of the other Wren officers, Dob, was asked to go with 2 people she knew and another girl was needed. The idea was to come down here on a recce for a rest camp for the soldiers, so the day before yesterday we got up at 5.45, packed our things, took a boat across the canal and picked up the two men and the truck the other side – So off we set; to begin with it was very chilly, as it was then only 6.30 and the road which is a track in the desert, flat and uninteresting, the further south we got the hillier it became with an occasional oasis here and there, a few palms or trees. Now and again we met a bedouin on a camel, or one of the Sinai police, also on a camel, but otherwise there's no one about – half way down, we met a truck with an officer in it who told us his general and staff were at a camp in Abu Zenima where we wanted to stay, and that all his division were scattered about somewhere – however, when we got here, we befriended the sole survivor of the mining company, the only European for 80 miles, a Yorkshireman, and he opened one of the disused bungalows for us, so we have done very well after all. This morning we motored down the coast to look at this proposed camp – a disused stone house built for an ore company long since defunct, on top of a hill overlooking the sea – There are marvellous mountains all round, sandstone but of the most curious strata – they seem to have been eaten away by rains, which have cut deep gullies into the rock, producing a triangular effect on the mountains – They are a deep cream colour and look heavenly against the blue sky and deep deep blue sea – We had 2 heavenly bathes and once on a calm shallow beach and the second time we climbed round the headland the house was on and bathed on the windward side and rode lovely breakers – After lunch, which was the most wonderful fish, just caught, cooked by Mr Baugh's cook, a most remarkable Sudanese boy, Mac and I decided to augment our tan, so we oiled ourselves and sat on the beach till it became too hot to be bearable so we walked along to the jetty, where we spent about 2 hours diving in and out, and watching the fishes – the water is very clear, you can see right down to the bottom and watch shoals of bright emerald fish dart here and there, larger grey ones, and even bigger white ones with huge black eyes. It has been a fascinating afternoon and we are a <u>marvellous</u> colour – I have to confess that the backs of my legs are burning somewhat! The bathing really is perfect – no current, soft sand underfoot, a marvellous bay and mountains all round – I believe there are sharks, but we haven't seen any. I wish you were here to enjoy it all – tho' it's hot you don't notice it, because of the breeze, it's dry too – more later. Love Sheila

Of the boyfriends, only John is nearby but she suspects she is in his 'black books again'. She is cheered when, out of the blue, Robin sends her some Jane Seymour Peach Skin Food, 'I couldn't help smiling when I opened it and am longing to know its history as Robin is so shy I can't imagine him going into a shop and buying face cream!'

A week later John gives in and pays her a visit; they 'spent the afternoon sunbathing. He was in good form and we got on very well. Poor man – he says he will still hang on – for as he says, you never know – but I told him I really couldn't marry him, and he said, well if he didn't marry me, he wouldn't marry anyone, so it looks as if I have made a permanent bachelor out of him.' He has volunteered to serve his final months in India; as he has already been abroad four and a half years, Sheila thinks he is mad as 'once there he'll never get home'.

She and John go to Cairo overnight to do some shopping and to see Esmé Cameron, who is going back to England too, as she has been unwell. Diana Booth is also returning to England and Sheila is increasingly desperate to find out what will become of her. The Eastern Fleet seems as 'remote as ever', the UK is 'uncertain' but there are some possibilities for the Mediterranean. They have also been told that no one at their station is being relieved to go 'home' until after the Second Front, which was continuing with Operation Overlord and the D-Day landings on 6 June. She thinks they have something 'in mind' for her as she had to have yet another medical.

Her last few meetings with John were fraught: one of the rows was over Sheila wanting to go to Ceylon and John's disapproval: 'really he is quite impossible'; and a few days later he appears unexpectedly at the French Club, having turned down her invitation to a dance there. So Sheila had gone with a girlfriend and her party – and guess who was sitting at the neighbouring table after all:

Tewfik 30/5/44

Old John was furiously jealous because I was at the French Club in another party, and also because of the trip to Abu Zenima, which he was very rude about! All this time Owen Meade, who is a clown, was making the most terribly funny remarks – the band was playing Night and Day (you know what the words are) and there he was encouraging John to 'spend his life making love to me', etc. to a very black looking non responsive John who informed me that his faithful girlfriend from home will be out here soon and from then I shan't get a look in! 'Don't be pompous John', commented Owen and really it was all so funny and yet maddening, because it's hard to speak out your mind with a whole host of people round who would wonder what on earth we were thinking of! However, I gather John has gone off to Palestine in a huff – and I am to see him no more! It's rather strange really, as I was beginning to wonder if one day I wouldn't marry him after all –

he'd been so much better lately and strange as it may seem, I am very fond of him! Still, I've no time for stupid people like that!

Needless to say the 'high and mighty John came down from his pedestal on high last Sunday, when he deigned to pay me a visit – Really, what babies men are!' and in mid-July they go to Palestine together, the travel writer's eye taking it all in:

c/o Fleet Mail Office Suez
11.7.44

John and I had very pleasant leave in Palestine, punctuated by a few quarrels, of course! We travelled up to Haifa by train, spent a night there, and then took a bus on to Jerusalem, via Tel Aviv. Jerusalem is among the hills, and stands very high so we had a beautiful journey there, and weren't too hot. We couldn't get into the King David, which is the best hotel there, a modern place, awfully nice, so we went to a small pension in the German Colony, where we lived like fighting cocks, on the fat of the land, which is black market of course. Everything is rationed, and sugar absolutely unobtainable. We'd brought a bag of our own, so we were all right. I very much enjoyed visiting the old city – a terribly smelly place surrounded by the old walls of Jerusalem. We visited the church of the Holy Sepulchre – a terribly commercialised affair, the old wailing wall, where as it was Friday, all manner of Jews were bemoaning their sins, and eventually wandered out of the city by the Via Dolorosa. The following day we went to the Garden of Gethsemane, a glorious spot outside the walls, on the side of a hill. Above stands a most picturesque Russian church, with many minarets rising above the Cypress trees, and in the garden itself is the Church of All Nations, a quiet peaceful spot, with glorious purple stained glass windows. We also visited Bethlehem (where I lost my identity card!) and saw the stable and manger where Christ is said to have been born, a lovely old church is built on top – dating back from the times of the Crusaders and there are some beautiful mosaics. Eventually we returned to Haifa and stayed in a small Jewish village called Nahania [Nahariya], some miles away. The pension was delightful, owned by a German Jew called Weidenbaum. From Nahania, we went to Acre, the Crusaders' town, which is still enclosed in old walls and battlements and seems exactly like it must have been hundreds of years before. We climbed to the top of a minaret in a famous old mosque there, and viewed the city – a jumbled mass of streetless buildings, wherein, in a square kilometre, live 17,000 people. It's unbelievable! I was more impressed by Acre than by any other place in Palestine – it really is worth a visit!

Heaven knows whether I'll come home or not, but maybe I'll turn up some day. Lots of love, Sheila

By this stage Sheila had made up her mind that if she doesn't go to the Eastern Fleet by the next convoy she will never leave Suez, so she decides to apply, via Alexandria, to come home, which would mean arriving back in England in August. Stung by the news of her former junior colleague's appointment with Admiral Ramsay – even if this is after the D-Day landings – she wants to be there so she may 'do likewise in the next show'. She believes she could still get a job abroad if she 'wangled hard' at it.

John in the Garden of Gethsemane.

On return from Jerusalem she is 'annoyed' to find that in her absence she was given an appointment in Colombo which was turned down by FOLEM 'in view of the fact I had applied to go home'. It was as Principal Cypher Officer and would have entailed promotion. Showing remarkable humility she says perhaps it was a 'good thing' as it would have 'worn her out' and made her 'swollen headed'.

Despite having promised her a place on the next convoy she is let down again:

c/o Fleet Mail Office Suez
19.7.44

… I do hope you get the wire I sent off to you yesterday also telling you that I have literally missed the boat this time. I am really very annoyed about it. They promised me I could go in this trip – otherwise I should have made more effort to get to Colombo and now they have let me down – only 2 Wren officers are going this time, and both with their husbands, tho' neither have been out as long as I have – I have pulled every thing possible, but of no avail – my relief is not here yet. However, I may try and get an air passage in which case I may arrive fairly quickly. Otherwise, don't expect me till the end of September. Maddening isn't it? I am firmly resolved to have another shot at Colombo from home after a little leave.

Nevertheless she begins to prepare for the trip home despite feeling extremely unsettled. Her luggage is a major concern: 'I have got an awful lot of stuff I am afraid.':

c/o Fleet Mail Office Suez
24.7.44

My dear Mummy – I haven't been doing very much of note lately – In fact I've rather gone into a recline on hearing they are not sending me home yet – they are devils really – a whole lot of Wrens from S. Africa have recently gone through on the way home who haven't even served their two years! Still, we are on a different station and it seems to make all the difference – However, I have packed up my trunk and my large black box, and have sent them off to the Navel Stores Officer, who will embark there over the next ship going to England. They will then be sent to the N.S.O. [Naval Stores Office] at Newcastle, who will either send them down to Durham direct, or write to me and tell me they are there for collection. It certainly saves me a lot of bother, as I am now only left with one suitcase and a small bag for if I have to fly. If I do this, then I shall give my big case to anyone who is going by sea next time, and they can bring it home as part of their luggage – I've hardly got anything to wear left at all – all my whites, of course – 1 suit of blues with everything to go with it, greatcoat, 3 summer dresses, 1 evening dress, 6 pairs of shoes, underwear, 1 afternoon dress, 2 shirts and 1 pair of shorts and that's about all, except for a bathing dress – at the minute I am knitting wildly at a thick red jersey, as I am sure it's going to be awfully cold! I've got very used to the heat, that, tho' whilst I am sitting now, I am all sticky and little channels of water are running down my legs, I don't mind a bit – I like it! It must be about 90 degrees in this room at the minute – somehow it doesn't <u>seem</u> hot at all – Have you told the family I am coming home? If not, for goodness sake keep it dark – as I don't want to have to do a ton of relations on my return, and exhibited as an interesting specimen from the M.E.!

Love, Sheila

It seems strange that Sheila never writes of any war news, but I suppose it was all so far away and she felt very distanced from any of the action. She doesn't even mention Italy, where both John and Bruce had been fighting, and D-Day comes and goes, then the liberation of Paris in August. She remains completely focused on getting out, but continues to work hard. Her relief has finally come and she is free to leave when the opportunity arises. So she and her friend Aenid Brothers decide to seize the chance, have some fun, and get some last-minute leave in Cyprus. First they go to Ismailia to see Aenid's family who live there:

Sheila and Aenid in Suez, shortly before her departure.

c/o Fleet Mail Office, Port Tewfik

5.8.44

My dear Mummy – … No further news of my coming home yet, except that everyone seems to think I'm definitely going.

On Wednesday Aenid and I went up to Ismailia with 2 Naval people we know from here. Her family lives there, so we stayed with them – A grand change we went up in a truck – a frightfully bumpy one – and stopped at the U.S. Club at Ismailia for a bathe first. I hadn't been there since the Flap – I was just filthy – however, it's salt, so we came to no harm! In the evening we dined at the French Club and returned to Suez the next morning. Ismailia is the best place in Egypt for mangoes – and the Brothers have 3 trees in their garden – lovely things! These two Naval people are quite fun – one, called Tony Cox, is a New Zealander, and if he can get in a row or scrapes, he's always right in the middle of trouble – Tonight we are motoring up the canal and coming back down here in an 'R' boat – a sort of landing craft – There's a full moon – so should be rather fun. Last night I went out to a duty dance in a South African Sergeant's mess – we had a sit down supper first, and danced after – but it's really too hot for dancing especially as it was inside. They had a band of Italian P.O.W.s – there are hundreds of them round here. Personally I loathe the Iti's – oily creatures. We have on occasions been asked on board Italian Naval ships which sometimes come down here, but I wouldn't go on a matter of principle, tho' I should be most curious to go and see what they are like.

Our S.O.O. [Senior Operations Officer] has been drafted away recently, and as he was Signal Officer, I was asked to step in and take the job over – which I said I would do. It doesn't entail much extra work, but I am now in charge of the W/T [wire/telephone], coding office and S.D.O. [Staff Duty Officer] – as well as the telephone exchange. However, having been personally asked by NOIC if I could and would do the job, the first time I sent a signal, he made me look a frightful fool by stopping it, altering it so that it wasn't intelligible, and then telling me that I have no authority to make signals and am not to do so in future. If I wasn't leaving, I should kick up a hell of a fuss – whoever heard of a Signal Officer with no powers to send signals, especially when she's the only person who knows anything about it!

Aenid and I are going to Cairo on Monday to do a wee bit of shopping – All the boy friends seem to be getting on OK. Robin and John are both in Italy – and Bruce has now gone to France but says he hopes to be back on leave by the time I get home. John hopes to be back in UK by October – things will be very complicated! Have you got your evacuee yet? I hope she will be nice. Molly Rendell hopes to be down here next weekend. I do hope she can come, she is such a dear.

With heaps of love

Sheila

This is the last ever mention of John Pritty in any of Sheila's letters; we will never know if they met again in England, whereas Robin and Bruce continue to play an important part in her life. I found some of Robin's letters to Sheila penned from Italy, tucked away in her writing case; tiny, spiky writing, not at all romantic, talking mainly about opera. They were written after her return to England in the last part of 1944.

Finally, at the end of August, Aenid and Sheila go on leave, which turns out not quite as they plan, but it is a great adventure. The photographs show them disporting themselves among the ancient ruins at Baalbek, clad in their whites, complete with hats! Remember it is compulsory to wear uniform at all times in public, except when 'at dances or sporting events'. A recent rule has just tightened up the wearing of civilian clothing, which causes great ire among the girls:

c/o Fleet Mail Office Suez
30.8.44

My dear Mummy – I have just completed the most hectic week – a grand one, too. I hastily turned over to my successor, a rather wet individual and Aenid and I bailed off to Cairo last Wednesday to try and fix an air passage to Cyprus. Yes, Sub. Lt. Collis said he could fix us up, would we come back in the morning? Next day we went down to the RAF people near Shepheards to be weighed, yes we had a passage! Where too! Oh to Habanya. Where's that? Oh, somewhere in Palestine I think said Lt Corporal. Then up came a Fl. Lieut whom we also asked – it's in the Persian Gulf, he replied – they do send you to some funny places, don't they? More and more we insisted we asked what would we do when we got there? Oh, get in a boat and sail down the Euphrates, he replied. We really did jib at this, and said we only wanted to go to Cyprus – he nearly had a fit and said that he'd no idea, but anyway, he could do nothing for us, so we stormed back to Collis who took a very maleish [meaning 'so what?' in Arabic] attitude and said well, we'd have to go by train. We did! Our companions to Haifa were an Indian sister, and an Italian, presumably married to an English soldier, and her 2 children – one of which had a cold and the other spots. We have since caught the cold, but not spots to date! When we arrived at Haifa we found the last way to get to Beirut was by military diesel, which took 4 hours, but as it was such a lovely

'A Romanesque Group':
Aenid Brothers and friends at
Baalbek, August 1944. Note
the full uniform and hat!

Sheila with a gargoyle, Baalbek.

journey on the edge of the sea we didn't mind – on arrival at Beirut we fixed accommodation facing the sea and collapsed into bed – The next day we went up to Tripoli with the Naval M.O. [Medical Officer] – another lovely drive by the sea – we took with us an Army M.O. who was scared stiff of the driver, or at least the way he drove! He sat up in his seat muttering away and could even hear him heaving his breath when we shot past anything as we invariably did! However, we arrived OK and soon we were pottering round the souq and exploring a castle on a hill. It seemed to me to be a smaller edition of Beirut, unfortunately we didn't have time to go down to the harbour which is most picturesque they say, full of caciques. We returned the same way, but over the Chekka Pass, a new road cut in the mountains by 9th Army Engineers in 100 days – a great feat. The other road invariably gets blocked in winter by land slides. The Army M.O. nearly had a fit, but the Naval M.O. insisted we should go across! Anyway, we got back in time for a grand bathe. Next day we planned a spot of hitchhiking and eventually arrived at the crossroads for Baalbek and Damascus after 4 lifts including one with the Greeks, and another with the Poles, who could speak no English at all. However, one of the priests spoke a little French and we got on marvellously, chatting away in the most frightful grammar! They were thrilled to the marrow when they heard I knew Romanowski, a S/M [Submarine] Captain, and there was much frivolity – all in Polish, Russian and broken French. I was most sorry to leave them. Aenid had a bright idea we ought to go up to the nearby NAAFI, so we did and soon a truck drove up with about 4 army officers and 3 O/Rs [Other Ranks], on a recce of sorts. They were off to Baalbek and soon we were off with them. Those people had set their hearts on a good lunch, so we drove up to a hotel in Baalbek with the grand name Villa Kaoum – Hotel de la Source, where we had lunch under the trees. Baalbek is a fascinating place, streams of clear water running everywhere, even under the houses, of course, we visited the ruined Roman Temple a magnificent affair, and we pottered round for over 3 hours – when we'd seen all there was to see, we drove back to the NAAFI, for tea, and as Aenid and I were keen to get on to Damascus that night, the senior member of the party fixed us up in an ambulance that was just going on, so we pompously sat in the front and simply tore through the mountain passes until we approached the city when it was dark. You drive in through a narrow pass with a river running beside the road and there were lights everywhere. We were most impressed and although very tired, had to have a prowl before going to <u>bed</u>! The following morning we set off for the Souq – probably the most famous in the world, 3 small boys besieged us to guide us round – each accusing each other of being liars, bad boys, not Boy Scouts, tho' what this had to do with it we couldn't guess! However, we saw all there was to see including the silk factory and the place where St. Paul escaped from the well in a basket. We left Damascus at 4 and arrived in Beirut at 7 – after a lovely drive over the hills and very cold it was in places! Alas, almost as soon as we had arrived, I received a message recalling me to Tewfik, so we hared down to Haifa the next day and I caught the 3.20 train to Ismailia where I now am – sitting in the French Club awaiting my car to be sent from Suez. I must really run over to Navy House now and see if it has come – so no more.

Tons of love – Sheila.

This was the signal that Sheila had been waiting for – that she was to prepare for departure.

However, this letter was written just before an almighty row blew up, which was never revealed to her mother. Tucked in her writing case, I found a memorandum written on 1 September to the Chief Officer, WRNS, Levant and Eastern Mediterranean, defending herself from a charge of 'deliberately disobeying the Maintenance Commander's instructions'.

After arriving in Suez at 0550, where she wrote the above letter, she was ordered by the Maintenance Commander to catch the 16.15 train to Alexandria in preparation for sailing. However, she argued that she had 'no luggage' and he gave her permission to travel early the following morning, whereupon she took her uniforms to be 'dhobied'. Permission was rescinded, however, and she was then re-ordered to catch the afternoon train with a couple of hours' notice

– which of course she could now no longer do as she had not 'even begun to pack' and her uniforms were being laundered. She then called the Chief Officer in Alex and cleared that it was 'in order' to travel the next morning.

However, this message did not get through to Suez, and the Maintenance Commander's Chief Petty Officer arrived to fetch her; when told she was not going until the next morning, she was hauled before the Naval Officer in Charge, Suez, who 'severely reprimanded' her and told her she 'was not to be trusted' and that he was 'very disappointed'. To add insult to injury, she was 'confined to quarters'.

Naturally she was devastated as she felt she was leaving Suez 'under a cloud which is not justified and, in view of the fact that I am leaving this Command for the United Kingdom, an adverse report would be most prejudicial to my future career in the Service'. We will never know whether she was exonerated or whether this was indeed to form a blemish on her perfect service record. That she kept this letter – in pristine condition – hidden away, demonstrates how serious a matter it was.

Sheila's joining instructions, carefully pasted into her scrapbook, show that she was travelling first class on the *Highland Princess*, departing from Alexandria. What a difference it must have made to be able to sail back via the Mediterranean rather than round the Cape! She was 'Officer-in-Charge' of all the Wrens on board.

On arrival in England on 2 September she received her 'discharge certificate' and one assumes she then received her leave entitlement and went home to Durham. There are no letters until they resume in May 1945, right at the end of the war, when she was sent to Germany. The only ones that survive are those from Robin.

She was instructed to report for duty in Harwich on 4 November, where she worked as a Cypher Officer. Unsurprisingly there are no scrapbook entries or letters dating from Harwich in 1944. It must have been quite a come-down after the excitements of Egypt.

She had been away from home for four years, and abroad for the best part of three. During that time she had been closely involved in probably the most important military campaign of the war, the invasion of Sicily, whose success triggered the further invasion of Italy and was the turning point for the Allies. At last they could begin to see that the strategy of encircling the Axis forces in Europe with a pincer movement could work – starting in France (the Normandy landings), down to North Africa and extending back up via Italy to Russia.

She had left England a newly commissioned Third Officer, still rather green and naïve; she returned a decorated Second Officer, with a wealth of experience, who had rubbed shoulders with some of the greatest of the naval commanders and admirals as well as countless dashing and sophisticated army officers. In other words, she returned home a sophisticated and worldly woman and a senior officer. Quite something for a girl from Norfolk.

But for Sheila, it was a homecoming with mixed emotions: the circumstances of her departure must have caused her great anguish; her love-life was in disarray and, while she would have been delighted to see her father and other friends and family, one suspects that she dreaded the inevitable criticism from her mother – in particular over letting John, Bruce and Robin slip through her fingers – that would no doubt be meted out, now that distance was no barrier. Once again she would have been champing at the bit to regain some excitement in her life through a final posting.

1945

'Oh it's all such a stupid muddle'

The war ended on 7 May 1945, a few days after Hitler and Eva Braun committed suicide. The Allies had the enemy surrounded on all fronts and Auschwitz and the other concentration camps throughout Europe were already being liberated as early as January of that year. The Yalta Conference, the second meeting between Roosevelt, Churchill and Stalin, was held in February to discuss the future of a post-war Europe. It was agreed, at Russia's insistence, that Germany was to be divided between the Big Three and France to prevent it from re-emerging as a unified power. Victory, in other words, was a foregone conclusion.

This division of Germany was to lead to great rivalry between Russia and the US, in particular, over the 'brain drain' of German scientists at the end of the war and, a few years later, to the Cold War. As soon as the war ended, the US controversially bagged eighty-eight rocket scientists including Wernher von Braun, inventor of the V2 or 'doodlebug', who later made a great contribution to the Space Race on the US's behalf.

Germany was in a terrible state after the war, with as many as 5.2 million displaced persons and 20 million homeless, due to the ferocity of the Allied bombing raids, which had left Germany a smouldering ruin. In addition, there were over 12 million Germans living in non-German territories and 6 million of these were expelled in the most barbaric conditions, by the Russians and the Poles in particular; as many as 1 million died – frozen and starved in slow-moving trains taking them 'home' – and millions of others were used as forced labour in Russia as retribution for the terrible damage inflicted by the Nazis during the war.

The Allies had destroyed transport, infrastructure and industry, along with some of Germany's most glorious buildings, such as Cologne Cathedral and the city of Dresden – some say with a vindictiveness that was disproportionate. Agriculture had come to a standstill and much of Germany was starving as the Nazis had relied on imported labour and prisoners for producing food. After the war, the US was importing food for over 7 million POWs, but this went not to Germans in Germany, but to those that were displaced by them during the war. Imports of food were therefore banned and, after the war, adult death rates increased by a factor of four, and those for children by a factor of ten. The International Red Cross was banned, and even German agencies such as Caritas could not distribute imported food. In the cold winter of 1946–7, calorie intake was down to 1000–1500 per person per day.

The interim governing body was called the Allied Control Council, and it is referred to in Sheila's letters home, as she is toying with working for them in Germany (she calls them Mil.Gov or Control Commission). Their objective was the de-Nazification of Germany, mainly its ideology and symbols such as the swastika. Reading her letters, it is hard to get a handle on what the post-war occupiers did: but piecing together the evidence it seems the navy was involved in mine-clearing and sweeping; all services were involved with the surrender of the German armed, naval and air forces. My father, for instance, in 1945, played a senior role in the operation to transfer the German navy, anchored at Wilhelmshaven and comprising some 500–600 ships, to the Russians. After commandeering the ships by waking the German commanders at 2 a.m. to prevent them scuttling their boats, the fleet was sailed to Riga in Latvia where it was handed over to his sailing companion, the Russian Admiral. Interestingly, many of the German sailors opted to remain in Russia, preferring the ideals of the communist state.

Sheila, as a Cypher Officer, must have been in charge of directing the messages in relation to the naval operations, but it seems it was not that busy: she often refers to having little work to do and finds time for knitting while on watch. The contrast with the high life lived by the occupying forces and the destitution of the local Germans is something that troubles Sheila greatly.

Sheila's main objective in 1945 seems to be deciding which of her suitors to marry and, as in Egypt, this dominates most of her letters in the latter half of the year. She realises that her time in the WRNS is coming to an end with the war, and that her admirers will be dispersed. Apart from not wishing to return home unwed, I get a sense she wanted to beat her sister to it!

The first letter from Germany is not written until 19 May. I have tried to piece together what her movements were in the meantime. We know she went to work in Harwich on HMS *Badger* in November 1944, and can only assume she stayed there until posted to Kiel sometime in May. Her scrapbook contains several Christmas cards for 1944, including one from Jaap, who is 'with your people again … which is all for the better'. It is from HMS *Maidstone* and VII Submarine flotilla; another from Aenid who is still in Egypt, two from Robin in Italy and one from Bruce, who encloses a train ticket for Berlin 'for use on your next leave – will book your room in a hotel later!!!' There is nothing from John Pritty.

On 8 January Sheila attends the memorial service at Westminster Abbey for her old boss, Admiral Ramsay; her scrapbook contains not only the order of service but also cuttings of all the tributes from the newspapers of the day. In February she is made Head of Department at Harwich Cypher office, and is booked on a course to take place on 7 May. Given the date (the date Germany surrendered!) I imagine it was delayed as she attends a course in Petersfield in July.

I can only guess that she was sent to Germany some time before VE Day [Victory in Europe Day] on 8 May and that only one or two letters are therefore missing. As she was Mess Secretary it implies she was there for at least a month, plus she had time to buy and send a cheese, which arrived before 19 May:

Kiel

19.5.45

My dear Ma –

I can't remember when I wrote last – it was ages ago I believe …! I'm glad the cheese arrived O.K. – Yes I knew it was in 6ths – I bought it myself!

I do like being here; the old boy I work for is a dear and also the other Wren in the office, Betty Mackenzie. I have just turned over as Mess Secretary to her and I was only 3/1- out in the accounts – not bad!

We had our housewarming party here on Wednesday – it was a great success – we danced till 2 – I met such a nice person in the 8th Hussars – the Adjutant, one Richard Dill on Saturday – last night with the 4th R.H.A. [Royal Horse Artillery] who are stationed here, gave a special dance for us in their Barracks – we had a sit down dinner which lasted till 11 o'clock!! And then we danced till 4 am – It was such fun, all on Champagne too, but my goodness, I had a terrible hangover today. The worst I have ever had! Only gin with the Captain at midday saved me, and in the afternoon I rode with 2 of the RHA (who are experts) over the most <u>heavenly</u> country – lovely fields and lanes, and this evening I had an hour's tennis! Consequently I am worn out now and have been dozing in front of an open log fire.

Oh, the parcels have never arrived yet – I do wish they would come – I really do need some clothes very badly, my red evening dress has got <u>pitch black</u> round the hem where it dragged on the ground last night!

I went to see the Kiel Gov. people and lodged some new papers, my others having been lost. Is this Col. Stewart contacting me, or am I to phone him up? Let me know.

No news of R. for 2 or 3 weeks – I hope all goes well – must stop as I am honestly nearly dead. Dawn was breaking and birds (nightingales I think!) were singing, when I got to bed. We have hosts of owls – Heaps of love, Sheila

Kiel
25.5.45

My dear Ma –

Many thanks for the parcel which arrived intact 2 days ago – don't
forget to let me know what I owe you for the blouse – I always seem
to lose your letters when I write to you – I can't find your last at all
– I hope you are sticking to your diet and thus getting better. At the
minute I am filling in time before going out to dine at the Yacht Club
– I have spent most of the day in the pouring rain at a local gymkhana
– It was such a shame because it would have been such fun. I went
with a crowd of people from the ship – but the thing was run by the
Air Force – Naturally enough, most of the events were won by the
Army. I met my gorgeous young Hussar there – he's too beautiful for
words – tall, dark, blue eyed and very good looking. Awful faux pas –
he was wearing a wonderful Hussar greatcoat piped with yellow and I
thought he was a Pole!! Later he came and greeted me, I didn't recog-
nise him at all! There is a super gymkhana at Hamburg on Saturday
which I hope to go to with him.

   This dinner in the Yacht Club is in aid of meeting the Chief
Country Commission Signal Officer who's coming up here for the
weekend, damn he's here –

———•———

26/5
Well, it's now tomorrow, as you can see. I went to this dinner party last
night but am now of very mixed opinion about joining Mil. Gov. To
begin with, the party consisted of the whole P and T [posts and tel-
egraph] Dept. of the Mil. Gov. here and the Chief man and his PA
– The latter turned out to be a civilian, and his P.A. a braw Scots lassie
from Dundee – The P and T dept. of Kiel proved to be mostly civilians
of the Post Office clerk variety, mostly without a 'haitch' in their 'eads –
I don't think there would be any difficulty at all in 'getting in' – but the
thing is, I honestly don't think I could stand working with and for such

people – they're all very nice and all that – but not to work with and live with – They were all Sergeant and Chief Petty Officer type – the fact that one had been an officer in the Wrens meant nothing to them; it's all so hard to explain, but you'd know exactly what I mean if you had met them – This P.A. girl had been an OR [Other Ranks], I believe in Mil. Gov or A.T.S. [Auxiliary Territorial Service] and was very bouncy – No idea of how to behave or anything. Yet she has this frightfully good position – This, of course, is so typical of the new government, all these people are probably excellent at their respective jobs, but have absolutely no background and no savoir faire at all – and this is the typical class of Englishman you find out here in Mil. Gov – a very bad example to judge England by, I feel – The thing is, that they all seem very keen for me to join as soon as possible and I don't know <u>what</u> to do at all – I'd have to sign on for a year – I believe I could go wherever I want to; this old boy is the complete head of signals for Control Commission in Germany, and if he likes you, they say he will fix you up immediately. I must say he seemed very keen to take me – I should have to join as a Cypher Officer – a thing I told him I had no intentions of doing – but he said I'd only nominally be a Cypherer – but would do other jobs – he also asked me where I'd like to go – I murmured Berlin – but think I'd plump for Austria if asked again. I do wish I knew what to do – If only I knew what prospects, if any, there are of getting the type of job I have in mind. It might help me to make up my mind. As you know, I wrote to Daddy to enquire and I have filled in and returned the form he sent me – I don't know whether I am flying too high in my desires – I have a horrid feeling the Navy will decide to get rid of me quite soon as we get signals daily saying we must cut down staff. Rosemary had some wonderful idea that I should go out to Egypt again as they are very short of people there, but I'm not sure if it wouldn't be better to come back to UK and try my hand there for a bit. Frankly, I'm completely puzzled –! And even all my young men have vanished one by one!! How are the mighty fallen!!!!

I had a very nice ride this evening, we played tennis in the afternoon, but it was far too windy – however, it cleared up later, and 2 of us went out …

I really must stop. I shall be interested to hear what you and Papa think about this CCG [Control Commission]

She was indeed offered a job with the Control Commission as she calls it – at £390 p.a., but they wanted her to start straight away, so she turned it down. 'They are a queer crowd and have an awfully bad reputation.' Obviously her middle-class upbringing has rubbed off on her; her mother would indeed 'know exactly what I mean'.

In the same letter, of 23 June, she goes on to say that she and her friend Betty Mackenzie – who was to remain a friend for the rest of her life – went out 'sailing all the afternoon with Tom Unwin – he has had some frightful rash, and hasn't been able to shave for about a week – looks quite fierce!' This is the first mention of her future husband and my father. He doesn't sound very attractive! They must have met at the yacht club as my father was a keen sailor. She doesn't see much of him until about a year later, when she returns to Kiel. In the same breath she talks of a letter from Robin, in Italy, who is riding-mad.

July sees Sheila back in Petersfield for her Signaling course, and it appears she spends the weekend at Deddington in Oxfordshire, with Lady Hobart whom I assume is Robin's mother, as she has news that Robin will be home the next month and is leaving the Signals to join the Royal Armoured Corps (RAC), although it means dropping a rank to lieutenant. She will be seeing her parents before going back to Germany: her father has a new job: 'It must be very interesting. What fun if he is able to save a little petrol for when I come – I do hope it won't <u>all</u> have gone on Rosemary!!!' The rivalry is never far away, even if the sisters spent some time together in London seeing an Ivor Novello show. She 'dined on curry' at Veeraswami's [sic] after seeing another show with her fellow course attendees.

On her return to Germany she is posted to Hamburg. Now closer to home than Egypt, the lack of suitable clothes seems to be a major preoccupation, but at least mother is on hand to oblige:

Sheila, in her late 70s, travelled to Baluchistan as part of an archeological team; she was the ethnographer.

Rosemary with Granny Proctor in Downham Market c. 1930.

Grace with Sheila and Rosemary as babies.

Captain Percival Findlay Mills, MC, Royal Engineers, Sheila's beloved father.

Sheila on the left, with sister Rosemary, as teenagers.

Sheila and Rosemary while at St James's in London, 1940.

Official portrait of Sheila in her uniform.

Warrant card for 3rd Officer Mills.

Name MILLS
Sheila Margaret F.
Description 3rd. Officer.

Unit W.R.N.S.

Height 5' 8½"

Colour of Eyes Blue.

Colour of Hair Lt. Brown.

Signature of Holder Sh.M.Mills.

Miss Boyd, Director of the WRNS Dundee, carrying out an inspection.

Formal OTC photo at Greenwich, Sheila is the fifth on the right, second row up, her height obscuring another girl's face.

Alexandria, the
Cecil Hotel;
looking down
the Blvd Saad
Zaghloul.

Sheila, taken on the morning of 29 June
1942, as plans for 'The Flap' were being
executed.

Sheila and Mary Dugdale, 'the night we left Alex in a hurry'.

'Old' Kay Way, also waiting for evacuation orders. Kay was with Sheila in Methil and for much of her time in Egypt.

Sheila in Ismailia.

Paddy.

Kay Way and Ann Halliday on the balcony of their shared room at 11, Rue Rassafah in Alexandria.

The Mohammed Ali mosque and citadel.

Catacombs and Pompey's Pillar.

Idwal and Sheila on top of the Great Pyramid.

Above: Sheila on a camel at Giza.   Below: Polyphoto of Sheila showing off her whites.

'To Sheila: with love from 13 Corps; for one who helped make it possible. Bruce (on behalf of all!)' – on top of Etna. Bruce is at the top left.

John Pritty's regiment, the 51st Highland Division, after the fall of Tripoli in 1943.

Beirut, looking towards the mountains.

Gezira race card.

John Pritty on his OCTU course; he is third left, bottom row, I think.

In the mess, 'the bar at lunch time', at Suez (l–r) Sheila, Mary Benton, Kay Chase and Monica Powell.

Sheila with two colleagues on the 'fearsome Tewfik camel'.

Sheila on one of the main streets in Damascus.

Beirut bathing belle.

Sheila (back row, left) and the WRNS at Plön.

Formal photo of Sheila in uniform,
showing her two stripes, taken in Germany.

Tom Unwin in his naval uniform.

Naval Party 1730 c/o BFMO Shading
7.9.45

My dear Ma –

Well, here we are at last in Hamburg! It was awful getting up at 0400 this morning but after we'd been weighed at the RAF place in St James Street it was soon light and we got to Croydon at about 6:30. The plane was a Dakota – all very comfortable with bucket seats and the trip only took 3 hours – we flew over the North Sea, to Holland across the Zuyder Zee [sic] and then North East to Hamburg. The airport is a very modern building – we checked in and went up to have a cup of tea, where an orchestra was already hard at work, even at 11:15am! Of course, there was no one to meet us, so we took a truck into the city to try and get some information. I certainly found it a very attractive place – of course there has been a lot of bomb damage which seems worse than London and I hear the dock area is just flat – but there are lots and lots of trees – and a lot of water – I haven't discovered whether it is all the Elbe or not – but it is certainly very pretty. It's extraordinary to see the people – none of them particularly well dressed and most of them look awfully pale and rather yellowish – lots of the men are still in uniform or parts of uniform – nobody takes any particular notice of you – tho' we did see some Naval officers in the Barracks this afternoon who just stared and stared. We eventually landed up at an RAF movements place – so I rang up Naval movements and an N.O. came round to pick us up – funnily enough someone I had known in Alex – we had tea in one of the NAAFI clubs and then he drove us out to our quarters. We live in the new Hindenburg Naval Barracks – which have only been built 10 years or so. They are large blocks of buildings all named after admirals (Ramsay is next to ours, which I believe is Grenville) there must be hundreds of sailors here – our office is just a stone's throw away, but we haven't ventured near yet. Our anteroom is awfully nice – beautiful carpets and chairs, and, at the minute, masses of flowers (we have a German flower decorator who does them for us!) food is army rations but seems quite OK – we get Danish butter and eggs.

Our stable companions seem a cheery crowd – they have only been here 3 weeks themselves from Brussels. Life is hectic and I'm afraid we can't help laughing at them as it seems to have gone to their heads a little. Even the plainest and fattest seem to have several boy friends to choose from! We have the Sadlers Wells opera here for 3 weeks, so we hope to go but you aren't allowed out at all without male escort. There appears to be hockey and tennis, all equipment provided – also in Hamburg is a wonderful leave hotel which is apparently the last word and where everyone comes for a 48 hours – we also have a country club as well. All seems to be laid on – I have just had a bath which was heated by a wood stove, like the one that burnt an F on Kay Way's behind, needless to say I was most careful! Should hate to be branded for life!

I hate my battle dress and should be so grateful if you could send me the better of my 2 uniforms at home and also my old navy shorts, I tried to get some in London, but couldn't – is the new zipp I bought anywhere around? For I must put it in – Did you get the towels and H.W.B [hot water bottle]? I had an HWB given me from comforts – I am enclosing £2 now with which I hope you will buy a library ticket and anything else you want – as a birthday present – I have provisionally arranged to draw £10 each month and have the rest paid into my bank – less the £1 allotment to your Bank. I don't know how it will work and I don't suppose I shall need £10 a month – but I shall leave it like that and see what happens.

Is there any chance of you getting some starch – none here at all, and all my collars are stiff?

Must stop now – with heaps of love

Sheila

In addition to the request above, on 27 September Sheila asks for:

… bedroom slippers – sheepskin would be nice – but I'm really not fussy – tho' I do draw the line at those ones with pom poms on the front – no, if you can't get sheepskin – then I think I'd rather have those felt ones men wear [she draws a picture] you know – we saw some in a shop in Durham for only 8 or 9 shillings – in a camel shade and I could put the warm soles inside them – Also – here is a plea for more clothing – could you please send me my navy pleated skirt, heavy brown walking shoes – navy suede shoes, like yours, with tongue. Some stockings (those 2 lacy lisle) and a couple of pairs of silk (not my best).

There is a leave centre at Bad Harzburg where they go for 72 hours rest and relaxation every three months or so, and where they are allowed to wear 'civvies'.

Meanwhile Hamburg life, like everywhere, is full of tennis, riding – 'only 2/6 per hour – very cheap!' – and socialising with the navy, the RAF and the army. There are gymkhanas and sailing regattas, hockey matches and skating in winter. But here, in Hamburg, there is also the ballet and good music and Sheila is delighted to go to *The Marriage of Figaro* and many other concerts, including *The Messiah* and a lieder performance with Elisabeth Schumann, who sang Strauss's *Three Songs*. We played one of them at Sheila's funeral.

I am amused by the reference to Anne Bridge in the next letter – my mother was to collect all her books during the 1940s and 1950s and I still have them today. The saga of the wool for Bruce's jumper is to be long-running: she mentions it no fewer than eight times in two months! In fact it only arrives in early December, leaving her scant time to finish the jumper and get it to Egypt for Christmas.

At last we have an update on Sheila's love life, and which boyfriend is in the ascendency, even if she is still enjoying the neverending round of parties and dances in the company of new friends:

Hamburg
23.9.45

My dear Ma –

As I expected a letter from you today which I was pleased to have – if Rosemary goes out to Egypt I have told her to try and get me

some more of my wool, but I should imagine it's a very vain hope
– If you do see any more that matches I must say I should like it –
in the meantime I am knitting a pullover for Bruce which is taking
great strides as I do it on watch – I need 4 more ounces of each of
the others to finish them.

…Yes, the parcel arrived OK and I wrote off a postcard telling you,
which I hope you have now had. The suit has been duly pressed and
has already been worn at a party on Friday in a Gunners' Mess – The
Anne Bridge book has also arrived, which I am devouring now – and
also the invitation to Aenid's wedding which of course I can't go to,
isn't it disappointing?

Bruce has not yet decided what he is going to do, but will have to
make up his mind soon – In the meantime things are progressing <u>most</u>
favourably, so for heaven's sake keep your fingers crossed!

… I have met some people today who have been to the Belsen trials
which are held at Lüneburg, near here – Horrible and beastly as they
must be – I must say I should very much like to go to see what these
people really are like. I believe there is a slight chance I might be able
to –

I have moved upstairs to a new room with Kay Pollock, an Irish girl
whom I like very much – she is awfully pretty, gay and amusing, so
we get on very well. She makes me laugh so – she is longing to meet
a heart throb and wherever we go we seem to meet the dullest of the
dull! Did I tell you Betty Sinclair, a girl who was on my course, is a
great friend of John Pritty's sister, Maureen, the deaf one. I said nowt,
but quietly asked if she knew where her brother was, and she said she
thought he was going to Australia but had never heard whether he
had or not. He's probably demobilised now anyway, Hope so! Heaps
of love,
Sheila

27.9.45

My dear Mama –

Thank you so much for your letter which arrived all unexpected-like – what a lot of news, more than I can supply from here – I think.

... I think I forgot to tell you that the First Lord was over here the other day, and we all had to turn out for an inspection – He gave us the usual pep talk – doing a wonderful job etc. etc. but I don't think many people were very impressed – everyone out here is very chokker as there is so little work to do and they all feel they ought to be demobilised quicker – we also had the C in C over here and he came to our mess for drinks. I'm afraid I didn't make a very good impression as when he asked me where I came from I said Durham in an absentminded sort of way he nearly passed out, as of course he meant what ship – However, we righted that and then the conversation varied to hats versus berets – and I was informed that my hair was on my collar and all too true it was, too! We have the Director coming to visit us tomorrow – but as I am off to the hairdresser this morning, don't think I should offend!

We played tennis yesterday on a simply lovely court where I believe the German Championships used to be held – It had an excellent surface and was surrounded by poplar trees. On Saturday I am going to the Sailing Club's regatta dance and a cocktail party on Monday. I've not met anyone at all I really like – hence, when one hears stories of so and so having a marvellous time, out with a different man each night – it just don't mean nothing! Actually most people here are out the whole time – I must say I do like those people in the mess very much – everyone gets on so well and there's an enormous amount of fooling around –

Thank heavens the electricity is on again and I can do my ironing – twice it has gone off on me and I've been held up 2 days – No hot water this morning either – stokes must have gone on strike.

So, no more now – away to the iron!

Heaps of love
Sheila

Sheila did get to the Belsen Trials as she had intended and they made a strong impression on her. I can feel her discomfort growing in these letters at the standard of living enjoyed by the services, not only far beyond that of the vanquished Germans, but also way above those at home who were to struggle with rationing for some years to come. It perhaps goes a little way to explaining why she and my father hit it off when they finally met properly: a shared disillusionment with the price of peace:

Hamburg
7.10.45

My dear Ma –

I don't think I have written for quite a time – due to the fact, I'm afraid, that I never seem to have a moment to spare, and a disinclination for letter writing on a night watch … Your letters lately seem to be full of the dead and dying and you will get me all depressed!

I have had a very busy week, to a cocktail party on Monday, on Wednesday out to dinner with Daphne Satchell, another 2/O, to a Sappers' mess, whom I have met – for a quiet evening, consisting of a huge dinner, and sitting round a log fire in the twilight listening to music, Chopin mostly. It was heaven, see we have no time at all.

On Friday I went down to Lüneburg to attend the Belsen Trials, we have been given a pass for 4 till the end of the trials, and it was most interesting. Lüneburg is about an hour and a quarter run from here – through the outskirts of Hamburg, where I have never seen such bombed streets in my life – they have to be seen to be believed – rows and rows of rubble lined roads – not a thing left standing, with grotesque twisted girders here and there – and perhaps a fragment of a house every few hundreds of yards. Absolutely frightful. However, we got to Lüneburg in the pouring rain (most fitting) and were led into the court room, which was not at all full – it was arranged in a square – the Judges, 2 Army brass hats, and a bewigged gentleman, sat opposite the accused, 50 of the most bestial and terrible looking people I have ever seen – who had large numbers hanging round their necks. They looked more like animals than people, and as we walked in, most of them stared with curious bravado, to which we stared hard back. Irma Grese[8] was No. 9, and true to descriptions, she is a glamorous bit of work with very long ash blonde locks hanging down her back – We heard 2 statements made by her on capture read by the prosecution – and all the accused were intently following from the papers they all had – they chattered to each other and some of them even smiled in conversation – it seemed extraordinary. A similar statement by Dr Klein, the Belsen doctor, was also read out and statements by 2 officers of the accused, but I don't know who they were.

Anyway, what they said was enough to send the whole pack to the gallows – We thought we were going to hear one by Kramer, but it was held over till the following day. He looked a thug pure and simple, very much like a monkey, with close set eyes, and dark cropped hair. I shall never forget how they all stared at us, it was just horrid. I am hoping to go again next week after some of the others have been – and I think everyone round here should be made to go once, so they can realise what has been going on. We have all been having fierce arguments about the Germans, really, one doesn't know what to think, they all say 'oh I was not a Nazi - but was powerless to do anything' but it seems to me a pity that someone didn't rise up – I'm afraid I just don't believe they didn't know what was going on in the concentration camps, which they say they didn't. However on the other hand, I can't bear to see them all so hungry, as they are doing – with so much food which we leave over, being just thrown away. Our German cook here was caught taking away scraps of food from the barracks, and has been sent to prison for 6 months or more – that seems to me wrong – We are not allowed to feed our German stewards, and last night we were being driven to a most sumptuous party by a German driver who said he and his wife got 4 bits of bread each a day which they gave to the children – much as one realised how wrong the Germans

8 Irma Grese was one of the most notorious concentration camp guards, who started off at Ravensbrück women's camp. For a harrowing account of life in the camps I recommend Sarah Helm's recent book, *If This Is A Woman*.

have been and what they are responsible for, it does no good starving them when there is the food for them to have – especially the children as they are the ones that are going to be the Germans of tomorrow. It's all a very complex question which we are forever arguing.

This party I went to last night was amazing – such food I've never seen the likes of – with ices and cream – anything to drink you wanted, including a wonderful egg and mild flip with brandy all mixed up in it. There were a lot of German civilians there – who I don't know. I'm all against mixing with them at social occasions!

To go from the sublime to the ridiculous – I have got you 5 packets of jelly which I will either send or bring – Must stop now,

With heaps of love,

Sheila

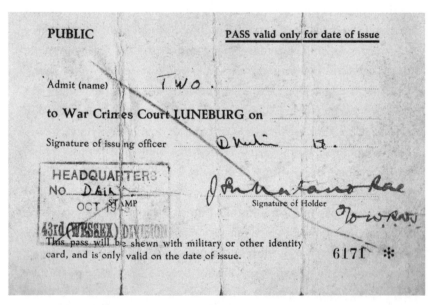

Sheila's ticket to the War Crimes Trials at Lüneburg.

The party-going continues. So impressed was she by this party in early November that she stuck the menu in her scrapbook, but she remains torn about the morality of such excess:

> I've had another busy week – on Monday night I went to a dance given by the local Navy in the hotel where they live, a luxury place where nearly everyone has a suite plus private bathroom – When it came to the buffet supper I couldn't believe my eyes, a room with tables on their sides laden with every possible kind of delicacy I've ever known, caviar, lobster, smoked salmon, chicken, pork, venison, ham, in fact nothing was left out – everything was most beautifully served, mostly in aspic; hams had anchors painted on a coating of white jelly, lobsters arranged on a plate whole with small cases of dressed lobster all round – an in another room close by there was nothing but oysters! Small wonder that I, in my excitement, tossed a whole dish of lobster down the front of my best suit!! (luckily we scraped and rubbed it off straight away and it's none the worse!) Added to this, there was everything you can think of to drink – from champagne to liqueurs – I also saw to my horror, eggs, not by the dozen, but by the score, being shelled and whipped into cocktail. I also drank the cocktails, the whole thing was incredible – fantastic – and to my mind should never have been allowed to happen – I cannot think that it's right to have such sumptuous feasts while the rest of Europe starves, but what can one do about it?

The next letter is written from the hairdressers; it appears Rosemary is being posted to Egypt with the WAAF, much to Sheila's envy, as that is where Bruce is currently stationed. It seems that Sheila's mother's parcel of civilian clothing for Bad Harzburg did not arrive on time!

Cold Buffet

Fresh Oysters

Lobster en Bellevue

Lobster Mayonnaise

Canapees assorted
(Salmon,Eel,Sausages,Ham,Sardines)

Canapees with Caviar

Medaillons of Soles "Marguerite"

Smoked Salmon

Smoked Eel

Russian Eggs

Stuffed Eggs

Poached Eggs

Venison Pasty with Cumberland Sauce

Chicken "Neva"

Roasted Chicken and Russian Salad
and Mixed Pickles

Legs of Pork and poached Apples

Ham

Hare "Carmen"

Legs of Mutton roasted - Mint Sauce

Pork Tongue and Russian Salad

Frankfurt Sausages

Sliced Venison "Rossini"

- - - - -

Monday,

Cold Buffet

Salad assorted

Beetroot
Potatoes
Russian Salad
Cabbage Salad
Herrings Salad
Meat Salad
Tomato Salad

French Cream Tarts
Petitfours
Freandies
Fruit Salad with Maraschino Sauce
Peaches Melba

Cheese Pastries
Roquefort Cheese
Camenbert Cheese

Brown Bread - Rolls - Butter - Biscuits

----

after dancing: Clear Turtle Soup

Coffee

5.11.1945

HOTEL VIER JAHRESZEITEN · HAMBURG

Menu from the 'incredible' party at the Vier Jahreszeiten.

Hamburg
17.10.45

My dear Ma –

I don't think I have written since I had my first ride last week – It
nearly killed me – I can't remember ever having been so stiff before
– I couldn't even stand up straight! However, I have now been 4
times altogether, and think I've found my horse legs all right now –
Incidentally, the horses are really very good and the country round
here good for riding ...

I've just returned from my 72 hours leave in Bad Harzburg, which
I simply love – I went with Kay Pollock and Caroline Hawksworth
who are awfully nice. Kay and I share a room and Caroline (who
is old enough to be our mother) is the wife of an Admiral and
knows the Navy through and through, she is also an expert German
linguist, so was a great help to us – we drove down in a most comfortable Buick with rugs, wireless and even central heating – with a
German driver and a marine with gun to guard us! The country was
rather flat most of the way – but well cultivated and wooded – we
went first through Lüneburg and the next big town was Brunswick
which we skirted, it seemed to have been badly knocked about
– Eventually we arrived at Harzburg which is a sweet little town
nesting on the side of the Harz Mountains – which are not very
high really, but completely covered with trees – pines, beeches, syca-
mores, birch, chestnuts, and the whole aspect was as if they were on
fire – so marvellous were the colours – The maples were wonderful,
ranging from red and gold to pale yellow – the whole place is a leave
centre for troops and we had nothing to pay except for any drinks
we might wish to buy, ironically enough the whole place is run by
30 Corps. Bruce's old H.Q.! We stayed in a very nice hotel called
the Harzburger Hoff – there were very few girls there, but quite a
lot of men – everything was very well arranged – a tea dance the
first day and a musical concert in the evenings, and then to bed for
we were tired – Then the next day we set out for a long walk over

the mountains – going up by the mountain railway which was one of those horrid things on a string, we were petrified! However, we walked some miles over hills and through the most glorious woods till we came to a tiny village where there was a red white and blue barrier and 2 or 3 soldiers hovering over a fire –

Now when walking you have to be most careful not to get into the Russian Zone or you mightn't get out – the Russians being a bit queer – so having seen a notice, 'you are getting near the border – be careful or you may be shot' we asked a gunman in the woods and he said it was some way away – However, it all boiled down to the fact that we had been through the Russian Zone and hadn't known it – anyway, we landed up on the wrong side of the barrier and the soldiers were so surprised they thought we were Russians – me in my red jumper and all!

Naturally we returned another way!

Kay and I rode twice, but horses weren't up to much – we met 2 very charming boys in the hotel in the Westminster Dragoons. They were sweet and we danced with them on two evenings – one of them was Jameson's whiskey, and the other heard while we were there he was being class 'B' released to go up to Oxford – It was lucky meeting them as most of the others weren't up to much – also staying in the hotel was a Naval man from a HQ near here, and he brought us back in his Mercedes Benz also in great comfort – and took us for a nice drive round one afternoon when it was wet.

On the way home Patrick Jameson asked us to have lunch with him in his mess just beyond Brunswick, which we did – They were an awfully nice crowd and had a dog I coveted terribly – a half cocker half golden labrador that looked like a hound – It belonged to their C.O. unfortunately – We eventually got back to Hamburg at about 1815 – to find a terrific conference going on to decide our future – apparently a lot of us will soon be redundant and a bit of re-allocation is going on – I hope they don't send us home, though it wouldn't break my heart, I should like to stay on a bit longer.

Oh, I have volunteered to stay on in the Wrens till the end of next September – otherwise I might be out next Spring – I had a medical and have been pronounced fit.

With regard to the German problem – there was a very good article in the Telegraph last Thursday or Friday – I don't know which – in the centre page – If you read that, you will get a very true picture – of what conditions are really like out here.

Robin writes to say that he thinks he has got his transfer to the RAC [Royal Artillery Company] but will have to undergo all sorts of training and exams –

Has Rosemary gone yet? I am enclosing 2 P.O.'s for her, and my clothing coupon book for you – if you can will you please send her on her P.O.s as I don't know where she is not having heard – Bruce's comment was that words completely failed him and that it seemed to be the last straw for fate to offer!!! but he said he'd look her up and report to me if she was behaving OK! ...

Tomorrow Kay and I are going out to a nearby place to dinner and dance with a Tank Regiment.

I believe they are Desert Rats (I hope so!) She is a dear, but rather shy and retiring, rarely ever saying a word. But she is so pretty and rather Irish – I find I'm not at all shy these days, and if people don't like me, well I'm sure I don't care – so I'm trying to get Kay to be the same!

I think I must really be dry – I've had a whole heap of hair cut off as it got rather unmanageable, I do hope it won't look too much of a mess! I'll send you a p.c. of Bad Harzburg. It really is lovely –

Oh, thank you for the parcel which arrived not on time!

Heaps of love, Sheila

By the end of October Sheila and Kay had elected to be transferred to Plön, the headquarters of Flag Officer Schleswig-Holstein, near Kiel. The WRNS were already beginning to cut down on staff and I think they felt it good to be out of the way:

It will be very cut off in winter, but it is supposed to be very beautiful. Plön is on a large lake – with hilly wooded country all the way round – lots of sailing to be had in summer, and skating in winter. I expect there will be quite a bit of riding too, which will be fun. Also, skiing, we hear. It is the HQ of 8 corps and lots of Army around. Lots of people say we are fools to go, but as we like country life, and the other 2 are keen to stay on here, I think it is the obvious answer.

Before they left they watched the demolition of some U-boat pens in Hamburg harbour: the photos are stuck in the album, but as she says it was 'such a dull day, I don't think it will come out.' They didn't.

Just as she is about to leave Hamburg for Plön she meets Ken Millar, who is about to muddy the waters vis-à-vis Bruce, who is now a lieutenant colonel and an even more attractive catch. The fact that he belongs to a tank regiment of Desert Rats from Egypt brings back many happy memories:

Hamburg
29.10.45

My dear Ma –

Life here is most pleasant – really we are lucky and this week has been just grand. To begin with, I have been riding three times, and now feel completely at home when mounted – all most horrid stiffness and black and blueness has now gone – Secondly, Kay and I have fallen for the Tanks in a big way – (at least they seem to have fallen for us!) – however they are an awfully nice crowd, and we had a good party at the Atlantic on Tuesday – followed by a simply marvellous day out at the Itzehoe yesterday. Ken Millar, who is Squadron Commander, arranged to pick us up at about 10 am, take us out to Itzehoe, which is about an hour's run away, have lunch at R.H.Q., ride in the afternoon, and finish with dinner in 'A' Squadron mess – so he duly arrived, accompanied by Duggie Smith, who comes from Newcastle and the Colonel, Rory Leake, who is a terrific charmer – Ken and the Colonel are both regulars. Ken has been a P.O.W. for 3 or 4 years, but the Colonel seems to have been in every show there was starting from Desert Days – and he is a D.S.O. and 2 M.C.'s the better for it as well as a whole string of other gongs. I'm afraid the 3 of us together immediately became the most tremendous bores – 'do you remember old so and so' and 'did you go to such and such a place?' Cries of maleesh, aiwah and saida rent the air (all wog terms!) and added to all this, everyone seemed to be wearing corduroys, which were Shepheard's rig – After a very excellent lunch of wild duck, we discovered the horses were off the road, so we decided to go sailing instead. They have a beautiful seagoing yacht, the 'Jarmo' which they keep in the small nearby river, so six of us set off in the car, plus Jock, the Scottie, and proceeded down stream with a motor boat behind us to tow us if the wind gave out, it was very calm – eventually it did, so we transhipped, chugged down to the Elbe and came back at dusk, vainly trying to shoot ducks, of which there were many, but all too elusive – the country round there is flat and wet, with windmills rather like Holland I should imagine – We eventually landed up in Ken's mess, where Betty and I bathed and changed and then on to a sumptuous dinner by candlelight. Laugh, laugh, laugh, that's all we did, until Betty and I had to leave about 2200 – It really was a perfect day. On Wednesday Ken and I are supposed to be going to a symphony concert and on to a dance at the Atlantic – but as we had some altercation on the way home – I wouldn't be a bit surprised if it falls through! However, on Saturday, the regiment is playing the 53rd Welsh at Rugger and have arranged an enormous party afterwards, for which I am performing to at least a dozen Wren officers – It's going to be such fun.

On Saturday I went to a Symphony concert with a certain Bill Philpotts, Lieutenant RNVR, whom I have recently met [in Bad Harzburg]. We went on to the country club after and danced. Today we have been out driving in his Mercedes Benz (yes awfully posh isn't it?!!) right into the country to a place called Großensee, where there is a most lovely lake, all surrounded by trees – the trees are nearly all bare now, but some of them are still golden, and with the sun on them. Still look pretty. However, it was a most pleasant drive, and we ended up at the Atlantic for tea.

We still don't know when we are going to Plön – the rival firm, 4th Tanks are up there; they also have a desert rat as their emblem but a black one – not a red like the 5th Tanks – Ken is going up there with a guard funnily enough, at the beginning of the month.

I can't remember whether I told you that Bruce has got the M.B.E. – I know I forgot to tell someone, but it may have been R. Isn't it marvellous? for services rendered in Holland and Germany – There'll be no holding him, I'm sure – so I wrote off and told him I hoped he wouldn't be wanting a larger size in hats!! However, I'm thrilled about it, as you can guess. Has R. gone yet? I had a letter from her last week while she was on the verge – and I have already written an Air Mail out there. In spite of the marvellous time I am having here, I should simply <u>adore</u> to be out there now – and most of the Desert Rats I have met say they would too – in fact, they expect to be back again next year – am I jealous? Rory Leake knows Diana and Peter Booth well – he's been all over the M.E., Iraq and Persia – lives in Kenya and really is too good-looking for words! Such fun, too.

Must stop, or you'll think I'm dotty, a good-time Gertie who never does any work at all! (Hush, I'm writing this on watch, but don't tell anyone – now if I'd got that wool I'd be knitting).

With lots of luv

Sheila

Sheila hasn't heard from Bruce for a couple of weeks and she is concerned, 'wondering what's in the air – as he is usually so good in writing … Methinks there may be some glam Wren down there – but certainly hope not! However, time will show, but it's maddening having to wait, he still expects to be back in Feb, he says.'

It is love at first sight for Ken, but she urges mother not to breathe a word to Rosemary about this: 'I don't want Bruce to know, he might get hold of the wrong end of the stick':

Naval Party 1730
c/o BFMO
Reading
4.11.45

… In the meantime I'm afraid I've made a conquest here, and after 5 meetings a proposal of marriage was offered to me last night! The gentleman in question is one Ken Millar, a Captain in the Tanks – very tall, <u>very</u> military, and really quite nice – but <u>not</u> the kind of person I'd like to marry – As a matter of fact it was all most embarrassing – but I'd better begin the tale at the beginning – last Sunday we went down to Itzehoe, and it was arranged to have a colossal party this Saturday – I to produce the girls – Ken and I in the interim went to a concert at Broadcasting House on Wednesday, and ended up at the Atlantic for dinner – Kay was there with 2 of the subalterns, David and Duggie, who are keen on her, and really it is priceless to see the 3 of them together. Ken has been most attentive since the word go, but I thought he was joking and consequently laughed off all his remarks, until he suddenly asked me if I was engaged, to which I replied, most unofficially, yes, I was (thought this was the best thing to say in the circs!) So we left it at that. Now at this tremendous party last night it transpired that he was violently jealous of the Colonel, Rory Leake, who is absolutely grand (and the answer to any girl's prayers!) and as we were dancing round the scrum of the dance floor, he asked me if I would forget my unofficial engagement for an official one – to which I replied I was sorry, but couldn't – All the time a most riotous party was going on – The Colonel and I really split our sides we were laughing and joking so – all most harmlessly – but Ken got crosser and crosser (another John P. I'm afraid) and it ended up by his not even saying goodnight to me – so that's how we stand! The proposal, by the way, was enhanced by bribes that I should be back in Alex by next March with a flat of my own, and Millar as my surname! Isn't it strange that everything seems to lead to my eventual return to Alex – John P. would probably be out there by then, Bruce would probably still be there – No – I just <u>couldn't</u> do it – I do wish Bruce would come up to the mark and everything would be bettered! Life is complicated isn't it!!!!!!

They moved to Plön and now, with a new admirer, it's time to renew the wardrobe again, although she is still worried about the delay in getting the wool for Bruce's jumper:

NB Naval Party 1734
13.11.45

So sorry but delay due to going to Plön and being so busy thereafter no time for letters. Marvellous barracks and excellent job, and everyone very pleasant. I'll have to tell you all about it later.

I've had your letter, for which thank you. Also the 2 bed jackets and slippers which are all heavenly – thank you so much.

<u>Please</u> send me some decent wool, those odd scraps are useless and I must have it immediately if I am to get the garment finished. Also – when you have a moment, please may I have my skates and also my brocade evening dress, shoes (gold) and gold bag, as we are going to be allowed to wear evening dresses at Xmas – Hooray!!

Ken is up here for the week, and we are firm friends – I do like him immensely but he is rather pukka – However, he seemed to have a fixed idea that it has to be me, and is willing to wait and see as he knows all about B [Bruce]. I do wish B would do something. The mail has been shocking lately and he hasn't even had any of mine – nor me his!

R. is living in the YWCA I used to live in in Cairo – I was deeply envious of her, all my troubles would have been at an end if only I could have been there!

It's now 0:40, if I hadn't written this now, heaven knows when I should have done so –

Heaps of love,

Sheila

Thoughts of marriage are beginning to loom large in Sheila's – and the family's – imagination. Aunty Dorothy has offered to 'give' Sheila a wedding; Sheila thinks the 'obvious thing' would be to lay in a stock of champagne from Germany 'as there is lots about – also good wines and liqueurs – However, it's no good counting one's chickens etc, as the gentleman has yet to come up to scratch (awful if he didn't!!)':

Plön
18.11.45

Yes, it is all a great pity things should have worked out like this – It's now 2 weeks since I've heard from Bruce and it was 2 weeks before that letter. None of my letters seem to be getting through to him either, and with this Palestine trouble one just doesn't know what's happening – I wish I could send a cable and find out but you can't from here. Rosemary has met several people who know Bruce, but of course I wouldn't dream of asking her to find out anything about him, especially as Rosemary has never been a very discreet person – Anyway, the position with Ken is that he is very much in love with me, and so prepared to wait and see what happens. I must say I do like him enormously, he's great fun, sensible and levelheaded, intelligent to talk to, likes music, has run his own dance band and has knocked around a good deal (being of an Army family) which I think is a very good thing – for at least he knows his own mind. He is 29. To look at he is 6ft 4 ins, very thin, large, blue eyes – in fact, if I didn't say so before, he looks like the man in the Rose's lime juice ads! A typical English Army officer – His people live in Scotland near Stirling, where his father, a Colonel in the Cameron's (I think) is stationed – He has 2 sisters, one, an ATS, is called Sheila, and is in Ceylon – one thing worries me rather, he is rather a snob (self admitted!) – but I have teased him about it quite a bit, and also told him that we have no money, and live quite quietly and humbly in Durham. If he would rather I was anything different or would let a thing like that worry him – well then I don't think he's the right man for me – I think he's going to get his majority in December, and become a squadron commander – In January the regiment goes to Berlin to do guard duties there and I think they expect to return to the M.E. in the spring – It looks to me if I am not careful, I shall fall between 2 stools – I do wish I could hear from Bruce, when he is coming home, and so on – I don't even know if he's just not writing or whether it's the mail – The whole thing's a very tricky problem, which, I only hope will sort itself out for the best soon – I will keep you fully informed in all the latest details – but in the meantime, please don't mention it to Rosemary or anyone, because it's so easy to get those sort of things distorted, especially through the post – Pa knows of course, doesn't he? …

Robin is leading a very gay life in UK – he is definitely joining the Tanks – all I can say is I bet he lands into the 5th and I bet that I, and all my swains, all land up the M.E. together sometime next year, with John P. thrown in the background! Quelle Vie!!

Must stop now – get up, dress, have tea, and stagger to the office for an hour or so – (yes, I do feel honoured about Ken – having just re-read your letter – all after three meetings – too!)

With lots of love

Sheila

In the very same letter she says:

I've realised what a help to me it's been to have been in the M.E. and to have knocked about a bit – I also realise how green I must have been when I went abroad, I'd certainly like to have that M.E. time all over again – for I feel now I could master most situations – even of the John P. variety!

It seems to me, reading these letters now, and comparing Ken and John's characters, that they seem pretty similar, both liable to fall into terrible rages and fits of jealousy, and that she has learned very little! The phrase 'we are now firm friends again' rekindles memories of her on/off affair with John Pritty and does not augur well for this little romance. She seems strangely attracted to this kind of man, my father being of a similar type; Robin and Bruce were complete opposites, it appears, real gentlemen; but perhaps not sparky enough? The really rather pathetic thing is her obvious and utter desperation to find a husband – to be 'honoured' by Ken's courtship is a strange way of looking at it – and not to fall between the proverbial 'two stools' as she puts it.

The very next letter says it all:

1945 (12) Plön
22/11/45

My dear Mum –

No mail from anyone for three (repeat) three days, as apparently there has been a bad fog at home (no planes!). Anyway, it has caused a depression to fall over most of us, which I hope will be returned by the arrival of something tomorrow!

Well, after my last exuberant effort (I was feeling like a million) I feel slightly deflated as there is still no news from Bruce (nearly 3 weeks now) and I have had the stupidest bust up with Ken imaginable! The former may be due to the bad mail system – who knows? The latter arose as follows – Kay and I drove down to Hamburg on Monday with 2 Army people to the 21st birthday party of 2 twins who are stationed here – Ken and David (Kay's admirer!) were also there, and we arrived at about 7 o'clock – Ken and David had, however, been there some little time, and had passed a good hour in the men's bar prior to going to the party and Ken was well away. We got on famously till half way through dinner after numerous cocktails, white and red wine, followed by champagne, when Ken's jokes became too much of a good thing, they were, fortunately, only understood by me and another man who had been in the M.E. and annoyed me intensely. Finally he stuck his monocle (reserved only for special occasions!) in his eye, and started a frightful lineshoot, which infuriated me all the more – especially as we were surrounded by dozens of people we didn't know. In a party of our own it would have been quite OK. So I gave him a black look and decided to ignore it all – from thence after he refused to be in the slightest bit friendly – in fact, went out of his way to be unfriendly and cold. I was furious, in fact the party was ruined for me, especially as when I quietly asked him if our date in Hamburg on Saturday still stood, he raised his eyebrows and said he was probably going to Wilhelmshaven, but would let me know – I wouldn't have cared two hoots if I hadn't been fond of him, but unfortunately I am, and it did hurt rather. However, if he doesn't cool down, he can just go to hell – and I shall still go to Hamburg on Saturday if Ken Pawson is still going down there. Really, isn't it all too childish for words?!!

I went up to Kiel on Tuesday for lunch. It really is in the most terrible state – sunken ships, twisted steel, salved boats lying high and dry on the quay, and hardly a building left standing. I lunched on board the Naval depot ship, which was a liner the Germans were building for Turkey before the war. She was sunk and had her stern blown off by a bomb, but we salved her, and she really makes a very good accommodation vessel – However, I was pleased to get back to Plön.

We rode again yesterday, me on the Admiral who was really quite skittish – and I even managed a jump (there was no alternative I hasten to add!) However, it was all very thrilling and we hope to learn properly…

Robin is still being very gay, and says he really hopes to get his transfer soon. He hopes to get out to Palestine next year in time for a spot of trouble. What did I tell you, everyone will land up in the M.E. ere long, with the exception of me, it seems!!!

Another request (I know – I'm always asking for things!) could you please send me out an E. Arden lipstick CINNEBAR or CYCLAMEN – refill will do – as I have lost mine! A letter from M. Dugdale yesterday, saying that she and Eleanor are coming to Hamburg next month – Hamburg knows nothing because I asked them this A.M.! We do track each other about, don't we?

Heaps of love,

Sheila

Riding the Admiral.

Nevertheless, she is not put off and continues to pursue Ken, despite keeping her options open with Bruce, who is driving her mad with his silence. As the Christmas party season approaches, she is still worrying about what to wear; her scrapbook contains no fewer than seven invitations for the festive season: women were obviously in demand! And a card from Ken signed 'with all my love and very best wishes':

Plön
2/12/45

My dear Ma –

Many thanks for your letter and also for the wool, which is perfect, not to mention the hatpin which I only found by accident! I see another parcel has arrived for me today, I wonder if it is from you and whether it is my evening dress. If you haven't already sent it off, I would like to have it soon, please. Do you think that ancient old floral one would do as a second thing, as I believe we are going to wear them 2 or 3 times and naturally would rather not wear the same dress for every party – I don't think there's anything else really suitable for winter as I've no intention of wearing the flame one here in Germany, the old floral one is most attractive, but very decrepit and not suitable for bright lights! Still, it suits me – look at it and see what you think. I also want shoes and bag – that you know though.

The usual busy round here – I think I probably told you we went to Kiel on Tuesday: I went again on Thursday, with quite a nice person in the Gunners (ex ME all my proteges are!) we went to see a circus – but minus the animals – at the local theatre and ended up at the yacht club after. It really is a beautiful place. It was the Kaiser's own yacht club, and the equivalent of Cowes in England. The only thing is that it is nearly always empty, except at weekends, Kay and I dined with the Admiral on Friday, and saw a picture after – all rather boring.

Ken Pawson and an awfully nice friend of his, Donald Yeats, motored me down to Hamburg to meet Ken – unfortunately we started late, ran out of oil and didn't arrive till after 9:30. As I feared, Ken had spent most of the 2 hours he had to wait in the bar (who could blame him really?) it's always horrid when you don't start together I always think – so the party wasn't the howling success it should have been. The rest of his squadron had a huge party (stag) at a table nearby, and were teasing the life out of Ken – What to make of Ken I really don't know. I think Caroline's advice of not to take him too seriously is the best. I'm not really much good at judging people under those circumstances – but it certainly loosens the tongue! Oh well, the next week or two will show! Yes, I have thought of writing to Bruce once and asking him what his intentions are – it's a thing I'd much rather not do, but would prefer to dwell in patience, till I see him. By doing this I should probably lose my chances with Ken, especially if his regiment gets recalled to the M.E. as they think it will. But Bruce stands out a mile ahead at the minute, having seen Ken in such a light recently. Oh it's all such a stupid muddle. I am going to wait and see what happens. I'm really feeling very much 'off' with Ken in view of his recent behaviour – as you say, those men are all the same, blast them!

Kay and I went for a long walk in the woods this afternoon. No riding today as they tired the horses out 'hunting' yesterday! I hope to go myself tomorrow – There's very little other news – quite a lot of invitations for Xmas parties have come in – I don't think I shall go to any of the ones that are a long way away.

I must stop and go to sleep. This is rather a jumbled mess, but I am feeling rather mixed up and annoyed, and wish that February was here to solve all my problems!

With lots of love

Sheila

Ken is mad keen to have a son to send to Eton and into one of the best regiments. (I think he was at Eton himself) One minute he's all for getting married and being a success in the army, the next, never to marry, have a couple of women up his sleeve, and probably leave the army a disillusioned Major. See what drink does for you!!!

Sheila keeps her options open – her mother sends her a book to give Ken, *Orientations* (by Somerset Maugham I assume, although how this relates to the fact that 'He reads a lot … is mad keen on Omar Khayyam', I'm not sure), and she also asks her to send the following cable to Bruce, whatever the cost, 'I don't care'. It costs her about £2, which she sends to her mother in Postal Orders. She also sends one to Rosemary as well, and complains that it is '1/3*d* a word! Ugh!':

LT-COL BOOTH-MASON
STAFF COLLEGE
HAIFA
A VERY HAPPY CHRISTMAS AND NEW YEAR TO YOU.
HOPE TO SEE YOU SOON. LOVE SHEILA MILLS

It appears to be difficult to meet up with Ken over the Chrstmas period, however, as he is based in Hamburg. As Kay is on leave, she is even unable to go to his squadron party; given that they 'hardly do any work at all' it is all very boring.

Finally she gets the news from Bruce that she has been waiting for, regarding his home leave. He is hoping to meet Rosemary in Cairo. Ken is still very much on the scene, and preparations for the Christmas parties are underway,

'Countless invitations still pour in. I really must enter up my diary – we had a good one in the senior officers' mess on Monday and Wendy gave a farewell party this evening. Tomorrow it is the chief's and P.O.'s and also the Army Signals, which I feel I must go to – all in the game etc.'

Meanwhile Robin is doing a course at Catterick and she has invited him to stay with her parents in Durham:

Plön
17.12.45

My dear Ma –

… Well, I have had a letter from Bruce, saying he is definitely coming in February, and asking about my leave etc. He says that we must definitely see as much of each other as possible and must really come to a decision as to how we feel about each other with which I heartily concur – So I have written off suggesting that we meet in London, and then he comes up North and stays with us for a bit. I think he will probably be staying in or near London – I must say I am awfully glad the cards are now on the table, as I hope it will make things easier for me to decide – before not knowing quite what was happening it was extremely difficult – at the minute, I do feel that I know Ken very much better than Bruce – as really I've seen very little of the latter in the last 2 1/2 years – all rather a fantastic situation, really – I've had such a pleasant weekend in Hamburg with Ken, Dennis Coulson (the 2 I/C of the regiment) and Betty Crocker – things couldn't have been better – I stayed in the Atlantic hotel; Ken and Dennis were there too and it was so nice – we lost the rotor arm of the jeep unfortunately and had rather a job getting another as it is an essential thing to make the jeep go – However, we got one in the end and lunched at the country club, then they drove Betty and me up to Plön in the afternoon, stayed for tea and dinner and drove back to Itzehoe – They are definitely going to Berlin next month – so goodness knows what will happen after that – Ken is coming down here on Christmas Eve and I am very keen to find out exactly what he feels about the situation –

We are all rushing round getting ready for Xmas – the Senior officers have their party tonight – a full dress affair for us – the dentist and I are having a great time cutting one of my wisdom teeth for me – It won't do it by itself.

I must stop now – sorry this is so scrappy – It does look mama, as tho' one of your daughters will be "off" soon – but chickens mustn't be counted ere they hatch, and heaven help me to make the right choice!!

With heaps of love

Sheila

On 19 December she writes again to her mother, clearly anxious about the February meeting with Bruce:

I am going to try and get my leave on the 18th Feb, arriving in UK about the 20th, and have written to Bruce to this effect – he says he will be home anyway at the end of the month, and possibly by the 11th so it should fit in well. Do you think it is a good idea for me to go direct to London and see him there and then return North with him as I suggested to him? If so, I should want a bag of clothes sent down to London, as I don't want to have to stay in uniform all the time. I think my pale blue woollen dress had better be cleaned, don't you, so could you please arrange that for me?

She continues:

I have the most extraordinary task on hand, Michael Buxton goes home on Friday, and as he hasn't a UK license for his dog, and she is having puppies anyway, has left her with me – I have to see them into the world, look after them, and then bring Sally and one of them home on leave when I come in Feb. In return I am allowed one of the puppies – They are rough haired dachshunds very rare in England (I have never seen one and I don't mean the silky variety) Sally is a darling and has a little house of her own, which I have in my cabin, with her in it now –

Her annual Christmas letter comprises a list of all the festivities, late nights and feasting, with one of the highlights being the Boxing Day hockey match – the photographs survive but are not of good enough quality to reproduce:

Plön
25.12.45

My dear Ma –

A very happy Christmas Day to you – I expect you are on the way to church, if not already there, as it is after 1030 – I find I've missed our service here as it was at 0930, but I rose at 7 and went early –

Thank you very much for your last letter – quite by mistake I didn't send back the postal orders, so all is well – How most generous! The book arrived OK from Allan's, and was duly given to Ken last night – I only hope he will read it!

We have had a most hectic time this past week, out every evening, on Saturday I had to pack in at 11 o'clock as I was too tired to carry on any further – On Sunday several of us went to a carol service in the garrison church here. Unfortunately all the lights had fused and to begin with all was in darkness save for 2 candles on the altar – However, they did come on eventually, and we and an awfully nice service – afterwards we went to a party at the Admiral's House, given by the Chief of Staff –

Last night was our own party, and Ken and Dennis Coulson came – To my utmost **HORROR** Ken produced the sweetest white terrier puppy for me and so now I am saddled with two dogs, and the prospect of several more at any moment! Oh dear – it's really all most worrying – The party went off very well – it didn't end till about 2 and Diana and I were enveigled [sic] into going off to the 44th Tanks HQ mess for eggs and bacon and Champagne, off we went, but alas, no eggs and bacon – which was all too disappointing. So after a while we drove back but didn't land up here till about 0430 – oohh – as I was up again at 7 you can guess I'm exhausted now! Today we have lunch and dinner in the Senior Officers' mess and a party there after, but I don't think I shall go to the latter tomorrow, one at the Junior Officers' mess – Thursday at C mess in Plön – I was also asked to an RAF party up near Schleswig for that day by an awfully nice Wing Cdr, Allan Theed, who knew Aenid in Egypt. He was going to try to come down here to collect me, and fly me back the next morning – but as I'd already said I'd go to this other thing, I can't go – Rather a pity. Friday, a party at the 44th Tanks, not awfully keen; they aren't half as nice as the 5th – Saturday, Ken wants me to go to Hamburg – Sunday nothing, thank heavens, and Monday another Army mess party in Plön – The Corps Commander is giving a large dance on the 5th – all the army from all around will be at that, so you see, life is very full and added to it all, Kay is on leave and so I have quite a lot of work to do –

Yes, I too think B. is an ass not to have done anything ere now – His whole idea while the war was on that being separated it wasn't fair to either of us, and then of course he didn't know he was going to Haifa when we last met. It certainly makes me wonder if he really <u>does</u> want me – still, I must be patient till Feb. As for Ken – well I don't know!

27th

I'm afraid I never got down to finishing this 2 days ago – life has been most gay – in fact, I'm afraid I'm dead sick of going to parties – we had the most enormous lunch party in the senior officers' mess on Xmas day – everyone sat down to lunch together from 1.30 to 3.30 – we didn't have turkey – but pork and goose – very good we ended up by playing parlour tricks – and singing wildly – After that I came home and went to bed! In the evening we had a buffet supper and dancing again in the Senior Officers' mess. Yesterday, back to work, but an extraordinary hockey match 'men' versus 'women' was played. I made a very swash-buckling pirate, complete with beard and moustache, hair tucked into my beret – all the men were wonderful Grecian tunics of yellow and white – one had an enormous balloon tucked underneath for a bustle – others wore bonnets, turbans, lipstick, and the referee a Wren shirt, with 4 pairs of blackout pants on underneath which he proceeded to divest himself of until he had to make a sudden dash for his car halfway through – some had hockey sticks, others brooms; a blow lamp burned rigorously in the middle of the pitch – someone had a violin – others squatted and played cards, in the end we drove round in jeeps scream-ing madly – Needless to say the 'men' (us) won!

Another dance in the Junior Officers' mess last night – again tonight with the army – and so it goes on. Both evening dresses have seen good service – The puppy is really behaving very well, but I shall have to give him away as I really can't cope – it's a shame as he is rather a darling, but it can't be helped.

While Kay is away I have her wireless fitted in my cabin – it's an ordinary service wireless receiver with loudspeaker attached of which the puppy is all too keen in biting the lead –

I do hope you have managed to have a good Christmas – do you ever listen in to the British Forces Network radio from Hamburg – it really is awfully good –

I must stop now, ere I have to put this down and it doesn't get finished –

With much love and a very happy New Year – Thank you for your wire, by the way you must enquire about the Naval private telegram system for us in Germany. Then you needn't send to Reading – They come direct to us by teleprinter.

More love,

Sheila

1945 draws to a close with no resolution in sight to Sheila's affairs of the heart – just more waiting and anxiety. Bruce, Ken or neither – which is it to be?

1946

'These men!'

It is almost impossible to get more than a glimpse of the real horrors of post-war Germany from Sheila's letters. There is the occasional passing reference to the privations faced by the German staff working with the British, or the band who tried to smuggle food from yet another sumptuous British feast in their instrument cases. There are also examples of small kindnesses shown to staff and children, as well as compassion and debate around the subject.

For the occupying forces the images of the recently liberated concentration camps, with the charred bodies, the emaciated survivors and the mass graves must have influenced their thinking about the German people. They find it hard to believe that German citizens did 'not know' what was going on, and so what might today seem callous behaviour has to be seen in that context.

Nevertheless, Allied policy was brutal against the vanquished between 1946 and 1950. It is thought that over two million women and girls were raped by the victors[9] and that up to one million German POWs were deported as forced labour, while up to three million of them died in camps.[10] Naturally few begrudged the Allies the Nuremburg Trials in order to see the architects of the Final Solution brought to justice and sentenced to death.

9 The victorious Russian army even raped survivors of the concentration camps, according to Sarah Helm.

10 Peter Stuyvesant, National Journal 20/3/2012

The Americans, in particular, with Russian backing and British acquiescence, in return for a large loan to rebuild Britain, not only divided Germany into four zones but also dismantled, rather than rebuilt, industry and rationed food to subsistence levels. The Cold War, it could be said, in many ways saved Germany as it forced the Allies to look more favourably on it as Russia became the enemy.

But for Sheila 1946 was a year of seemingly endless parties, sport – especially riding – and concerns about her future, from a work perspective but, more importantly, in the quest to decide upon her husband. At the end of 1945, she was being wooed by Ken, but holding out for an answer from Bruce, whom she is to meet on leave in February, and with whom she hopes to settle the future of their long-running 'understanding'.

'Life is very full', she writes from Plön on 6 January:

Did I tell you about our New Year's Eve party in one of the army messes here? I haven't laughed so much for ages, and tho' we drank of the very best (marvellous champagne cocktails) unlike my sister I remained compos mentis! I even had another proposal from a very glam and beautiful young man called Peter Shaw-Pullen – who is frightfully frightfully Mayfair and theatre, who was expert at saying the most charming things one likes to hear, but rather prone to dancing to cheek to cheek!!

The parties continue apace, including 'one very high-level one given by the Corps commander Lt General Sir Evelyn Barker [the invitation survives] … we had dinner beforehand with the Commander and 3 Lt. Colonels from the 7th Armed Div., bespeckled with DSO's and MC's – but rather nice.' She wore her old floral dress and was admired by the Admiral. The photograph, also pasted into the album, shows her in it.

Meanwhile Robin went to stay with Sheila's parents:

… he really is such a dear, but very quiet … I couldn't help smiling – your only comment with regard to him was 'he's rather a lamb' – twice!! Well, yes, he is – and, of course, very young for his 25

Lt General Sir Evelyn Baring's party – Sheila is in her floral dress.

years, even tho' he has been about a lot – of course. I think it's merely shyness because he's like that to everyone – most retiring and often says very little – I think he's probably very good at his job – very much ruled by the army, of course, which is natural, but a pity – He's terribly thoughtful and kind – with a distinct opinion and mind of his own. He's very honest and direct, too, and so sweet with his mother and sister – He really wants about six bombs behind him, tho' – one never quite knows what he is thinking.

In news of her other swains, Rosemary has met up with Bruce in Cairo; apparently 'she likes him very much and heartily approves'. As usual, torn between her lovers, she asks, 'I wonder what Robin really thinks of me now?' She has not heard from Bruce for over a fortnight and is 'almost getting cold feet that we shall miss each other, or something terrible like that'. By 16 January she is losing patience:

I really am rather annoyed with Bruce – it's most strange that he never wrote to R. about not turning up that time and do you know the last letter I've had from him was written on the 19th Dec – I just can't make it out. I usually hear from him about every 10 days and his last letters have been full of plans re our leave and when he may be home – but the trouble is every letter says something different and I do want a reply to a particular letter of mine which says I can't get leave after the 16th – That's only a month from today and I do want to know soon so that I can make plans – I loathe cabling as it always seems so climatic – but if I don't hear from him within about a week I see no other alternative. Oh <u>dear</u>! Perhaps he's got cold feet!!! Well, if he has, I'd far rather know, and plan accordingly than be on the end of a sting!!!

This does not prevent her from keeping her options open and Ken has been to Plön to visit; he wanted her to share his imminent leave with him in Paris – 'woohoo' – but she has to decline. She is also given the chance to go to Chamonix on an official rest and relaxation break, but again she is 'completely messed up owing to no news from B'.

To add to her chagrin, 'in the latest bombshell', Kay has announced her engagement!

Sheila's leave is to dominate her letters over the next three weeks: 'I will let you know soon as I can when I am coming – I hate to seem too "keen" or "chasing" but I must know whether B. is coming or not to make my own plans. <u>These men</u>!!' Her frustration is tempered by reports of the fun she is having – skating on the frozen lakes, the addition of another new admirer, Sandy Sibun, with whom she and Kay visit Aarhus for some shopping, despite 'everything being terribly expensive', the birth of the puppies – and of course, more parties.

On 27 January she writes:

Yes, I have heard from Bruce now (these men!) the letter took 17 days to reach me, and the following day I had a cable in reply to mine – a very nice one – so all is well. He still doesn't seem certain of when he is coming, but wants me to try for leave about the 20th – go home – and then wait and see when he arrives if he hasn't already done so.

She is in a state of high anxiety and leaving nothing to chance:

Plön
7.2.46

Well now – about my leave – if I haven't told you already – it is all fixed – I leave here on the 19th, sail on the 20th, and expect to be home sometime on the 21st – I only get 12 days, much to my annoyance, as VJ leave has been stopped. How nice of Papa to take some leave when I am home so that we can go about – At the minute alas, I am all at sea with my plans, so heaven knows how we will fit in – mine are, very roughly this – As you know the whole reason for having my leave in Feb is to see Bruce, and I am determined to do this. At the minute, he still doesn't know when he will be coming, but the form is that when he arrives in UK he will either write, phone or wire, and we will make plans – Now if any communication from him arrives before I arrive back (you know his hand writing, don't you? Very childish probably!) I want you to find out his address and phone number and I will phone you up from Hull whenever I arrive to find out what's to be done – I shall come straight home from Hull, and probably go south to meet Bruce later. I do want to get this settled (I feel so nervous!) and think it would be better to meet him alone in London rather than lug him all the way up north only to find we hate each other on sight!! After all a year is a long time and I am petrified that he may have changed his mind! When in London, I also want to see Robin, and (<u>whatever</u> the form is with Bruce) try and clear the air there – After all, there is a limit to everything, and either way he's got a few home truths coming to him – This may seem rather ruthless, but I feel I must know where I stand! I don't think I shall see Kenneth before I leave as he is having an extra 2 weeks in the UK and won't be back till the 16th – At the minute I am having rather a trying time with Sandy, who seems to have got it rather badly, but this simply <u>can't</u> be allowed, and I am going to be very firm. Oh dear, why is it that it's never the right one?!! What a curse men are!

Robin seems to be held in a 'first reserve' position and she is determined to see him as well on her leave, as she records in her last letter
before her departure. I am amused that she calls her mother 'mum'
in this letter, something I was not allowed to do when I was a small
child. It had to be 'Mummy':

Plön
13.2.46

My dear Mum –

I'm so awfully sorry I've not written before – I've been waiting for my
final dates and arrangements to be made – well now, the position has
somewhat changed since I last wrote – but it's now quite firm – so this
is what it is – I am flying over in a Stirling from Schleswig to Bury St.
Edmonds, on the 19th and from there I shall come straight home by
the Harwich Express (going backwards!) – The only trouble is that no
one has a UK train timetable and I don't know how the trains run – so
if you think you can get reply back to me by p.m. the 18th, do write
and tell me how they go – It takes 2 1/2 hrs – the air passage, so I
should arrive in ~~Schleswig~~ UK (must be going mad) by about lunchtime
– Anyway, on arrival, I will send a wire saying what I am going to do,
and then appear! I can bring unlimited baggage too, it's a mail plane.
    Well, about Bruce – I think it's quite definitely that he is cooling
off, but anyway, we shall soon find out when we meet – he is arriving
in UK about the 19th and will doubtless write or ring – if he rings,
please get his address or phone number, and I will contact him on
my return. I have had 2 very pressing letters from Robin, who will be
on leave at the same time and who is very keen to take me to a large
dance at Westminster Hospital on the 22nd, so what I think I shall do
is to go down to London for it and hope that by that time Bruce will
be back, and that I can see him whilst I am down there. Dear oh dear
oh dear!! I always seem to get into such complications and muddles –
what will happen I can't say – but I can only say I hope it will be for
the best!! It really seems <u>awful</u> to rush off as soon as I am home – but

I am sure you will appreciate what a dilemma I seem to be in – one which really must be solved! At the minute it rather looks as if I shall be back home again within the next month or two anyway – a thing I will tell you all about when I return – As I am going by air, I am going to try and get 14 days instead of 12 – but mum's the word.

So glad you've managed to get the house done up – I hope it won't be cold when I am back, as we are so used to central heating we are quite tender little flowers! You seem to have had a good time in Yorkshire. I'm so glad –

Sally plus puppy I have to take down to Kiel to an M.L. [Motor Launch] who is taking them back to UK. I do hope they will be OK. We now have 3 left. Did I tell you I have lost Desmond! [the dog that Ken gave her] Diana and I took him out for a walk and he disappeared, last Friday. I am désolé – we searched high and low too.

We had a good party last night, organised by me – we decorated the place with catkins and it looked awfully nice. I had such fun tasting the drinks and arranging the food – at the very end the German band got arrested because they were walking off with food in their violin cases – what a world!

Mummy, I must stop, as I must write a wee line to Robin – I do hope you won't be cross because I am going off to London so soon – you do understand don't you? If Bruce does ring – I'd rather you didn't tell him I have arranged to go to London. I want to tell him myself. I shall probably have to go down for an interview anyway – I don't mind you telling him that in the slightest – Personally, I think he has got cold feet – I know I have myself! Still, time will show –

So au revoir – hope to see you on the 19th or 20th – I will wire as soon as I arrive.

Heaps of love,

Sheila

The next letter home is not written until after the leave, on 7 March, reporting her safe arrival, and a 'pleasant evening with John' at the Mirabell. Could this have been her last meeting with John Pritty? We will never know.

There is no mention of Bruce in the following letter – indeed Ken seems to be on the scene again: 'it was grand to see him … we tea'd and dined and went into Itzehoe to the new Officers' Club – Shepheard's – of which we are new members. Reluctantly, I came home at 4 o'clock – they wanted me to stay the night, and as I've not done a stroke today, I wish I had! What it is to have a conscience!' She is going up to Hamburg to see him during the week, and then he is coming to see her over the weekend, when they plan to go to the officers' club at Travemünde and stay the night.

The Hamburg meeting was not a success as Ken:

… had one of his 'moods' on – which he says he can't explain him-self – It never struck me before but they are probably something to do with him having been POW. I then find it very difficult to under-stand him and just can't make out how we stand. We are supposed to be going up to the officers' club at Travemünde on the Baltic for Saturday night – I wonder if we will?'

It really does sound like John Pritty all over again.

She still has not heard from Bruce by 14 March and she is 'at a loss to know what has happened – but I haven't written – after all, unless he's fallen very ill (most unlikely) he could easily write to me'. She has in the interim applied to join Control Commission, the military gov-ernment running Germany. She is obviously very concerned that she will either be demobbed or posted back to being a Wren in England, neither of which she is keen on. 'I hope to hear on Tuesday what is to become of me. I want very much to stay out here – I just <u>couldn't</u> come home and do the kind of job Daddy thinks I ought to do (don't show him this!!) unless one is married or engaged or got some defi-nite commitment in U.K. I think it's far better to be out here – so I do hope someone will take me on!!'

Finally she hears from Bruce, as she reports to her mother on 20 March:

Plön
20.3.46

My dear Ma –

Thank you for your letter – I am so glad that you are better, but don't forget to take care – why <u>don't</u> you see a doctor – Yes, we had another bout of snow, but it has gone now – In one week I was ski-ing, riding and playing squash – not bad! Ski-ing was fun, but rather difficult – I kept falling down to begin with and got some horrific cracks!

Well – ! A letter from Bruce today – full of apologies and con-science-stricken feelings – certainly cold feet was the answer – he's not fallen for anyone else – He returns to Haifa today, and will be out there till next November, when he comes back to UK possibly to a job in War Office – I feel rather annoyed with myself really, for not realis-ing all this before – I did actually know it, but didn't want to believe it, I suppose – I felt the same, but thought that a meeting would clear it all up! However, he hadn't got the guts for that – so what!

Hope R. gets on all right with her Winter – we seem to strike suites of young men who can't make up their minds! Ken is the same – he suffers badly from ex-POW-itis – consequently he can't make up his mind what to do from one day to another. He seems to have made up his mind that he doesn't want to get married, but is in no way sure of himself. On the other hand he is in love with me – but he can't make up his mind. He's frightened because he's poor and this new pay thing[11] is even worse than before – He even has no confidence in himself – I find it so hard to get to the root of the trouble and find out what really is the matter. We went to Travemünde on Saturday for the night and had quite a pleasant time, but this uncertainty seems to cast a cloud

11 The army had introduced new pay scales, which in fact left personnel worse off than before.

over everything. He has grown rather morose which consequently has a bad effect on me – so we aren't the gayest of couples after our hilarious times before Xmas – He was going to Brussels tomorrow, but has cancelled it and is coming up here for a dance in Plön and on Saturday we hope to meet in Hamburg for a Tank party at the Country Club and stay at the Atlantic. I wonder what we will do?

You have made no comment on my proposal to join Control Commission – I hope to go down and have an interview next week – I only hope they will take me, as I don't want to come home one bit – !

Some of the people are horrible but doubtless they will improve later on – if they accept me, I want to transfer direct without coming home, as it will be much easier –

Robin is going off either to Italy or Austria any day now – everything most involved as his original appointment has fallen through. He seems to be in great demand, and at one stage was asked to be 2nd Cd. of 2nd Tanks, much to his surprise – it appears now that he will only probably get a squadron and become Major again, but considering Ken, a regular tank man, hasn't been able to achieve this himself, he's very lucky to do this as a newcomer to the RAC – what influence and friends will do! Must stop now as I am going for a walk – It's a heavenly day –

Heaps of love,

Sheila

p.s. I've just remembered it's your 30th anniversary some day soon (I never know which day!) Many congratulations – now you must have one of those bottles of Champagne – I insist – a very fitting occasion – I can easily get more – Now mind you do!

S.

At the dance in Plön, with Ken.

Poor Sheila – the champagne is laid down for the wedding, and she is still keeping Ken and Robin in play although, as her next letter reveals, life is far from satisfactory on the boyfriend front. She manages to derive some enjoyment from her work at least, while waiting to hear about her application to Control Commission:

Plön
25.3.46

My dear Ma –

What's the news from here, now? I told you I'd heard from Bruce, didn't I? If it's not one it's the other! Ken has now been playing up and Sandy has completely deserted me for another mess member – this latter I don't mind about a bit – but it seems a bit strange. However, to revert to Ken, he cancelled his Brussels trip and came up here for a dance last Thursday. We had such fun and both thoroughly enjoyed it – As you know, we were meeting in Hamburg at the weekend – there was to be a party and we were going to stay in the Atlantic. When he came up Ken said the party was off as there was no accommodation in the Atlantic and that he thought he'd have a quiet weekend for a change. I was disappointed naturally, but said no more. Later I chanced to ring up Betty Crocker in Hamburg, who mentioned that Ken and Dennis had been arranging a party for her and 2 other Wrens in Hamburg for Saturday night! <u>Was</u> I mad? And now Ken has had the cheek to ring me and ask me to another do in their mess on Wednesday, to which he said 3 Hamburg-ites are going – I have been distant and vague and certainly don't intend to go. Transport is almost impossible, anyway.

I had a most interesting day yesterday and entertaining too. I went out to lunch with the French Naval Liaison Officer in Kiel. A sumptuous affair – wonderful food and drink – I felt absolutely bloated after it – Then Priscilla and I were taken on to tea with half the German nobility. Princesses, counts, countesses, generals etc. I must say it was most interesting and I did enjoy it very much. They were all charming. Well mannered and cultured. Interesting and amusing to think that their sons had all been arrant young Nazi officers. Photographs of them emblazoned the walls all round – we were principally entertained by a General who had led the Germans against us in SW Africa many moons ago. A dear old boy. His wife and daughter, also charming, were also there, and a newly demobbed colonel who was chopping wood on the estate. Conversation was naturally limited – they all have a very narrow outlook and no appreciation of what is going on outside at all. They are all evacuated and there are about 90 people living in the Schloss, of course all denounce the Nazis madly, but would have been among the first to acknowledge them had they succeeded. All spoke English well, and most had been to England. Yes, it was most interesting. In the evening I went to a party at the Admiral's house, which funnily enough I enjoyed immensely – the food and drink again, were excellent.

Riding has started again in full swing. I have been out a lot in the last week and this morning before breakfast – but it was too much for me. I fell off and have got acute lumbago!!

Any news of Rosemary? I really must write to her – I wonder if she saw Bruce – Hope all will be well in that direction.

As you can guess I feel a bit depressed with life, but doubtless some-thing will materialise. I hope to hear about control commission next week.

With much love

Sheila

Still smarting from Ken's duplicity, she 'refused to go to Ken's party on Wednesday. Nothing would induce me to go on principle – I won't be two-timed!! However, I think (and hope!) we shall meet this weekend – he suggested it, and rang me up today, but I was out.'

Obviously put out by Sandy Sibun's perfidy, she adopts an equally high-minded posture over the next slight as she notes on 28 March: 'I am at the minute having a most amusing time – there is a big party in Kiel tonight given by Sandy's mess from which I was omitted – apparently they are now one girl short – and (can you CREDIT it?!!) have asked me if I will go to take her place!! I had great pride in saying, No, I was doing nothing, but wouldn't dream of going! I have now invited a guest to dinner at the time when les girls are going to be picked up – and I hope they all feel darned uncomfortable – really – what do people think I am?' Sandy was married as it transpired, so she was not averse to getting her own back.

Ken seems to have wriggled back into her good books as she goes on a short leave with him to Brussels in early April:

Plön
6.4.46

My dear Ma –

... I expect you are wondering what I was doing in Brussels – well I will tell you – to begin with I will say that I think I was foolish to go, but everyone else here has been off somewhere or other, and I wanted to as well – Kay was up in Copenhagen with the hockey

team – everyone was away – Ken rang up and said he was going
to Brussels on short leave – would I like to go too? Like an ass I said
yes, if I could get a pass – I could get a pass – I went – The journey
was long and tedious, and I didn't like Brussels much – we quarrelled
rather and in fact didn't really make it up till the day we came back – I
have never known anything quite like the prices – absolutely fantastic,
they were – On the way back we had 24 hours in the train and passed
through Ruhr district, I have never seen anything like the bombing – for hours and hours we passed nothing but flattened out towns
and factories – and when we slowed down, hordes of small children
crowded round the train begging for food – It wasn't a pretty sight.

Her anxiety about her future is in no small part due to the fact
that the barracks is closing on 15 April and she has nowhere to go.
Originally she thought she was 'possibly' staying to do an 'interesting
and unique job – Staff Communication Officer to NOIC Cuxhaven
– the snags at the minute are (a) there are no Wrens there at all –
only 4 or 5 civilian welfare women workers in the whole place and
(b) NOIC has to be asked whether he approves having a girl Signal
Officer over his men' – but it was not approved, as she not allowed to
be the only woman on station:

> [I am] completely in the air in every respect and feel rather depressed
> – I should like to make a clean sweep of everything but it's difficult to
> know how to set about it – The one thing to avoid as far as I can see
> is to be a Wren in England, which would be just deadly – If I can get
> in to Control Commission I should like to go to Berlin or Austria if
> one gets a choice – I wonder? Anyway, I shall probably land on your
> doorstep with all my bags in 3 weeks time!

To add insult to injury she discovers that her application to join the
Control Commission was sent to England, 'so there is nothing to be
done for me out here'. In fact, the military government was in the
process of reducing staff, but she is determined to pull all strings possible, despite the welcome news that she is to be transferred to Kiel,

in a secretarial capacity, dealing with German property. Ever optimistic, she says:

> Soon I hope to get my Control Commission idea sorted out and if
> it's OK, I shall then transfer – If not, it will give me a chance to look
> round for something else – The barracks close down tomorrow – all v.
> sad – I am going to a horse show – Gymkhana in Itzehoe with Ken –
> and go to Kiel on Thursday.

Sheila, as mess secretary, was in charge of organising the farewell party; an event dutifully recorded in her album with a copy of the invitation and formal photo:

Plön
11.4.46

My dear Ma

We gave a most successful party on Monday organised by Mills – it consisted of a cocktail party for about 120, then a dance with buffet for about 60 afterwards – The Admiral and General came to say nothing of old Brigadiers etc. We got most of the food from Denmark – drink was good, gin cocktails and champagne cocktails – Our staff are wonderful all ex-Hamburg-America line stewards who know exactly what is required – the food they made was just wonderful, too. The German band from the barracks played and we had the dance in the club room, which is a huge and very pretty room in the block where we live – we decorated the room with sprigs of young trees and daffodils. The whole thing was a great success – I asked Ken, but we had another of our famous rows – (I always seem to quarrel with my boyfriends!) However, we made it up in the end – the trouble seems to be that certain things I do annoy him – but instead of telling me, he bottles it always – Of course, he annoys me, but then I overlook these small things, which to him are mountainous – I used to be like that with John Pritty, but have grown out of the habit, Ken, having been

302

a POW for 4 years, is that much behind me in age, even tho' he is 29, and still a very young in many ways – I feel sorry for him, because unless he grows out of these ways, he will be very unhappy –

So, my position seems to get worse and worse from every point of view!! Heaven forbid that I return to UK for keeps!

R. N. H. Q.
PLÖN

H.M.S. "ROYAL ALFRED"

4th April 1946

Paying-off Party

DANCE PROGRAMME

1. Fox Trot
2. Quick Step
3. Paul Jones
4. Modern Waltz
5. Slow Fox Trot
6. Fox Trot
7. Tango, Beguine, Rhumba
8. Eightsome Reel
9. Slow Fox
10. Strauss Waltz

SUPPER

11. Quick Step
12. Slow Fox, Waltz, Tango
13. Strauss Waltz
14. Fox Trot
15. Eightsome Reel
16. Beguine, Rhumba
17. Modern Waltz
18. Quick Step, Slow Fox Trot
19. Tango
20. Final Waltz

Dance card for the farewell party at Plön, organised by 'Mills'.

Another farewell party on 6 April; Sheila is seated with Ken on her left.

Ken stayed up for ten days and they did all kinds of things: 'dancing, walking, rowing and even went to a Gymkhana given by his Bde [Brigade] – on Easter Monday – The stupid thing is that we really don't hit it off much as we'd like to so I'm not quite sure what we are going to do – Our characters are really most similar – perhaps that's why.'

She is finally seeing that he is probably not the one for her.

Sheila is sorry to leave Plön, but felt she was getting in 'a rut'. She has no idea what the social life will be like in Kiel, but they brought their horses with them and the swimming and sailing in summer might be 'quite fun'. They are living in a large house 'midst trees and bomb damage (which is frightful)'. She loves her new room – 'it's rather small, with light furniture, green carpet and looks into the morning sun – It is next to Diana and we have a small balcony – Beyond the bomb damage is the harbour – on either side, both houses are one dreadful conglomeration of rubble – funny this one missed it. People live in the basement of one of them.'

A new place requires new clothes, and she is soon making lists of things for her mother to send:

26.4

I think that I shall have to do a transfer of clothes – I would like sent out 3 cotton dresses – red floral, coloured stripes, green beige button through, my silk blue and white print, blue housecoat, old red Syrian sandals, white wedge shoes and white cleaning stuff. Also, pink cardigan – Yes, I should love the red airtex too. There is another high level dance at the Corps Commander's mess on the 6th so I shall need another evening dress – I do wish you hadn't sent the blue to Rosemary, as I need a change badly – I think I had better have the red brocade this time – I also need badly some hair grips from my gray case and some shampoos – Please could I have the last 3 things by return as I need them rather urgently?

P.S I have thought of more things I need – one, face powder – a box of Cyclax from my cupboard please – Damn – can't think of the others.

Just remembered – I sent 2 parcels (reg) home with material for dresses – could you pse send them back unopened and they won't have to be paid for again –

———

8.5.46

It looks as if I shall be here for some months yet, so please, I should like my things fairly soon. Oh, I got the shampoo and clips. I was most pleased with them.

———

10.6

Thank you for my evening dress and cardigan which I believe will have arrived as I see there is a parcel for me to collect.

It's not all one-way traffic, however. From Denmark she sent almonds, nail varnish and swansdown powder puffs. In Germany she is buying wellingtons, sheepskin gloves, a tin of tongue and cheese for her mother, as well a 'beautiful' Roquefort for her aunts Rose and Dorothy to share.

In Kiel her mood lifts; social life kicks off well and she has to work hard which I think she enjoys. The yacht club seems to be the social hub, and she, Diana and Betty ride frequently. The change of scene also gives her a chance to think more clearly about her relationship with Ken. Rosemary seems to be having similar problems with her boyfriend, Winter:

What's happened to R? ... How is the big romance progressing? I feel that if he doesn't do anything now he never will – You know what these men are! I am frightful – I can only have interest in one person at a time and thus never bother about all the people around – so that when I suddenly find all is not well in that direction (vis Ken) I discover how few people I really know or care about. I get in a very bad habit of not bothering about people who don't particularly appeal to me, which is really a very bad thing indeed, I'm sure it's better to be everybody's friend, than to keep one's circle select and small as I seem to do! I really must turn over a new leaf!

Which is indeed what happens.

Kiel

8.5.46

My dear Ma –

… I can't remember when I last wrote but I think it must have been last week – life here has really been very gay and promises to be so in the future. I went out 5 nights running, and could have gone tonight as well, but felt I must get on with mess a/c's and sordid things like that. We have a mess meeting tomorrow, and I want to prepare for it, as I shall have no time in the morning, as I shall be working. I am kept hard at it from 9 till 6, quite a change. My boss is a delightful old boy, most hard working and conscientious – but he <u>does talk!</u> He's also a great tease and never lets an opportunity pass. But I do like him and enjoy working for him very much. The Corps Commander's party in Plön was on Monday and Diana and I went up with Capt. Morse in his car. En route, the petrol tank dropped off and we had to get another car! The party was a great success. I knew such a lot of people there, I found. I wore the red check again, for want of something better. It has been much admired – I must say I like it too – The guards have a very good Officers' Club at a place near here which I went to on Saturday. Food and drink are just <u>excellent</u>. It's frightfully select and only a few regiments are allowed to go – the joke is they seem to let all kinds of women go – I believe half of them are Germans or displaced persons!

A nice letter from Robin this week – he seems settled in up there and is doing a lot of riding in Gymkhanas too. I always thought he must be good, but I think he really must be first class.

I think the Ken affaire will die a natural death. I am sick of being treated in a casual sort of way. It appears to be too much of an effort for him to come up here to see me. (It takes 3 hours) and his gliding seems to be all important to him on Sundays. So I damned if I'm going to rush down to Hamburg to meet him, as he suggests. I've turned a blind eye to many things but I can't go on doing it. I'm sure there must be better fish in the sea somewhere! Rosemary seems to be

getting on like a house-on-fire. I so hope he comes up to scratch – I
rather feel that if he doesn't now he never will.

We have been all decorated up for VE day – flags all over the ships
– I wish you could see our new house – it is such a nice one, and could
be even nicer if the furniture fitted in better. We have a beautiful
Steinway piano, too. You don't notice the terrible bombing all round
now that the trees are out – at the minute we have no curtains – very
awkward in the bathroom! …

Lots of love,

Sheila

On Victory Day, she 'took half the morning off and went riding –
in the afternoon I went out sailing with an awfully nice young Sub.
here – Tom Unwin – we had such fun'. In the evening they went on
aboard the destroyer Zenith, and then on to a film. 'I reckon I had as
good a day of Victory as anyone.' So my father enters Sheila's orbit
again, but he is not without competition. In the same letter, that of
10 June, she writes of another admirer:

I have had such a pleasant week, and mostly all from mine own efforts,
which all goes to show it <u>does</u> pay to make the effort. I have asked
several people up to dinner and made up parties – have ridden a lot
– sailed once – one evening I went up to the Schleswig Officers' Club
with a rather nice Engineer I met in the course of my duty – Barry
Phillips – and last night I asked him back to dinner in the mess. We had
a hilarious time as 2 old old friends of mine ex. Hamburg and Harwich
(Wrens) came up en route for Denmark and did we chatter? In the end
Barry drove us round to his little ship 'Nautik' where he lives all by himself and we finished the evening on champagne and Nautik specials,
gazing over the rails at the water, in true troop ship style. It was fun.

She adds as a postscript: 'not a word from Bruce, Robin neither for 4
or 5 weeks!!!!'

In mid-June, she writes about her impending leave to England in early July; she will go home for a few days and then spend some time with her cousin Hazel and her goddaughter Daphne, for whom she has knitted many a fine garment while on watch, and then perhaps spend a day or two in London.

Sheila is obviously going out with Tom a fair bit, although he doesn't sound very attractive as he has produced some 'frightful spots on his neck'. This on top of the terrible rash he had when she first met him in Hamburg. I put it down to his deep neurosis, which I shall explore a little later.

She tells a funny story about her lunch with some Russians. 'One of them asked Donald Wood [an interpreter and friend of Tom] whose girl I was – Oh she works for Captain Morse was the reply – Oh no – I mean who does she sleep with retorted the Russian!! They really are most odd!!'

Barry meets her on her return from leave in mid-July. She spends the rest of the day with him, and then on to Hamburg for the evening. In the next letter, she seems to be seeing a fair bit of Barry, as Tom is away:

Kiel

21.7.46

My dear Mama –

Today is your birthday – Many happy returns, once more! Tom has gone up to Denmark and I have asked him to bring back a cheese for you if he can get one on Sunday – so here's hoping! Thank you for your letter – I hope you are feeling less tired …

Life has been rather hectic since my return and I have laid off a bit as I felt rather tired. Two mornings running I went riding; one day we bathed at lunchtime – one evening Barry and I went to the Guards' Club at Eckernforde – the following evening three of us returned to our old barracks Plön and dined in Rodney block (where we used to live) with the guards – It was really rather fun – they were all frightfully guard-ee but awfully nice, really – Dinner was rather sumptuous – (caviar!) and afterwards we trooped off to their new Country Club which is in the house the General used to occupy – It was very nice indeed but very empty indeed as it had only been opened 3 days – They produced a cabaret and we danced – and didn't get home till 2.30 – ugh!

You can guess I was tired on Friday – but I rode in the evening and haven't felt at all stiff from my efforts at all, which is marvellous change for me – In the evening Tom came round after dinner and we walked and talked in the nearby woods – Yesterday Betty, Diana and I went out to Westensee to see where we have a country house for weekends – it's beautiful there – a large lake, with fields, woods and trees all round – we took Capt. Morse and a Norwegian with us – It was quite warm and we finished up in the Schloss drinking champagne on the terrace! Yum Yum! I ended the day by going to bed at 9.15 – heavens – Today I feel full of energy and Barry and I are going for a picnic – if it doesn't rain! This evening we are going back to Schleswig the club which we like best – Eckernforde always rather depresses me – there's far too much to eat – courses and courses and the band's not very good!

I hope you have had that bottle of champagne for your birthday – I bought 2 more bottles last week – 9/- a bottle! Could you please get me another small gold coin button from Coyne's – I should have got 5 – silly!

Rosemary seems bereft of all her friends – I wonder if she has gone to Italy?

I am very busy in my office – tons of bills to deal with which are rather complicated.

There's no news at all for now – I will leave this open in case anything happens.

Lots of love,

Sheila

Now Sheila is the two-timer. Only this year, 2014, I discovered a cache of my father's letters to my mother, stuffed in an old plastic bag, along with the wedding telegrams. This sheds a whole new light on their courtship and their relationship, and reveals much about my father that I suspected but could never prove, as by the time I knew him he was a hugely successful man, first in the Colonial Administration in Tanganyika and then in the United Nations.

The first letter is dated 4 July, and predates the above letter, in which he apologises for not being able to come to the UK 'after all as the "Cdr Aylen" gang have made other arrangements'. This refers to his work with Professor Walther and other German scientists in Kiel. He adds, 'do you know I miss you quite a lot.' This was getting serious only after a few weeks. His other letters contain a sketch of a bleeding heart and a long love poem on Naval Message paper, obviously written by him as there is lots of crossing out; here are the final stanzas:

It may just be a reverie
Of a sub on morning watch
But that's how you appear to me
That's what you'll always mean to me
At times when I am took with fright
I'd love to have you near to me
My light!

Forgive these lines
Writ down in haste
For beauty they have none
And all they really show to me
Is the damage
You
Have done!

Nevertheless she continues to see both Barry and Tom. Perhaps she was terrified of being left high and dry again as she was with Bruce, so kept her options open:

Kiel 30/7/46

My dear Ma – no news from you for ages. The mail seems to have gone all haywire. I hope all is well and that you are feeling less tired.

Life here is extremely pleasant, the highlight of the week seems to be Sunday. Tom asked me to go on a trip with him to try and look up some Russian cousins of a friend of his at home. White Russians – and with another young interpreter, Donald Wood as well, we all set off to find the place, near Ratzeburg, south of Lübeck, we had a bathe and a picnic lunch on the beach at Timmendorf and then sped on to find this place – After asking and asking and bumping over frightfully badly made up roads we found the house, a large old farmhouse packed with D.P.s [Displaced Persons] from the Russian zone and discovered the people we were looking for. They were charming, had lost everything in Berlin, were stateless as they were exiled Russians, but were still in hope that something would turn up. They had a sweet little girl of six years old who speaks German and Russian and we all three said how do you do to her in different ways in Russian (the only words I know!). After about 1/2 hour we decided we had better be on our way, but alas within a mile of the house we broke down – and had to go on foot to a neighbouring dairy to phone. This was all miles in the heart of the country. There we met a kind man who offered to tow us with his lorry into Ratzeburg, where we hoped the 10th Hussars would be able to help us. When we eventually arrived, we discovered they had no breakdown party at all and that we had to get another car from Kiel. However, they were throwing a small party for the local DP's – would we like to join in? – We would and did and spent a most amusing evening dancing and talking to the DPs – mostly Latvians, Estonians and Lithuanians. We met an awfully nice Lithuanian Colonel who was rather like a fish out of water – he spoke only French, and either Russian or German – Tom was marvellous as he is a very good linguist and the old man thought him marvellous. Eventually our car arrived at 1230 and we got home at about 0315! The dawn was rising! I was terribly tired as I had been late the night before.

Yesterday I took Barry out riding for the first time and it poured and poured with rain, we got soaked. This evening is a ladies guest night on board the ship – I am riding with Tom before, and then Barry is calling for me for the dance.

Oh, did the cheese ever arrive? I sent it off approximately a week ago in a big wooden box – cheese provided by Tom – box by Barry. I am rather worried about having two young men – both are dears – I really must be careful and not go sailing on head in air. There might be talk.

Tennis I played three times last week also, rode 2 or 3 times as well – danced 3 evenings and swam twice. It's a good life!

How is Rosemary? I've heard no news from her for 2 weeks or so. Oh, I am being taken out of the dryer so must stop. (Am having hair done!)

With heaps of love,

Sheila

And so it continues with her two young men, although Tom has a trump card in his favour:

Kiel Sunday 4th/8

My dear Ma – many thanks for your letter which crossed mine – I wonder whether you got the cheese? Your apples haven't arrived yet – George, our nice German steward, had some sent to him by his wife yesterday, and I found a plate by my bed – I felt rather awful taking them, but I always give him chocolate and cigs when he goes home – so I think he felt he would like to do something in exchange –

A very happy and busy week for me – Did I tell you how Tom and I went out riding and had a battle with an enormous cart horse stallion? We were galloping down a field to a gate, when this thing started to chase me and when we got to the gate, found it was wired up and padlocked – I got off to try and undo the wire, and left Tom to cope with the horse – luckily they weren't mares but the stallion didn't seem to mind, and I foresaw us all being trampled under foot. Tom was frightfully brave especially when the nasty thing got its foot caught in his horse's reins and he had to undo the strap – all the time there was bucking and kicking going on and I was battling with the gate which I had to take off the hinge – In the end I got it off, and my horse through, and repressed the stallion whilst Tom got his through – my goodness I was frightened, tho' we have had many a laugh over it since!

We went on to the ladies' guest night afterwards – I in my black dress lace earrings and velvet bow tied round my neck, which brought forth rounds of applause from everyone – I am glad I brought it back.

Barry has got to go home in a couple of weeks – a blitz from above has removed his job, and he is going home. It appears that he is married, but is another one who doesn't get on with his wife – this I don't doubt at all, but I must say what a typical male attitude not to tell until the last minute – all I can say is it's jolly lucky I hadn't fallen flat for his charms, because I should have been sunk!

Tom and I had a marvellous afternoon yesterday at Schleswig where we went over the Cathedral. It has the most beautiful carved altar screen – I have never seen anything so intricate – all scenes from the New Testament carved in oak, and in the contemporary costume of the 13th or 14th century – The ceiling and pillars are all painted delicately in buff ocre [sic] and brick colours – apparently all the paintings were white washed over at the time of the Reformation and were not discovered till 1938. N. Germany was the last part of Germany to be converted to Christianity and still on the ceilings are painted 2 witches on broomsticks, old pagan gods – an organ was playing whilst we were there, and I was terribly impressed by the whole place – Tomorrow is Bank Holiday and we hope to go on a picnic. In the evening we are going to a circus in the town – later on, we hope to go to Bad Harzburg together, and Capt. Morse says that I can go – but Tom (reluctantly I'm afraid) is going on leave in 2 weeks time – so we must try and go before he goes. He really is the sweetest person – but 3 years younger than I am!

The glamorous and beautiful
Sheila in Germany in 1946.
This is the black dress referred
to in the letter of 4 August.

I have had a very nice dinner dress made in almond green cotton-silk and I managed to get some very pretty painted wooden buttons to go with it – We got them at Eckernforde yesterday. It really is quite [sketch] sweet.

I really must stop and finally get ready for riding. It is a beautiful windy and sunny afternoon – I am going with Barry – Tom is out sailing as it is Kiel Regatta this week – They are going 10 miles outside the boom in cabin class yachts – I do hope he won't be seasick as he says he is terribly at times.

Heaps of love

Sheila

No news from R. for weeks – is all OK?

The next letters are all Tom (although Barry sneaks in when Tom is sailing) – dining, swimming, picnicking, visiting Lübeck, driving through the country. And then Tom goes on leave 'for a whole fortnight – Awful!' but they have arranged to go to Bad Harzburg for her birthday on 9 September. Barry, too, has left, but not before giving her a nice hand-made black handbag, but she's 'glad he's gone really – much as I liked him – Complications only ensue.'

Nevertheless, she has time for a rant about the notion that the British Army on the Rhine are to be allowed to bring their wives out, and it is revealing in what it says about conditions in Germany at the time, and her sympathy with the civilians:

Kiel
17.8.46

I think this BAOR [British Army of the Rhine] wives business is a scandal – Here, dozens of families have been evicted and there is absolutely nowhere suitable for them to go, as the town is so badly bombed – also, they have had to leave behind furniture etc. and feeling will I am sure, run very high, and rightly so – It is untrue to say that such luxuries await the wives such as the papers make out – we have hardly any furniture or anything to put into unfurnished houses and I don't suppose the NAAFI arrangements are any further forwards – There will be discontent all round – I am sure it is a mistake bringing them over here – they will have precious little to do except gossip and I don't suppose many will take an interest in the German problem today – Conditions in winter will be shocking – And as for giving them that luxurious train – that's the last straw, when you consider the trains we service people travel in – FILTHY – 2nd or 3rd class for officers, not enough lights – windows often boarded up – lavatories too smelly and dirty to even <u>enter</u> and I suspect, infected with all kinds of livestock – If they can produce decent trains for wives and families, what about the poor old service personnel who've won the war for them? It makes me sick –

I attribute this outburst partly to the stress she must have been feeling with Tom away, and to his growing influence over her, as he mixed freely with Germans as part of his job. He begins to bombard her with letters, ranging from extremely witty to downright depressive, many adorned by cartoon sketches.

Some of the sketches from Tom's letters.

Well, Sheila, let us hope that we, perhaps, shall achieve our paradise, our Shangri-la. If there is a god – and I don't think there is – he certainly should favour us. We have both deserved peace of mind & body.

I send you my love, darling.

Your Prosaic Tom.

The following letter was written on Salvation Army paper, while he was waiting for his train to take him on leave to England. She could not fail to have been amused by it, and this is my father though and through – limitless charm hiding a tormented soul:

Railway Stn
Bad Oeynhausen
15.8

Madam

May we interest you in corresponding with a lonely young man who is off on leave to England today?

He is a young naval officer – his plane didn't fly owing to the weather and so train is the answer. He is rather unhappy at the thought of going home and so, knowing you, we hope you will not mind the Xian [Christian] deed involved in writing to him.

He was rather bashful of writing to you himself, but appears to be very fond of you. In fact he forgot to take his change of [unreadable] and when asked why, said 'these bloody women, always on your mind' from which remark you will readily deduce the depth of his love.

In the hope, dear madam, that we have not offended you by our forthright request and wishing you the happiest possible of correspondences.

We sign ourselves

Respectfully

Josiah H Turmoil
Stn. Welfare Officer

NB the young man's address – his name is I believe known to you – is 17, Chamberlain St, Wells, Somerset.

These letters were to continue right up until their marriage in December, as Tom only returned to Germany at the end of August for a few weeks and was demobbed in mid-October. Reading them now, it seems to me that she was taking a huge risk in marrying him as he showed signs of great mental instability. It is hardly surprising when you know what he had been through, but neither Sheila nor anyone else, apart from his mother and brother, had any idea about the real Tomas Michael Ungar.

Tomas (Tomy) Ungar was born on 25 October 1923 to Hermann and Margarete (née Stransky) in Prague. His father was a writer and former Czech diplomat who had served in Berlin, where he had belonged to an elite group of writers – the 1925 Group – which included Bertolt Brecht, Alfred Doeblin, Albert Ehrenstein, Willy Haas, Egon Erwin Kisch, Robert Musil, Joseph Roth, and Max Brod.

In Berlin Hermann met Thomas Mann who was to become his sponsor and, later, Tomy's godfather. His books were *Boys and Murderers* (1920), *The Maimed* (1922), *The Class* (1927) and the plays *The Red General,* which was premiered in 1928 in Berlin, and *The Arbour,* which was published posthumously in 1930. He also wrote many short stories, including one about his son, 'Tomy learns to write'. He wrote about sex and psychosis in a manner that shocked the establishment and was probably the reason why he sunk into obscurity, not helped by the fact that Max Brod, Franz Kafka's executor, turned against him after his death – due, no doubt, to Ungar's unfavourable remarks in his diaries, which were also published after his death. Hermann did not know the meaning of the word tact, something his son inherited.

Hermann died when Tom was six and, despite the fact that he barely knew his father, his father's character was to influence him greatly throughout the rest of his life. As he writes in a letter to Sheila on 12 November 1946, 'I fear you will find me a difficult man to live with even as mother found father. The trouble is I am too highly strung … always dissatisfied, always dripping …' On 25 and 26 October (maybe his birthday made him so maudlin), he writes 'if you marry me you are marrying a madman … this is the typewriter[12] pa used to write his books on … He was mad too, mad and genial.' A few weeks before their marriage he says, 'it isn't too late for you to realise you are marrying a soft fool, a dithering and undetermined semi-lunatic … I'm quite serious'.

Hermann Ungar came from a very respectable, wealthy Jewish family in Boskovice, Moravia. In fact the name Ungar was only adopted when an ancestor, a Rabbi, probably Zebi Hirschl Ungar (1730–56), had visited Hungary to spread the faith (Ungar means Hungarian in German). Although they lived in the ghetto by law, they owned the largest house, the *Kaiserhaus*, or Emperor's House, and his father was a respected brewer and purveyor of spirits, some-time mayor and leader of the local Jewish community. One of my father's early memories is visiting his grandparents in the summer holidays and going round the vats of fermenting schnapps, running his finger under each tap, and licking it to get the taste of the spirit. The house dominates the square in the restored ghetto (Boskovice is now a UNESCO World Heritage Site), with a plaque to Hermann Ungar, and is still in use as a pub.

Emil, Hermann's father, was extremely well read, fluent in French and Russian, although German was their first language (my grand-mother used to say, 'Czech is for peasants') and his wife, Jeannette Kohn, would give French lessons to the *Grafin* (Countess) in the local *Schloss*. Jeannette was a direct descendent of the High Rabbi of Prague, R Schmuel ABD Prague Ha-Levi (1756–1834). One of Hermann's stories, 'Colbert's Journey', published posthumously with a preface by Mann, is a gentle dig at his father's bourgeois pretensions.

Hermann was sent to the local grammar school in Brno, where he was a nervous boy and was treated by a neurologist at the age of 13 for 'sexual urges'. In his late teens he fell in love with his cousin and, after the affair finished several years later – it was not suitable as they

12 I still have the typewriter.

Hermann Ungar.

were first cousins – he had the first of many nervous breakdowns. He went on to study law at the universities of Berlin, Munich and Prague, and joined the imperial army in 1914 to fight on the Russian Front. He broke his leg, and later suffered from various 'nervous complaints', including depression, and was declared 'unfit' for front-line duty. The terrible things he saw during the Russian campaign were to affect him forever.

As a young man he had been an ardent Zionist; his sister Gerta had emigrated to Palestine in the 1920s and, although he became disillusioned with religion to such an extent that his two boys, Tomy and Sasha, were brought up 'out of the faith', he was claimed on his death by the leading Jewish writers' groups, and has always been categorised as such. His tragic death at the age of 36 was as a direct result of being considered a neurotic hypochondriac – he died of peritonitis because no-one took him seriously when he said he felt ill. My father and his brother both inherited this obsession with their health.

Tom's mother Margarete, or Greta, was also from a respectable wealthy Prague Jewish family. She had already been married when she met Hermann, and the boys had an elder half-brother Hunza Weiss (John West). He and his father had fled to England before the war started, and later emigrated to Canada. According to reminiscences of friends and acquaintances, 'Margarete – in contrast to Hermann – was "a healthy, happy, powerful and earthy person", "statuesque, somewhat taller than Ungar, very attractive appearance", "a very beautiful woman, richly endowed with female charms", "a force of nature".'[13] She was an operetta singer, and held salons in their smart Art Noveau apartment overlooking the banks of the Vltava river. We scattered my father's ashes there in 2012, looking on to his family home.

Tom travelled to London, aged only 16, in 1938 to join his brother John and to study agriculture. In 1939 he used his last pennies to call his mother and brother to encourage them to leave immediately,

13 Excerpt from Dieter Südhoff, *Hermann Ungar: a Life and Works.*

Greta Ungar with her three sons, Sasha, Hunza Weiss and Tomy, *c.* 1927.

which they did. The Ungar parents and Hermann's younger brother, Felix, his wife and two children, dithered in Boskovice and Prague due to Jeannette's ill health, although his Stransky niece and nephew were among the last to leave Prague on the Kindertransport. They were only 2 and 4 years old. Their parents Otto and Louisa Stansky, along with Greta's mother, Paulina, and the rest of the Ungar family were not so lucky and disappeared in 1942, first to Terezin, and thence to Auschwitz, and were never heard of again.

Many years later I questioned my father about his denial of his Jewish roots, and he said his mother had told them that once they arrived in England they were to claim to be Catholic. She, and as a result my father and his brother, was terrified that if the Germans won and it was known they were Jews, they would face the same problems all over again. He never lost that fear of anti-Semitism, and it explains why he continued to keep quiet about his ancestry and why he devoted much of his life to helping refugees.

Greta and her two sons were evacuated to Wells, Somerset, where, aged 17, Tom joined the Home Guard. His mother worked in an armaments factory and Alec, as Sasha became from then on, managed to get into Bembridge school – both boys had been sent to the English school in Prague so spoke good English. Tom later joined Military Intelligence at Caversham because of his value as a German speaker.

In 1943 he joined the Royal Navy's Special Branch, training first at Skegness, where they were billeted in a disused Butlins camp, before joining HMS *Pytchley* at Fishguard, and then the *Hunter*, to provide Channel escorts, including for the D-Day landings. In 1944 he patrolled the Norwegian fjords aboard the *Grenville*.

Later in 1944 he was posted to Scapa Flow where he served under Admiral Phillips and his role was to interpret Luftwaffe and *Kriegsmarine* HF and VHF traffic. From there he served on various ships in the Russian convoys, often on the admiral's or commander's ships as the intelligence given was crucial to the convoy's survival. However, the closest he came to death was when he missed his footing jumping from a small lifeboat onto the HMS *Lioness* and ended up in the freezing water, sinking under the weight of his huge radio transmitter, which he was forced to relinquish, much to the fury of his commander. In early 1945 he joined HMS *Hart* under Commander Michael Sherwood on a mission to rescue valuable equipment from Germany of use to the Allies.

His finest achievements came towards the end of the war, when in 1945 he was posted to Kiel under Commander, later Rear-Admiral, Jan Aylen, who was commanding the *Walterwerke* project. In addition to targeting a list of the top forty or fifty German scientists, including the inventor of the doodlebug, the primary objective was to persuade the inventor of the high-speed, hydrogen-peroxide fuelled submarines, Professor Walter, to give over his blueprints and defect to the West. Aylen, who did not speak German, received the credit for the mission, but it was Tom's charm and fluency in German that was critical for its success and the eventual delivery of their equipment to the Vickers shipyard in Barrow-in-Furness. It was while Tom was working at Kiel that he met Sheila, probably at the yacht club, although it would have been normal for naval officers to socialise in such a small place as Kiel, surrounded by the former enemy.

By the end of August, Tom has returned from leave and it appears from his letters that they are contemplating a future together – in his last letter from Wells he writes, 'let us hope that we, perhaps, shall achieve our Shangri-La. If there is a God – and I don't think there is – he certainly should favour us. We have both deserved peace of mind and body.' However, none of this is revealed in Sheila's letters to her mother; symbolically she loses John Pritty's ring while out on a walk at this time:

Kiel 11/9/46

My dear Ma – Many many thanks indeed for your nice birthday card and letter – the only one I had! I had such a pleasant birthday but I will tell you all about that later on in the letter –

... I'm afraid I lost the scarab ring for good this time as it slipped off my hand 'somewhere' while out for a walk last weekend, and although we searched and searched we could find it nowhere – maddening.

Well, now for all my news – about ten days ago, soon after Tom came back from leave we had rather an unfortunate car smash, at 10 mph crashed into a tree – all so unexpected that I pushed my head through the windscreen and consequently got rather cut about. However, I was so beautifully stitched up by a German doctor that you can hardly see any scars at all even now and they say they will disappear completely with time. I may have to lose a tooth, that's all. Poor Tom, so upset about it all, got the best black eye I've ever seen! He's still got it too – after all this, our weekend at Bad Harzburg was doubly welcome, and we drove down there last Friday – It's as beautiful as ever – and we walked for miles over the mountains amongst the pine woods – we really didn't do much else and the weather was really quite nice –

We drove back yesterday without rushing it and went through Brunswick and saw what it is like – Tom had been there before the war; it has been very bashed about and some really beautiful churches and old buildings have been extremely badly damaged –

We stopped for lunch south of Lüneburg on a heath – lovely heather which isn't quite the same as ours – Eventually we had tea in the Atlantic at Hamburg, and arrived here at about 6.45, not wanting to be back at all!

I haven't signed on for the WRNS. Most of the Wrens will have gone from here after the end of the month, and, even if they accepted my volunteering it would probably mean going home to H.Q. – I couldn't be a signal officer, that's one thing certain – I think I have done right – life in the service I should think would be rather pointless in peacetime – I am thinking of applying to take domestic science course lasting a month in October, which can be taken out here – You take that as the main subject with 2 auxiliaries such as art history, economics etc …

Lots of love,

Sheila

My poor mother, the scars of that accident were to remain with her physically – her face was badly cut – and mentally as, in later years, she would blame my father for ruining her face and her teeth. Meanwhile, the Nuremburg trials are nearing the end, and Tom, who is being demobbed shortly, has managed to get a new job back in England:

Kiel
5.10.46

My dear Ma –

… Did I tell you about Tom's good job? The powers that be are trying to get him to stop on in the Navy as they say his work here is so important. It is, of course, but there's not much future for an RNVR sub if the Navy doesn't promise a permanent commission. He leaves here in a week; I shall miss him tremendously.

The last photos of Sheila before the car crash.

After the crash: 'Wounded warriors – unfortunately the printer has wiped out my white bandages, thinking they were a flaw in the negative. But Tom has a beautiful black eye and bump on his forehead.'

The results of the Nuremberg trials gave rise to a few precautions here in case there was any trouble from the ex. German Navy, who were very fond of Doenitz and Raeder[14] – we were all CB'd [confined to barracks] from Sunday to Tuesday and everyone rushed about with rifles. The ships here all sent to action stations in the harbour. In fact there was more Flap than that about it all! However, nothing at all happened.

We met a very interesting man here last week – an American scientist from California University – we had him to dinner in our mess and took him on to see 'Theirs is the Plan' a very shocking film. We had a visit from the 1st officer from Hamburg yesterday, she's rather the schoolmarm type – I went to an excellent concert with Tom in the evening, a bass from Berlin – The place was <u>packed</u> with most enthusiastic Germans, and he encored and encored at the end. We went on to the Yacht Club for dinner and got muddled up with a crowd of yacht crews, ending by singing 'Viola Viola' in company at the band stand. All very raucous and great fun. Tom hates dancing, but when he actually does it, gets on quite well and enjoys himself!

On Thursday we went to the Opera 'Falstaff' by Verdi, an opera I didn't know existed – it was excellent. The story of the merry wives of Windsor and so funny. Costumes and decor were very good too. Today we are going over to Travemünde to a party given to one of our young Lieutenants being demobbed, who is very keen on a German girl there. The party is being given by Germans, I wonder what time we shall get back – Tom went over last week, and returned at 6 am!!

I do hope you are well – It looks as if I shall be here for another month at least.

Heaps of love,

Sheila

14 Both Commanders of the *Kriegsmarine*; Raeder received life imprisonment and died in 1960, while Doenitz only received 10 years, despite briefly being President of Germany after Hitler's death.

Tom left Germany on 15 October, travelling by car to Cuxhaven, but before leaving he gave a 'bumper party in his office for all his employees, both English and German and what a collection appeared – The 3 officers themselves, 2 marine drivers, German drivers, German friends and so on – It really went off very well – only one of the marines got really tiddly – Tom and Jack gave a combined farewell drinks party on Monday. It is strange for me to be here without Tom as we have done everything together for the past 3 months. He starts his new job in London straight away.'

Sheila then goes on a three-week domestic science course at Bad Oeynhausen, to prepare her for the real world. She is planning to be back in England towards the end of November. On 25 October, she writes:

> I'm enjoying the course very much. Tho' a lot of the stuff I already know – I would be quite content to cook and dressmake all the time. However, one picks up quite useful hints on washing, ironing, cleaning and valeting, as with a how to repair fuses and tap washers etc. – we spent one morning on those horrid treadle sewing machines – so difficult to make them work – and I believe we have to make ourselves a garment or leave the place!
>
> I have cooked scones, shortbreads, a sponge cake and helped in preparing lunch of roast mutton and 2 veg, trifle and coffee – the shortbreads were a howling success – we cook entirely with <u>butter</u> as we can't get anything else!!

It is not until 30 November that she rather archly admits to her engagement. Many of the details she gives of Tom's life are wrong – not much of a surprise with hindsight:

Domestic Science Centre
Bad Oeynhausen
30.10.46

My dear Ma

... You will probably be surprised to hear that I am contemplating
matrimony – the lucky man being Tom Unwin – As you know, he has
returned to UK and is in London now, with his new job – we have been
thinking of this for some time now, but had to wait and see whether he
got the job or not, and various other considerations. Well now, the thing
is to get somewhere to live in or near London – and we're afraid it will
be terribly expensive – a small service flat in Town would be the answer,
in which case I should probably get a part time job to keep me occupied
as you know I hate London! If on the other hand we could get a small
flat or house just outside London – it might not be so dear, and I should
then have to stay at home and look after it – Tom's job earns him £600 a
year, which I think is very good to begin with – It is with a branch of the
N.F.U. [National Famers Union] and will probably move abroad in the
summer of next year – So we don't want to get any furniture.

I think you will like your future son-in-law, tho' you may find him
a trifle unorthodox – He is 3 years younger than I am – tall, fair,
gray-eyed and well built. He is Czech by birth, and lived in Prague
till 1939 when he came to England to study – now being naturalised.
Subsequently, his mother and young brother, Alec, came over and settled in Wells, Somerset. His mother is a widow, her husband having
been in the Czech Diplomatic Service, I think and who died of appendicitis when Tom was 9 – Of course, they have lost almost everything.
They have much property in Czechoslovakia, but of course that is all
Russian now.

As for Tom – he is an extremely clever linguist – and no one could
tell he wasn't English, as he gabbles away faster than we normally talk.
His German is the same – He is far-seeing politically, and deeply interested in world affairs, and – a Socialist!! A terrific peace-lover – almost
to being a conscientious objector! He is brilliant and almost fanatical

in his views and ideals, and everyone who knows him well says they think he will go far. I hope he will. He loves music and the country and has had to do everything for his mother and brother since they came over here. Alec is now studying forestry at a school in the south. They have a stepbrother in Canada.

I'm sure you will find him most loveable and easy to get on with – He's sweet with children and when in Travemünde in 1945, held classes for German children to teach them English under the name of Uncle Tom – This was stopped by the N.O.I.C. as being unsuitable (!)

He is temperamental and often gets fits of depression regarding the state of the world – But not the sort of temperament that flings frying pans about!

Anyway, having eulogised my Tom for a couple of pages, you will now have gathered that he is no ordinary person. His main worry at the minute seems to be, can we live in the comparative comfort we desire on £600 a year – I shall be interested to hear what you think – (he hates dancing, by the way, and seldom drinks!) He is so worried that he mayn't be able to give me all I desire, that he repeatedly gives me the chance of backing out if I want to. Personally, one has to draw in one's horns on leaving the Navy, anyway, and I don't think we should live in too much discomfort – The transition from service to civilian life is bound to be difficult, anyway.

There won't be any grand wedding, anyway, as Tom loathes ceremony and is all for rushing off to a registry office without any warning – a probable relief to you! A most unconventional young man! (But very sweet!) We don't think the difference in age matters as we get on so well.

No more now, must write to Tom.

Heaps of love,
Sheila,

DON'T MAKE A SONG AND DANCE OF THIS – PLEASE. You know the family.

The very thought that her mother would settle for a registry office wedding, and in London, is impossible to contemplate: I reckon Sheila was trying to get some of her own back for her unhappy childhood but, as we shall see her – and Tom's – wishes were overruled.

My father was a man who kept secrets: we know that he kept secret his Czech nationality from his employers, the National Farmers' Union (NFU), and then got in a real pickle because he could not get his naturalisation papers through; he had even kept it secret from Sheila until after their engagement, as this letter shows:

Wells
19.8

Darling

I've got something on my mind – a confession, in fact. I don't tell everyone because it only leads to millions of questions I have answered before: I am not really British, I am Czech by birth and my naturalisation is only just under way …

I had to keep all this quiet during war-time otherwise it would have been very dangerous in case I got captured. I didn't tell you from the first as I thought you might not 'go much on it'. Sorry if I underestimated you. Very few people at Kiel know as it is – it saves so many silly questions and is very much easier all round, but I do think you ought to know, if anyone …

It meant that he was extremely nervous about the wedding announcement lest there was mention of the name Ungar and his employers spotted it: 'if they insist on putting daughter of … and son of … it'll be a bit awkward in my case from the pt. of view of the aforesaid NFU problems, unless one lied a little and called it all Unwin … oh how dreadful all these formalities are – but do we care? DO we hell.'

His two much greater secrets, which he never revealed to my mother, were that he fathered a child in 1944, and that he was Jewish.

He had befriended Joyce, an attractive young woman with two small children, whose husband was away at war. Greta, who was not a particularly nice woman, lied about the baby that arrived after Tom had left for Caversham, and pretended it was the husband's, so Tom only got to know the truth much later. According to him, not until the 1980s when he and Joyce met again, and his daughter, Bonnie, became a part of his life (and mine in 2009); according to Bonnie, Tom 'visited my mother at her place of work in Esher, Surrey, in about 1946. He said he saw me in my cot asleep. Mother says he picked me up and referred to me as "our baby". Mother also tells of visiting him in his London flat – without telling him she was coming – and Sheila being there!' What they both thought of this meeting, history does not relate. Tom must have been beside himself with anxiety that this secret would come out; he only told it to me when he thought he was about to die and felt I should know about my half-sister, who is in fact older than my step-mother, who of course knew nothing about his first family either.

Suppressing his Jewish background and the terrible events of his childhood and teens was, I believe, to have lifelong repercussions on his character, and goes a long way towards explaining the tormented letters he writes to Sheila during their courtship and in the run-up to their marriage. Some forty-seven letters survive and while most of them have florid and intense descriptions of his love for Sheila, they are also mixed with serious doubts as to whether he is fit to marry her: 'my love for you has become a deep and lasting affection – as it is not the wild passion of fiery youth – not entirely anyway. And that is why I still feel, sometimes, that I may be doing the wrong thing in marrying in these circumstances of uncertainty.'

The passion is mixed with a penny-pinching pragmatism – probably born out of his refugee status – which was also to become more prominent in later life: 'for goodness sake don't buy too much bric-a-brac in the form of glasses and things. Much more useful if you buy sheets and pillow cases'; he then goes on to say his mother has advised him to dye his white shirts in to more 'useful colours' like grey and blue. As for wedding presents, they must be 'useful … iron; anything from carpet to lavatory brushes'.

His annual salary of £600 was equivalent to that earned by an MP but he suffered from angst throughout this correspondence about where and how they could afford to live on it. The letters are full of sketches of the various rooms he is considering and cost-of-living calculations, depending on whether they cook for themselves, take meals with their landlady, or even commute, which was an idea at some stage.

Like his father he had an 'ambivalent attitude towards middleclass standards, of which the marriage was part. Whilst Ungar theoretically promoted sexual freedom and also made use of it as his right, he proved to be a jealous spouse.'[15] Tom was desperately jealous of Sheila meeting up with both Robin and Barry in London just before they marry, but is shameless when he talks in an offhand way of other women he has slept with in the past.

Tom seems to accept being overruled on the registry office but is adamant that there is to be no fuss: 'I presume that it will NOT be a pukkha [sic] wedding where I would have to wear tails or something? Please darling, anything but that.' But when he finds out that it is to be a conventional occasion, he rails against the arrangements Sheila's parents are making for the wedding:

> Now why the hell do your people want to put it in the paper? I am very much against it. There can be no practical argument for it apart that we shall have a lot of mail to answer, and its just middle class pomposity and you can tell them I said so, or I'll tell them myself. NO I am ABSOLUTELY against it.

And in a later letter: 'oh you wretch, so we are going to have to be terribly suburban and have cards and cake …' Signs of his meanness come to the fore again in relation to the cake and the guest list

---

15 Excerpt from Dieter Südhoff, *Hermann Ungar: a Life and Works*.

when he says 'shall we just confine it to your friends?' and reluctantly agrees that spare invitations can be sent to German friends,
'but no cake, it would be like a mockery.' His socialism was very
much on display.

Again, like his father, he was obsessed with sex, or at least the
thought of it. He talks about their 'little problem' and says that
'self-denial and so forth is right but inwardly I ha'e me doots'. On
30 October he tells her he has consulted books and written to various
Harley street doctors to get advice on the best way of losing her vir-
ginity painlessly, and of preventing pregnancy. He goes into all this
in great detail, describing 'sheaths', 'pessaries' and the pros and cons
of condom use in married life: 'it's essentially an unmarried sinner's
method … and is unsatisfactory as you don't get the right "contact".'
He makes her an appointment with a specialist and reverts to this
subject again and again, exhorting her to visit the doctor before they
marry. On another occasion he says how 'wonderful it is we can talk
and correspond about these things without embarrassment.' I must
say I do rather wonder how my mother felt receiving these explicit
letters on sex education!

But his biggest neurosis by far was his anxiety over the state
of the world. Obviously depressed after being demobbed and
cast adrift, he was lucky enough to get a well-paid job with IFAP
(International Federation of Agricultural Producers, an offshoot of
the NFU) which 'square[d] with my ideas … a chance to do something to improve international relations and to provide food.' His
time in the navy, on the Russian convoys and in post-war Germany,
has made him into both a pacifist and an idealist, verging on
being communist. He dreams of going abroad and escaping this
'war, war, war' – he is haunted by Hiroshima and Nagasaki – and
living in a little cottage in New Zealand, or of 'teaching Negros in
Kenya', living a life 'of absolute goodness and, of gentleness and
non-violence and understanding others, of easy, peaceful leisure
and contentment. I do so passionately desire to be a pacifist and a
vegetarian … will you come?' It is a romantic prospect on paper,
and he writes very seductively.

These letters are long and rambling, and reveal a very tortured soul, who doubts until the very last as to whether he should marry or not: 'I have been pretty lonely since I was about 15 and got launched into the big alien world and I have therefore become rather independent', yet still he declares his passionate love for Sheila in every letter. Sadly, I think she must have been swayed by his good looks, his sense of humour and fun, and a sharing of ideals to such an extent that she overlooked the clear signs of someone who would, as he forecast, be very difficult to live with, and who never left behind the inheritance of his father's notions of sexual freedom.

She was not to know of the terrible damage that had been done to his psyche by losing his whole family, apart from his mother and brothers, in the Holocaust. One wonders how much he even knew about what had happened, as information was hard to get and verify. I am not saying my father was a bad man; on the contrary, he was a devoted and loving father (I adored him as a small child, in fact I was known as 'Daddy's girl') generous of spirit, witty and charming with a terrific, if sometimes cruel, sense of humour – that Germanic *Schadenfreude* – just an unsuitable one for my mother to marry. He retained a compassion for others less fortunate than himself throughout his life, working in development and with refugees for the United Nations after he left Tanzania in 1964. He passed on to me his hatred of inequality and gave me a social conscience, and for that I am forever in his debt.

Sheila's final two letters are all about the wedding, naturally enough. Given how much she came to hate her mother-in-law in the future, it is amusing to see her getting Sheila's highest accolade, 'a dear'. Even Tom is not always so polite about his mother, '… mother seems to be losing a little of her class … can that really be the woman who dined with Presidents.' He worries about her 'petty little swindles' (when I was about 11, I remember her teaching me how to shoplift in Canada, where she ended up after the war), but he does approve of her domestic abilities above those of the English housewife. 'Perhaps mummy could come up for a while and teach you how to cook and other housewifely achievements. And mummy is an excellent housewife, much better than yours probably, because English standards of housekeeping are shamefully inadequate. Polish the brasses, sweep the shit under the carpet and "Oh where's the tin opener, dear"?' In fact Grace was an excellent cook and housekeeper, far less slovenly than Grandmother Ungar, who had never had to lift a finger before the war. I did say tact was something he had not inherited from his father!

He obviously held out little hope for the benefits of Sheila's course as he urges her to learn how to cook 'meat – not stews except Irish stew, how to roast and stew as it is difficult; omelets and pancakes, custard and pastry; not vegetables the English way, awful, you will have to learn from mother'... and semolina as he 'loved it as a kid'. This bossy tone is present in many of the letters; he was a controlling man and he even admits to it in relation to work (he was a workaholic): 'I like to be an absolute dictator in the office.'

As for Sheila, he is torn between the need for her to work to earn money or becoming the vision of domestic bliss, 'once you have got a home to run you'll be quite busy, and if you're not you can always get a part time job.' The next minute he is sending her job advertisement clippings and seriously toying with sacking his assistant, Miss Fagg, who is older than him and useless, and employing Sheila as his secretary. In the end, unable to make up his mind, he says he would feel like a 'cad' if he were to do this.

B. Oeynhausen
8.11.46

My dear Ma – Many thanks for your letter. I was beginning to think you disapproved or were checking up on my Thomas. His name is UNWIN – Thomas Michael. It used to be UNGER [sic] but he had it changed by deed poll as in time of war and with the possibility of capture. Things would have been very hard for a Czech with the Germans – his mother is still Unger, I believe, but Alec has been changed – Tom's naturalisation is now under weigh [sic] –

Well, we have got a flat, or at least Tom has paid £5 deposit and I
have to say Yay or Nay on my return. It is in Maida Vale, in a house
belonging to a solicitor and his wife, S. Africans, whose daughter was
a Wren Coder in Alex – It is £4 a week (quite cheap for London) furnished, and has two bedrooms, sitting room and kitchen/hall. The only
snag appears to be that there is no running water, but I'm not clear what
Tom means – whether no bath or lav. only (and we share theirs down
below) or whether there isn't even a sink to do the washing up – I don't
mind the former, as he says there are illimitable baths to be had down
below – but I must have a sink!! Think of Tom shaving in the morning!
However, I think the latter will probably be the case in which case I
expect we shall take the flat as the rent is cheap – they provide crockery,
but want help with sheets – what quality can you buy these days? I am
keen to get coloured ones, are they obtainable? And of course is nice to
have our own blankets, which I prefer coloured also. Do find out about
these for me, please. I wrote to Draffens in Dundee, asking them to send
my beaver lamb coat down to Durham (it will have to be remodelled at
Jayson's) and asked them to get me new details of sheets and blankets
they had in stock – as they are an excellent shop, and it's possible that
Scotland may be better than Durham.

The flat has an electric cooker and the Theophilles will do our shop-
ping for us if I'm unable to – it means preparing breakfast and dinner
– I might get a part time job – Tom is keen for me to join him in the
N.F.U., as his assistant (a girl) is hopeless and in time he will have to do a
lot of travelling and naturally wants me to go too. I don't know what the
N.F.U. would say to a husband and wife combination – frowns I should
think – and again we may get tired of seeing so much of each other (!!)
But actually it's quite a good idea as the work is most interesting.

No comment from you on the actual wedding, pretty certain it
will be a registers' office affair and no fuss – (as Tom <u>loathes</u> fuss), no
family, friends, or relations, and no reception. OK by you? A few days
honeymoon in the country and then back to London – as things stand
at the minute, I plan to arrive in UK about the 21st or 22nd – go and
be demobbed in London or wherever it is – see you for a day (or 2 perhaps), come up North – dump uniform – and collect things together

for 5 or 6 days, return to London and then <u>either</u> go down to Wells to see Mrs. Unwin, <u>or</u> get married – I had such a nice letter from Mrs. U. by the way, (did I tell you?) She really does sound a dear, and writes letters very much like Elizabeth Vedgi – English and writing the same – I am certain we shall get on OK and not have any of the traditional mother-in-law trouble! She is very keen for us to get married, as she thinks her Tom needs someone to look after him, and she and Alec are going to Canada when the visas come through – She wants us to go too – but I don't think we will, unless Tom's job moves there.

I don't think I shall have much trousseau, either – another of Tom's unconventionalities! Not that he'd dislike me to have lots of pretty things – but it would never occur to him that lots of girls have an enormous bottom drawer and that I might do likewise! However, I have really got quite a lot of pretty undies – and my civilian clothes are in quite good condition – I only need a few new things – such as a really nice housecoat/dressing-gown for the winter – a twin set – if I can get one, and another cardigan – I think I'll wait till spring for another suit – which I really need, as that green tweed one I've had for 7 or 8 years – tho' you wouldn't think it. I've lots of stockings and R. is sending me a pair of snakeskin walking shoes from Cairo – I have also asked her to look out for camel hair rugs and carpets which are very cheap and attractive, and which she could have sewn up in sacking and bring home if she accepts a WAAF draft back at Xmas –

The cooking! Brandy snaps today, turned into flat moorish biscuits – but we didn't have brown sugar, which may be the fault –

Please reply to Kiel on receipt of this letter – I shall be back there by the 17th –

Lots of love

Sheila

Am off to Berlin for weekend tonight! Has my box arrived?

In fact they were never to move into the flat she describes, as they opted to stay in his digs where they got the very good value of 'breakfast and dinner (Irish of course) fish or chops, or bacon and omelet – almost as good as Kiel, no joking' as part of the rent. It must have hurt him to lose the £5 deposit! In the following letter, it sounds as if mother is remonstrating about the wedding arrangements. Tom's anxieties about his origins are obviously rubbing off on Sheila too, for different reasons:

B. Oeynhausen
11/11/46

My dear Ma –

Many thanks for 2 letters which arrived today – really, the mail has gone quite haywire – one of Tom's took 8 days!

Please don't make too much fuss about everything – Tom does hate it so – we really can't have a slap-up wedding – Tom can't possibly get away from his new job which he's only just started. We shall get married in London, and I expect in a Registry Office – I know it's not very glamorous etc. but much more sensible and suitable – I honestly don't think Tom would survive a proper wedding with hundreds of relations and guests – he'd probably get up and say something awful, or shocking and completely put the tin lid on everything. He's quite liable to!!! Don't put anything in the papers – not yet anyway – And (and I wouldn't have told you this if I'd thought you were going to tell everyone) please don't rush round telling everyone I am marrying a Czech. They will at once conjure up pictures of somebody akin to the typical Polish officer they have seen in UK during the war. I think Tom's father was in the Diplomatic Service – but I'm not sure. I'm certain I didn't make a definite statement – so please, again, don't go rushing round and tell everyone. Besides, why should everyone know Tom's ancestry etc? It's purely a family matter and I hate to think of all the busybodies in Durham clicking their tongues over the latest bit of gossip.

How sweet of Aunty Dorothy to ask if we would like Thurfield – I wonder how far it is from London? We would so much rather live in the country – but I don't want Tom to have too much travelling to do as he really works very hard.

A long letter from Aunty Rose today, who loved the cheese and (don't laugh!) wants to know if I can get her some more!!!! I <u>may</u> be able to have a day trip to Denmark on my return to Kiel, but I rather doubt it.

I had a very nice weekend in Berlin – one night there in a most luxurious YWCA, and a sleeper there and back. The first day I borrowed a bicycle, and sped around the ruins and on Sunday I went on a conducted tour arranged by CCG, visiting the Chancellery – now a shattered ruin, but it must have been an awe inspiring place – all marble – the bunker where Hitler is supposed to have committed suicide, and many other places of interest – It must have been a truly beautiful city, such wide streets as I have never seen before, one of them, the Kaiserdamm is a dual carriageway. Each road being far wider than Whitehall, for example – In comparison with other German cities, the people seemed better dressed, and there were a few little shops with trinkets and antiques, and one or two dressmaker's shops as well, with quite smart clothes in them.

Today we were let loose in the kitchen and each of us had to prepare a meal for 3 people – made shepherd's pie and marvellous treacle tart –

I'm not very expert at pastry, and it was terribly short, but most sumptuous! I dressmade this afternoon, and now, after all that, and a somewhat disturbed night in the train – I feel worn out! Only Tom's Turkish Delight is keeping me awake!

How far is Thurfield from the station and shops? It would really be necessary to have a car, which is entirely out of the question as we could never afford to buy – Tom hates being without me, but perhaps the I.F.A.P will turn up trumps!

Please don't be cross with me for my words of caution – I expect you are almost as thrilled as I am – and naturally when people ask questions – out it all comes. But I can't bear to be the subject of bridge party gossip and I know Tom would collapse if he thought he was causing such a stir.

No more,

Lots of love

Sheila

Sheila's letters to her mother gloss over the utter turmoil that was going on behind the scenes and which is revealed in the letters Tom wrote to her every day, reflecting his insecurity and anxiety, inability to make his mind up (something he never lost) and his deeply depressive nature. On a couple of occasions he was in fact contemplating suicide:

> … because life just didn't seem worth living … I now know what they mean when they talk of 'balance of mind disturbed'. I wonder whether these periods are not really not periods of very intense sanity, when one sees things so clearly, so unembellished by day to day palliatives that one takes the logical answer and draws one's consequences.

He was his father's son indeed.

It must have put great stress on Sheila when she came home for the wedding after leaving the WRNS. Presumably overjoyed at seeing one daughter married, and apparently charmed by her future son-in-law, nevertheless I suspect Grace, like most bourgeois British people, was a little disapproving of his foreign background and unconventional ways. Sheila would have had to do a lot of defending of her choice, especially when he was compared unfavorably, no doubt, with the likes of John, Bruce or Robin, all conventional and successful career soldiers, who would have been a much better match in the eyes of the bridge players of Durham city.

Several times Tom asks Sheila about the 'battle royal' and encourages her by saying, 'it wont be for long, she's losing a daughter now, so be nice to her for your last few days of iniquity.' After his first visit to meet her parents in early December, he writes that he 'rather liked your folks. Don't put their backs up the last week you are with them.

I think when your Ma talks about "Findlay says this" or "F says that" she really means SHE suggested it to F and he weakly nods approval. I don't suppose he gives a damn one way or the other.'

As the day draws nearer, he seems to be a bit more sympathetic: 'How is the battle on the home front? Don't let the buggers get you down, it's our wedding, our life. So even if they have their own way a little, well, Maleesh, sweetheart. Once we are out of that kirk, its just you and me ever after and damn the last man.'

They married at St Cuthbert's Church in Durham on 23 December 1946. They then went on a short honeymoon to the Lake District, staying in Coniston, before returning to the flat in Leinster Square. Tom soon became fed up with IFAP as he felt it was not aggressive enough, especially towards the Americans, who were hide-bound by the 'power of Yankee farmers who want more money and command lots of votes now … I will NOT work for an organisation whose aims run counter to the general prospects of mankind.' Marriage had not dampened his ideals.

He managed to obtain a position with the United Africa Company to be part of the Groundnut Scheme, the brainchild of the post-war Labour government, with the aim of providing food – groundnut oil – for ration-weary Britain. Sheila was to join him in July 1947. They spent the next three years of their marriage living in a tent in the middle of Tanganyika.

When the Groundnut Scheme failed in 1951, Tom managed to switch to the Colonial Service where he became first a District Officer, then a District Commissioner (DC), before becoming Permanent Secretary in the Ministry of Foreign Affairs, working for the new Prime Minister, then President, Julius Nyerere, until 1964. Sheila worked on and off from her arrival in Tanganyika, for the head of the Groundnut Scheme in Kongwa, in the District Office according to the opportunities afforded in the middle of nowhere and, later, for the British Institute (of Archaeology) in East Africa.

My parents on their wedding day, 23 December 1946, St Cuthbert's, Durham City.

I was born in Kilwa in 1957, where my father was DC; their marriage, already shaky, disintegrated completely in 1966 and they were divorced in the early 1970s.

There is no denying that Tom made a huge impact on Sheila's life, even if the marriage was unhappy. It enabled her to fulfill the wanderlust she had inherited from her father and had nurtured during the war; living in Africa gave her the freedom and opportunity to develop her passion for ethnography and archaeology and, most of all, to further shape her own compassion for others. Without him, she might have become just another army wife, living her mother's suburban dream. Instead she developed into a feisty and fascinating woman, loved and admired by many, from all backgrounds and races, young and old.

As her beloved cousin Hazel said to me as I was completing this book, 'she would have been so happy that you did this for her.' It is only thanks to Sheila and her mother, keeping this collection of letters over the decades, that I have been able to do so.

Bibliography and Sources

Primary sources

Sheila's letters form the bulk of primary source material, along with her photos and mementos from scrapbooks, including newspaper cuttings, dinner menus, service sheets and other ephemera.

Interviews with Sheila's surviving older sister, Rosemary, then 95, but whose memory was poor. She went to Egypt with the WAAF towards the end of the war, and met with some of Sheila's old boyfriends. She was also aware of the family history.

Interview with Sheila's cousin Hazel Dixon.

A recorded interview with my father shortly before he died in 2012.

Secondary sources

Artemis Cooper, *Cairo in the War: 1939–45* (John Murray, 2013)

Lawrence Durrell, *The Alexandria Quartet* (Faber & Faber, 2012 edition)

Sarah Helm, *If This Is A Woman* (Little, Brown, 2015)

Eric Lomax, *The Railway Man* (Jonathan Cape, 1995)

Olivia Manning, *The Levant Trilogy* (*The Danger Tree*, *The Battle Lost and Won*, *The Sum of Things* (Phoenix edition, 1983))

Alan Moorhead, *African Trilogy: The North African Campaign 1940–43* (Cassell, new edition, 2000)

S.W.C. Pack, *Operation Husky: The Allied Invasion of Sicily* (David and Charles, 1977)

Dieter Südhoff, translated by Angela Ladd, *Hermann Ungar: a Life and Works* (available to download from smashwords via www.herman-nungar.com)

Evelyn Waugh, *Sword of Honour* (Penguin Modern Classics, 2001)

Index

Visit our website and discover thousands of other History Press books.

www.thehistorypress.co.uk